The Black Hills and the Indians

A Haven of Our Hopes

MARTIN LUSCHEI

Niobrara Press/San Luis Obispo

ISBN-10 1-930401-55-8
ISBN 13 978-1-930401-55-6
Library of Congress Control Number 2007900989
Lakota War Shield courtesy of Minnesota Historical Society
MHS Acc. #335.E110

Cover design by Ginny Monteen

Niobrara Press
P. O. Box 15560
San Luis Obispo, California 93406
Orders: niobrarapress@sbcglobal.net

Printed in the United States of America

In memory of
Linda Luschei Hunio
1958-1994
and
for all who love the Black Hills

CONTENTS

The ground got very high at last, when we suddenly came to a steep pitch, from the top of which is one of the most splendid views I have seen. The whole valley of "Old Woman" Creek spread out at our feet bounded by steep crags, high rounded hills covered with pine, & in the distance the haven of our hopes "The Black Hills[.]" The country is most lovely, & I don't blame the Indians for wishing to hold on to it.

Colonel Richard Irving Dodge, 1875

Prologue

They rose off on the edge of sight in a bluish haze—the Hills, we called them. Sometimes they loomed black as thunderheads, a dark bulge on the horizon. From the backyard of early childhood, from my altitude of three feet, I had an unobstructed view of them from the rim of our little town. They called out to me across the intervening expanse, a dusty saucer of the South Dakota plains.

We longed for our excursions there, my big brother and little sister and I. We knew the Black Hills were holy ground. Within their sheltering valleys stood the log cabin built by the men in our family, the site of my earliest memories. As we neared the cabin we always counted the bridges along the way: first the high bridge, then the pigtail, a thrilling milepost, and on to seven, eight, all the way to thirteen, and there we were at our cabin, surrounded by tall pines on a terrace overlooking French Creek. When the lightning flashed and thunder reverberated through that granite canyon, we knew the meaning of awe.

We had two summers there before our father died and we had to leave our tiny prairie town. To this day the cabin he left to us remains, substantially unchanged; the alterations have taken place in me. As a small boy I never dreamed that on the Pine Ridge Reservation, just down the road, other children might be gazing at that dark rim from a different angle, or that only a little farther to the east a Lakota holy man was telling the story that would become *Black Elk Speaks*. Sometimes in winter the dark-skinned people, needy and poor, would come to our town in their wagons. If they came to our door, my parents would give them food. To me they were just "Indians." I never connected them with the Hills.

No such innocence could be claimed for George Armstrong Custer in 1874 when he entered those forbidden mountains with ten companies of the Seventh Cavalry, two companies of infantry, and more than a dozen wagons. He brought along two geologists, a zoologist, an engineer, and a botanist, as well as two practical miners, a photographer, and five newspaper correspondents.

Why such a large force, and why invade the very heart of Sioux territory? The Fort Laramie Treaty of 1868 specified that only "officers, agents, and employes of the government," in the discharge of their official duties, were authorized to enter the Black Hills. An Episcopal bishop had warned Custer against going. Custer's purpose ostensibly was to find a site for a military post in the region, but why the miners, the correspondents? Rumors of gold, of course, had long hovered over the Black Hills. To settle such matters, ventured the *Army and Navy Journal,* the expedition might clear up "the only mysterious site of great size" left in the United States.

Mysterious, yes. Lying off the main road west, the Black Hills were deeply shrouded in legend. Approached from the surrounding prairies, they loomed dark and brooding, an island rising from the plains. Less spectacular and more intimate than the Rockies or the Sierra, yet majestic and truly mountains, they had been constructed slowly, on a smaller, more human scale, and they were ancient, mellowed, old, old, older than the Alps or the Himalayas. Geologically distinct, mineralogically perhaps the most diverse area for its size in the world, these mountains had only a brief recorded history, a history marked by desperate conflict. Their treasures were the prime cause for the bloodiest war between the plains Indians and the advancing whites.

The Custer expedition's only contact with Indians was peaceful, even picturesque. Coming upon lodgepoles and a still smoldering fire, Custer expected trouble ahead. Instead his scouts found only a small hunting party of Lakotas, an encampment of five lodges along the floor of a beautiful valley. The Indians had no idea any whites were in the area. One of them, the daughter of the fearless Red Cloud himself, appealed to Custer: her store of coffee and sugar had run out. In a gesture of friendship, Custer had the Indian ponies laden with coffee, sugar, pork, and hardtack, but, fearing revenge from his Arikara scouts, the Lakotas slipped away. The promise of that encounter was blighted a few days later by discovery of the yellow metal that Indians said made the white man crazy: gold. The miners found a few grains of glitter on French Creek, and soon the news was trumpeted to the world. Within a year the Hills were crawling with prospectors. Where the Lakota Sioux saw in their *Paha Sapa* a source of food and spiritual sustenance, enterprising whites saw fabulous wealth, wonders epitomizing the American Dream. That clash of interests brought war.

The changes I myself underwent as I grew up came with an increasing awareness that the Hills I knew had been prized by others. I occupied a position of privilege; I'd lost my right to childhood innocence. Trying to sort it out over the years, the rights and wrongs of it, shadowed always by unmistakable injustice, I found confusion. Who *owned* the Black Hills? Many books had been written on the conflict, some of them very good books, but always partial, focusing on one aspect or another, or split down the middle—cowboys, or Indians? No single volume attempted to tell the whole story.

As time went on I became caught up in the conflict between my love of the Black Hills and a value I had learned growing up: a sense of fair play. And the Hills themselves, I wondered, what might their fate be under the pressure of escalating development? More and more I wrestled with those questions while engaged with domestic cares and the challenge of earning a livelihood. For years I'd wanted idly to do a book on the Black Hills. When I mentioned that to an old-timer, he said sharply, "Then you'd better get on with it!" I heard him. So for twenty years or more, amid the storms and struggles of life, I undertook to sift the available facts to find the story.

The Black Hills have been settled by whites for more than a century, but bitterness over their expropriation remains. The conflict is reflected in the monuments for which the Black Hills are renowned— Mount Rushmore, with its four presidents carved in granite, and the immense, uncompleted Crazy Horse astride his horse. In 1973 the clash helped trigger armed confrontation and the occupation of Wounded Knee by the American Indian Movement. In the following year the U. S. Court of Claims awarded the Sioux seventeen million dollars, plus interest, for the loss, a sum now exceeding six hundred million. The Supreme Court, while deploring the government's past dealings, affirmed the judgment. Yet the tribe, which occupies some of the poorest counties in the United States, refuses cash and continues calling for return of *Paha Sapa.*

In 1977 a mortal threat to the Hills surfaced in a book published by the federal government, the *North Central Power Study.* That menace brought together ranchers, Indians, and environmentalists, briefly, to thwart the designs of energy companies, who were heedlessly punching holes in search of uranium, proposing to ring the Hills with coal-fired power plants. No one wanted the Black Hills to become a "National Sacrifice Area," a region to be laid waste to supply electric power for distant cities.

The long struggle for the Black Hills between Indian and white epitomizes the core issues in settlement of the continent—American history in microcosm, much of it untold. Today that struggle constitutes the most formidable challenge of indigenous peoples to the immigrant population, proclaimed again and again, sometimes in shrill tones. The shrillest voices hurl charges of genocide, claiming possession since time immemorial. Countering voices, muted and often intimidated, ignore such claims, or scoff at them and fall back on "rcs judicata," a case already settled, or simply allude to "controversy."

Chief Seattle, in his eloquent farewell, prophesied that the white man would never be alone on conquered ground, but always accompanied by the invisible dead, the spirits of those there earlier. The Black Hills are not free of such visitants. Aggravating the conflict, the living parties scarcely talk to one another, forthrightly, or they talk past each other. Denial prevails, shrouded in misconceptions and ignorance.

The story of the Black Hills has never really been told, not in all its fullness—the larger story, apart from one facet, one point of view or another. Who could truly master all the elements involved, many of them scattered fragments based upon myth or speculation or biased testimony? The encompassing story too often must be imperfectly constructed from bits and pieces here, fragments there, selected in good faith from those sources judged to be most reliable, and critically examined.

So we have the tragic story of the Lakota Sioux, descendants of the Buffalo People who came out of the earth in their *Paha Sapa*, living in harmony with all creation until greedy whites stole their sacred mountains and herded them onto reservations. We have the triumphant story of heroic pioneers braving the hardships of frontier life and the wrath of "savages" to found a civilization in their land of heart's desire, the story of prospectors willing to risk everything in search of gold, of troops answering the call in defense of their countrymen. And we have the story of the poor wounded earth, scarred and pillaged by men and machines, now threatened by the pressure of more use and visitors than it can accommodate.

The old stories no longer work. This book is an attempt to tell the larger story, from the beginnings down to the present day. An impossible task, no doubt, but worth the attempt if you share the view of historian William Cronon: "We tell stories **with** each other and **against** each other in order to speak **to** each other."

PART ONE

Chapter 1: Beginnings

In the heart of the Southern Hills, where a stream snakes its way eastward through rocks half as old as the earth itself, stands a pegmatite knob frequented by bighorn sheep. This mound of coarse granite is a good place to start, if you want to get a feel for these mountains. From its modest summit the valley makes a loop two hundred feet below, the first in a series of crescents nesting one within another as the stream winds back on itself in the course it has cut over tens of millions of years. Winter is the time to go there, after a fresh snowfall. Turning to survey the prospect, you find yourself encompassed by one snowy range after another, pristine white to the last furry frieze standing out against vivid blue. In the hush over all, and the hush is total, you have a sense of why old Black Elk said power works in a circle and everything tries to be round.

Contemplating this snow-laden hoop of the world, you find it hard to believe the underlying granite once boiled in the earth's innards. As the snow melts, the somber green of the pines emerges, puncturing the white cloak. For a wider view of the terrain suppose we call on the power of wings—the eagle, say, to lift us on the wings of imagination to a height from which we can behold what lies below. From the eagle's realm we see that our little hoop is lodged near the southern end of a long heart-shaped dome bulging from the earth's surface, a forested island rising from a tawny expanse. Not far to the north an irregular gray ridge rises above its surroundings, the ancient core of the uplift. Beyond it the dome extends a hundred miles, tilting westward. Soaring high over the ridge, we can see a smaller oval bulging to the west on the far side of an invisible line in what we call Wyoming. Set off to the northeast stands an unobtrusive crest. From higher yet we see that the dome is flanked to north and south by rivers connecting on the east, like a cottonwood leaf joining at the tip. Around the ellipse of the dome extends a hogback ridge inside of which runs a band of red the Sioux and the Cheyennes knew as the racetrack, the setting for one of their creation myths.

On a clear day we can make out, far off to the west, the loftier ranges allied to the Rocky Mountains. To the east stands the multicolored wall of the Badlands and the great Missouri itself, and the big loop where it doubles back on itself twice, the Grand Detour encountered by Lewis and Clark, where their keelboat had to journey thirty miles to gain one. To the south, beyond the Niobrara or Running Water, lie the remains of the Great Platte River Road—the Oregon Trail.

Now we have entered *history*, as humans experience history. But to observe the Black Hills from such a height only deepens the mystery of their origins. How comes it to **be**, this verdant island in the plains? Why this vibrant green amid the buff and brown?

We might ask the first peoples. A Lakota legend traces the formation of these mountains to the Great Race, a tremendous, earth-shaking event to which all the animals of the earth were summoned for a competition to establish order out of predatory chaos. Gathering on the prairie, the animals joined in a race around a course laid out for them. The earth shuddered and groaned beneath their weight and pounding hooves until the ground subsided, causing a majestic pile of rocks to rise inside the track—*Paha Sapa*, the Black Hills. The blood from all the wounded feet left a band of red encircling the Hills.[1]

Geologists tell a different story.[2] The Black Hills have long fascinated them, though their findings have seldom been translated into language accessible to a lay audience. Here now, as we circle aloft, we might turn the clock back an eon or two, advancing by time-lapse photography to quicken the dawdling processes of geology, and witness something like this:

For most of the billion years preceding the first forms of life, the whole area lies beneath a vast inland sea. Molten rock boils deep below the surface while layers of sediment are laid down on the floor of the sea. From time to time—geological time—a bulge forms as the pressing weight of sediment forces magma upward, an alternating process in which a mushroom-like dome emerges from the sea for a few tens of millions of years and then vanishes, a bubble rising and bursting in a viscous stew.

Some hundred and forty million years ago, slowly, in stages, the dome emerges for good. Cooling magma is uplifted in two blocks, some of the oldest rocks ever to surface on the earth, raising an oblong dome two miles above its surroundings. Now as the seas recede, a mere sixty-five million years back, erosion works its way down through the overlying sediments to lay bare the granite core, forming a kind of layer cake, the older strata near the center yielding to successively younger strata near the periphery, leaving a record half the age of the earth.

Nearing the geological present, we find a crystalline core of igneous rock, fire-born, ringed by a zone of metamorphic rock transformed by immense pressure, surrounded in turn by softer layers of sedimentary rock and finally, again, by a looping, irregular ridge. Flowing eastward out of the core, a series of parallel streams cut their way through the ridge, depositing materials in the arid rain shadow of the range, where layers of sediment are dissected to form the Bad Lands. Amid its parched surroundings, the dome of the Black Hills blooms forest green. That smaller green mound to the northwest is their sibling, the Bear Lodge Mountains, just beyond which rises Devils Tower, a source of many tribal legends. To the northeast of the dome stands a more recent igneous intrusion, Bear Butte, a sort of afterthought to the uplift, a mountain sacred to the Cheyennes. From the inside out, the layer cake of the range has been designated the Central Crystalline Area, the Limestone Plateau, the Red Valley, and the Dakota Hogback. On a map, the Black Hills occupy the southwest corner of South Dakota, lapping over into Wyoming, an area some sixty miles wide, east to west, a hundred and twenty north to south.

This compact range, given its long time span, should leave a fossil record of life forms, from the first primordial algae and marine invertebrates up through fish and ferns, mammals and birds, to dinosaurs and mammoths, each in a formation recording its date of birth. And in fact the oldest known evidence of vertebrate life, the fossilized remains of fish, is found in the Deadwood Formation on the western fringe of the Black Hills. Recently unearthed on the southern edge of the Hills are the fossils of great mammoths from the last ice age, one of the most promising mammoth finds anywhere.

An overview during the last thirty or forty million years would show a shifting contest between forest and grassland and, in the most recent two million years, the advance and retreat of the continental glaciers that covered much of the northern hemisphere. The glaciers never quite reached the Black Hills but may have helped produce the unique grasslands complex and a distinct combination forest that mixes eastern and western species of pine. They also split the bird populations isolating eastern species from western, sometimes facilitating an overlapping of the two.

For man the truly fateful element produced by the uplift was the golden necklace around its core, though the commodity that first drew humans into these mountains would not have been precious metal but stone for spear points and arrows. While archeology in the region remains in its infancy, most evidence puts the earliest humans in the Black Hills about eleven thousand years ago—nomadic Paleo-Indians who came over the Bering Land Bridge from Asia during the Ice Age, twelve to forty thousand years ago, though the tribes today contest that view. For a few millennia these nomadic groups moved through the Black Hills area, hunting mammoths and huge prehistoric bison. Clovis sites, kill sites featuring mammoth bones and spear points dating from that period, have been found to the east and west of the uplift. Within the Black Hills proper, the disintegrating portion of a mammoth tusk has turned up, unaccompanied by human artifacts.[3]

About seven thousand years ago, following the last ice age, a climate change widened the subsistence base and the mammoths became extinct, leaving deer and rabbits and the smaller modern bison. Sites from this era contain more and more grinding implements. The warmer and drier climate seems to have diminished use of the uplift, which is not lofty enough to wear a snowcap year round, though recent findings show repeated occupation of a water gap on the eastern fringe, possibly for refuge from drought. The most intense human use of the mountains appears to have come later, with more long-term occupation—winter camps in the milder, more protected Southern Hills, enclaves sheltered from the biting winds.

The Indians, the first peoples, had been in this country long before. Yet what we know of those earlier visitors can mislead the unwary. Too often the facts about Indians, wrote Edwin Thompson Denig in the 1850s, have been gathered by "rude and half-civilized interpreters," or by foreigners who have "passed a winter or two at some of the trading posts in the country, seen an Indian dance or two," and returned to "enlighten Europe" about Indian character with what is "only the product of their own brains and takes its color from the peculiar nature of that organ."

"Hence," observed Denig, a fur trader on the Upper Missouri for more than twenty years who married into the Assiniboine tribe, "we find two sets of writers both equally wrong, one setting forth the Indians as a noble, generous, and chivalrous race far above the standard of Europeans, the other representing them below the level of the brute creation." In a cautionary note Denig added, "The strange sights and occurrences incident to the country, be they ever so truthfully described, are rejected by previously formed opinion, and the narrator stigmatized, even in the mildest language he could expect, as a teller of strange stories."[4]

How much the intervening century and a half has modified such distorted images remains to be seen. The emergence of Native American speakers may not always be helpful with the plains Indians, whose existence was so cruelly disrupted in the nineteenth century. The strategies and tactical plans of the Sioux were frozen in place by the Army. "The real Indians are gone," observed Frank B. Linderman, "and in the writing which will come from their descendants, we shall find difficulty in deciding between truth and falsehood concerning a life the writers could not have known."[5] Where received opinions are handed down as fact, Josh Billings, the Yankee wit, surely had it right: "It is better to know nothing than to know what ain't so."

Recent discoveries in the Southern Hills confirm the presence of native inhabitants along the eastern fringe that go back twenty-five hundred or three thousand years, possibly more than ten thousand. Among the earliest known inhabitants of the Black Hills country in the late prehistoric era were the Kiowas. A contemporary Kiowa, the poet and novelist N. Scott Momaday, offers a fresh perspective on the Black Hills in *The Way to Rainy Mountain*, his tribute to his culture and his grandmother. In this beautiful little book Momaday offers some guidance here, recounting a journey made with "the whole memory, that experience of the mind which is legendary as well as historical, personal as well as cultural."[6]

A mountain people of hunters, the Kiowas came into the world through a hollow log, according to their origin myth. They were small in number because when a pregnant woman became stuck the rest of them were unable to get out. Migrating eastward from the headwaters of the Yellowstone in the late seventeenth century, the Kiowas found their nomadic soul set free when they emerged upon the plains. Their first sighting of the Black Hills must have been of Devils Tower. "There are things in nature," says Momaday, "that engender an awful quiet in the heart of man." Kiowa legend envisioned Devil's Tower as the stump of a great tree clawed by a bear pursuing seven sisters who escaped to the sky, where they became the stars in the Big Dipper.

When they moved onto the plains, the Kiowas befriended the

Crows, a Siouan tribe descended from hunting people who had drifted down from the northern woodlands. The Crows taught them new ways. Along with the plains religion the Kiowas acquired Tai-me, their sacred Sun Dance doll, and a sense of destiny. Like the Cheyennes, they drew religious power from Bear Butte. They acquired horses and became fine horsemen and warriors. By 1682, on the testimony of the French explorer La Salle, the Kiowas had many horses, "probably stolen from Mexico," though they may in fact have acquired them by trade from the Lipan Apaches, who got them from the Pueblos after the Pueblo revolt of 1680. They lived east of the Crows in the Black Hills region with a small tribe of Kiowa-Apaches who had come down with them from the Montana mountains.[7]

Did the Kiowas truly *live* in the Black Hills, reside there within the uplift itself? Like other tribes to come, they made hunting forays into the mountains, perhaps sought shelter from time to time in the foothills. But the Kiowas "reckoned their stature by the distance they could see," notes Momaday, "and they were bent and blind in the [mountain] wilderness. . . . The sun is at home on the plains. Precisely there does it have the certain character of a god."[8]

About 1775, after a century or so in the area, they were driven out of the Black Hills by the Sioux or the Cheyennes. An entire band of Kiowas whose chief urged them to stand and fight was exterminated by the Sioux. The tribe drifted south to Oklahoma, where with the Comanches they dominated the southern plains for a century. But the buffalo represented the sun for them in the Sun Dance, and with the destruction of the wild herds the Kiowa will was broken. Their culture withered and died—perhaps the last culture to evolve in North America.[9]

The Crows were a Siouan people descended from the Hidatsas, who in the mid-sixteenth century lived in the "land of the lakes" of Manitoba. Migrating south and west, both tribes settled along the Missouri with the Mandans near the mouth of the Heart River, where they pursued a sedentary life. The Crows separated from the Hidatsas after a fight and moved west to the buffalo plains beyond the Black Hills.

Their origin story features Old Man Coyote, who creates the land out of a little mud brought to him from deep in a watery world by Hell-diver, a duck. Lonely, Old Man Coyote molds an image he likes from earth and breathes life into it—a man. The man comes first and will be first in all things. Still unsatisfied, Old Man Coyote fashions a better image—woman, who is to maintain the man's home while he is at war or off on the hunt. When a big fight develops and each of two mothers defends her son, Old Man Coyote divides the camp into groups made up of the children of each mother, held together like driftwood lodges. The succession is thus matrilineal.

A small tribe like the Kiowas, the Crows were all but constantly at war, outnumbered and usually defensive, but fierce. Always friendly with the whites, they were attracted to the religion brought them by Father De Smet, the legendary Jesuit who evangelized among the Indians in the mid-nineteenth century. In 1841 De Smet conducted a religious seminar for a large Crow encampment along the Yellowstone River. He promised to send them the "Blackrobes" they requested.

The Crows took their cue from that little black-capped bird, the Chickadee, who appeared in a dream to Plenty Coups, the last of the great Crow chiefs. Plenty Coups said the Chickadee taught him to be willing to work for wisdom. The Chickadee tends to his own affairs but listens, and never misses a chance to learn from others, both how they succeed and how they fail. Power, Plenty Coups decided, comes not from bodily strength but from mind.[10]

By the 1780s the Crows were engaging in raid and counter-raid with the Lakota Sioux. When they killed two Lakotas who were stealing horses from a Crow camp, troubles worsened. The Lakotas soon forced the hated Crows out of the Black Hills country, driving them west beyond the Powder River.[11]

Another early tribe moving in and out of the Black Hills was the Arapahos. Typical Plains Indians, they had come originally from woodland peoples to the east. The Arapahos were Algonquians of the same linguistic family as the Powhatans and the Crees. They shared the same deity, Manitou, whom they called Man-Above. Forced onto the plains perhaps by hostile tribes, they may have been agriculturists before they crossed the Missouri to become the Bison Path People. They too became sun worshipers whose life on the plains depended on the buffalo.

One Arapaho cycle story concerns Found-in-Grass, who caused the buffalo to issue from a hole in the ground. All was water, their creation myth holds, until Flat-Pipe the Earthmaker shaped the world and living creatures out of clay brought from the depths by a turtle. Flat-Pipe first made the Arapahos, goes their account, and then the other Indians and finally, "beyond the waters," the white man.[12]

The Arapahos had probably migrated to the Northern Plains by the seventeenth century or earlier. Until the close of the eighteenth they led a wandering life untouched by European civilization, roaming widely to hunt buffalo. They spent the long winter months along the headwaters of streams on the eastern slopes of the Rockies, eventually splitting into Northern and Southern bands. When they encountered the Cheyennes in the Black Hills, the Arapahos considered them enemies at first and sought to exterminate them, but then, recognizing a kinship as fellow Algonquians, accepted them as friends. The Arapahos were initially friendly to whites, but by 1830 the Northern Arapahos in the Black Hills region were threatening the life of any white man who ventured west of Chimney Rock, a hundred miles to the south on the Oregon Trail. Frequenting campgrounds in the Medicine Bow area of southwestern Wyoming, they left trails through the Laramie Mountains on their way to and from the Black Hills that are still visible. Ultimately, most of them followed the Kiowas southward, where in 1864 some Arapahos encamped with their friends the Cheyennes were slaughtered in the infamous Sand Creek Massacre.[13]

The Cheyennes, another tribe of the Algonquian family, came from far to the east, where they had once lived in established villages, cultivating the soil. Cheyenne tradition tells of living on the edge of a great body of water, most likely one of the Great Lakes, before migrating west to a flat country around the Red River. Driven further west by tribes possessing firearms, they crossed the Missouri and worked their way out onto the plains. There they met a band of the Suhtais, who spoke a variant of their language, and joined with them as one tribe. Drifting west, some Cheyenne bands encountered such abundance along streams running from the Black Hills that in time most of the tribe was drawn there.[14]

The area became their spiritual homeland, the center of their wanderings, which ranged from west of the Black Hills to the Missouri and from the Little Missouri to the Arkansas. Like the Arapahos, they split into Northern and Southern bands. Like the Sioux, they had a legend of the race around the Black Hills. "That race," says John Stands In Timber, the late keeper of Cheyenne oral literature, "gave mankind the right to use animal flesh for food and to be the master . . . . If the animals had won they would have lived on his flesh instead."[15]

The sacred mountain of the Cheyennes to this day remains Bear Butte, where Sweet Medicine, their prophet and culture hero, is believed to have found the Four Sacred Arrows. Traditionally the Cheyennes have been a very religious people. All the plains tribes, says Father Peter J. Powell, had "profound spiritual depths in the older sacred ceremonies, with their constant theme that man's vocation is to live in harmony with the creator and with creation as a whole," but of them all the Cheyennes "most completely centered their lives" on those ceremonies. Their creation tale has similarities with the Arapahos', but the story of Sweet Medicine is specifically connected with the Black Hills. As told in recent times, it shows strong parallels with Judaism and Christianity.[16]

Sweet Medicine was born to a young virgin, conceived in a sequence of dreams. As a boy he performed miracles, but after hitting an old man, knocking him unconscious, Sweet Medicine was sent into exile. During his exile he traveled "deep into the heart of the Black Hills country," where he seems to have been called by some great power. He came to Noahvose, the Holy Mountain, known today as Bear Butte. There he entered a lodge within the mountain where he found the Four Sacred Arrows, where gods in the forms of old men and women taught him the ceremonies and the ways of ordering good tribal government.[17]

Along with the Sacred Arrows, Sweet Medicine brought the ceremonies to his people, especially the ceremony of renewing the arrows, required if one Cheyenne ever killed another. Murder was to be punished by banishment, a law that kept feuding to a minimum and may have given Cheyenne society greater stability than was enjoyed by other plains tribes that had not achieved the same measure of control.[18]

Sweet Medicine lived a long time. When he was old and helpless and knew he must die, he called the people together. Enjoining them to remember what he had taught them, he left them an ominous prediction: A time of great change was coming. Light-colored strangers would appear among them, Earth Men, with powerful ways. "Follow nothing that these Earth Men do," he told them, "but keep your own ways." The buffalo would disappear, to be replaced by "a slick animal with a long tail and split hoofs, whose flesh you will learn to eat." They would need to use another animal with round hooves that could carry them long distances. But in time, he was sorry to say, their ways would change. "You will leave your religion for something new. . . . You will lose track of your relations and marry women from your own families. You will take after the Earth Men's ways and forget good things by which you have lived and in the end become worse than crazy."[19]

In the popular mind the world over, the typical North American Indian is the mounted warrior of the plains, clad in a loincloth or in full regalia. Of them all, the one that comes most readily to mind is the tribe of Red Cloud, Sitting Bull, and Crazy Horse—the valiant and warlike Sioux. More precisely the Lakotas, a division within the tribe, the Teton or Western Sioux. The prevailing stereotype hinders any attempt to see the people behind the image, but the *Ikce Oyate*, or Real People, as the

Lakotas call themselves, are inseparable from Black Hills history, and we need to see them clearly.

Testimony of the Lakotas reveals a powerful connection with the Hills. Luther Standing Bear, a Lakota chief who returned to the Pine Ridge Reservation in 1931 after an absence of sixteen years, extols that relationship in *Land of the Spotted Eagle:* "Of all our domain," he says, we loved, perhaps, the Black Hills the most. . . .

> In wooded recesses were numberless springs of pure water and numerous small lakes. There were wood and game in abundance and shelter from the storms of the plains. It was the favorite winter haunt of the buffalo and the Lakota as well. According to a tribal legend these hills were a reclining female figure from whose breasts flowed life-giving forces, and to them the Lakota went as a child to its mother's arms.[20]

Gifted with highly articulate writers and orators, and the center of interest to a wider audience, the Lakotas have been the most talked about of all Indian peoples. Their mythology has captivated thousands. Oral tradition holds that they originated within the Black Hills, the Heart of Everything That Is, where they dwelt underground as the Buffalo People, the *Pte Oyate*, until they were enticed onto the surface and migrated outward from there.

A good avenue into the Lakota way is *Black Elk Speaks*, the remarkable life story of a Lakota holy man told through John Neihardt, a white poet, in 1931. *Black Elk Speaks* is more than just a Lakota story; it may be the most influential document of its kind. To the generation of young Indians searching for roots of their own today, asserts Vine Deloria, Jr., the Hunkpapa scholar and unofficial dean of American Indian intellectuals, the book has become a "North American bible of all tribes." Deloria believes the principal works of the Black Elk theological tradition "bid fair to become the canon or at least the central core of a North American Indian theological canon which will someday challenge the Eastern and Western traditions as a way of looking at the world."[21]

Black Elk's long life, from 1863 to 1950, spanned a period of profound change for the Lakotas, from free life on the plains to confinement on the Pine Ridge Reservation. In the Lakota narrative scheme outlined by the anthropologist Ella Deloria, Vine Deloria's aunt, *Black Elk Speaks* would fall under the category of *woyakapi*, stories accepted as actual happenings of comparatively recent times, "occurrences that may happen to someone aided by supernatural powers." Stories that include fictional elements would be *ohunkakan*, some of which, the "real *ohunkakan,*" are situated in a mythic past—tales intended to amuse and entertain, but not to be believed."[22]

Historical evidence identifies the Lakotas as the advance guard of seven Sioux bands moving south from the headwaters of the Mississippi and then out into territory occupied by other tribes on the Great Plains. When the French first encountered them in a region of lakes and marshes around the Mille Lacs in northern Minnesota, the Sioux traveled in bark canoes and subsisted partly on wild rice. In the late seventeenth century, attacked by the Chippewas, or Ojibwas, who had obtained firearms, they were driven from the woods. The Lakota bands led the way, followed by the Dakotas and Nakotas, the other Sioux dialect groups. Lured by the abundance of buffalo and the promise of the beaver trade, they moved south and west onto the prairies east of the Missouri, beginning a sustained movement into country occupied by other tribes.[23]

By the time they appeared on the Minnesota prairies, the Lakotas were armed with guns from the French. They followed the buffalo during the summer and trapped beaver in winter, traveling to the trade fairs in spring. By the late eighteenth century they had become the dominant trappers and traders on the prairies east of the Missouri and had depleted the populations of buffalo and beaver. Notwithstanding the fierce reputation they acquired later, the Lakotas "were no conquerors," says George Hyde, when they first came down into the great valley of the Missouri, "but poor people afoot in the vast plains." They had yet to acquire horses.[24] As buffalo robes replaced beaver pelts as items of fashion, their need for horses became pressing. Most likely they obtained horses from raids on the Arikaras. Then as they prepared to migrate further west, they found themselves blocked by those same powerful Arikaras, who prospered in fortified villages along the Missouri.

Lakota hunting parties nevertheless made forays into the west. It is generally accepted that at about the time of the American Revolution a party of the Oglala band ventured far enough west to discover the Black Hills, though Lakota creation stories say they originated there.[25] For a time the Lakotas settled with the Arikaras and began to adopt their horticultural economy, but their evolution into sedentary villagers was cut short by the arrival of European traders and European diseases even as the buffalo enticed them westward, fortunately, because the smallpox epidemics introduced by the whites—deliberately at times, by some accounts—devastated the villages along the Missouri. The Arikaras, Mandans, and Hidatsas were reduced to a desperately weakened remnant. Wandering in small groups, the Lakotas were less susceptible to the contagion. They drove the other tribes farther north. When the surviving

Arikaras moved back downriver, they became virtual serfs of the Lakotas. By the turn of the century the Lakotas had crossed the Missouri and were contesting the plains out toward the Black Hills with the Kiowas, Arapahos, Crows, and Cheyennes.[26]

By 1804, when the Lewis and Clark expedition was launched, the reputation of the Sioux had reached Washington. Jefferson's instructions to Meriwether Lewis were explicit: "On that nation we wish most particularly to make a friendly impression, because of their immense power, and because we learn they are very desirous of being on the most friendly terms with us." After a challenging encounter with the Sicangu Lakotas—or Brulés, as they are widely known—who controlled the Missouri above the Big Bend, Captain Clark came to a harsher view of the Lakotas: "the vilest miscreants of the savage race." They would remain "the pirates of the Missouri" until they were reduced to dependence on the government for their supply of merchandise. Until then, citizens of the United States could never fully enjoy the advantages presented by the Missouri. Coercion would be required. "Persuasion or advice, with them is viewed as supplication, and only tends to inspire them with contempt for those who offer either."[27]

The Lakotas had become known for harassing traders, pilfering merchandise, and demanding gifts of merchants coming upriver from St. Louis. The Yankton Sioux downriver, a tribe distinct from the Lakotas, had warned Lewis and Clark that "those nations above will not open their ears." In private, Jefferson himself had confessed that in its new western lands the United States was "miserably weak." The negotiation with the Lakotas, with all its tangled complexities, may have been the most demanding piece of Indian diplomacy assigned to Lewis and Clark.[28]

In the interest of St. Louis traders the expedition was determined to make direct contact with the villages upriver. The Lakotas, who as middlemen profited by control of European goods to the villagers, saw the expedition as a threat. The two parties met where the Bad River joins the Missouri, on the site of present-day Pierre. Without an adequate interpreter, and utterly naïve about rivalries within the tribe, Lewis and Clark made the classical error, standard practice in government attempts to deal with Indians, of selecting their own "chief."

When the client chief's rival jostled Captain Clark, warning him the expedition must not proceed further, Clark "felt My self warm and Spoke in verry positive terms." Drawing his sword, he informed the Indians that his men "were not squaws but warriors." Lewis had the swivel guns aboard the keelboat readied to fire. Bloodshed was only narrowly averted.

Three days later, on the expedition's departure, a confrontation again brought trouble as the client chief and his rival each sought to vindicate his personal claim to authority within the tribe. In the end, a bloody clash was averted with a carrot of tobacco. Having failed in their mission to advance friendly relations, Lewis and Clark continued upriver, unaware that the final moments of the encounter were less a conflict between Indians and American explorers than "a tussle between rival band headmen."[29]

The Lakotas pushed out onto the plains west of the Missouri in seven bands—Oglala, Sicangu, Minnecoujou, Siha Sapa, Itazipko, Oohenumpa, and Hunkpapa. Prospering, obtaining horses, roving widely to hunt buffalo and fighting enemies on all sides, they gained population rapidly. Their reputation for daring and success began attracting the "bolder spirits" from Sioux bands lingering east of the Missouri, says George Hyde, and the Oglalas "soon learned to love their new home with its high, dry, and windy plains—a hard country where men had to be fully alive to avoid perishing."[30]

The conventional view that history on the Great Plains was one continuous process of Indians driven from their homelands by the remorseless advance of whites fits poorly with what actually happened during this period. Only in the 1840s, when white migration turned the Platte River valley into the American road west, did the whites come to pose a significant threat to Lakota interests. After their initial conflict the Lakotas found the Americans "useful, if dangerous allies." No tribe ever manifested "a greater degree of friendship for the whites in general, or more respect for our Government, than the Sioux," observed the American agent for the Upper Missouri in 1838. For most tribes of the north and central plains—Pawnee, Mandan, Hidatsa, Crow, Omaha, and others— the "crucial invasion" during this period, says Richard White, "was not necessarily that of the whites. . . . These tribes had few illusions about American whites and the danger they presented, but the Sioux remained their most feared enemy."[31]

The final phase of the Lakota advance south and west began with their struggle to wrest the area between the Missouri and the Black Hills from the Arapahos, the Crows, the Kiowas, and the Cheyennes. The Oglalas and Sicangus drove the Kiowas south and the Crows west. Ultimately the Lakotas formed an alliance with the Cheyennes and Arapahos that would dominate the north and central plains for half a century. The Lakotas, "who by the 1850s were mourning their own dispossession," one historian observes, "forced others into the mountains as they fought to control the bison herds on the northern plains." As the buffalo were slaughtered in ever greater numbers, the Lakotas followed the diminishing herds beyond the Black Hills into the Platte River country, where in 1833, to capture their trade, the Rocky Mountain Fur Company established the post in southeastern Wyoming that became Fort Laramie.[32]

George Hyde, who has chronicled more of their history than anyone, places the golden age of the Lakotas from about 1805 to 1835. "They were now plentifully supplied with horses, game abounded in their territory, the camps were usually overflowing with fresh and dried meat, and the call to come and feast was heard all day long." From the Oglala camps the Black Hills were almost always within view. The winter camps were sheltered in stream valleys near the eastern edge the Hills. "[S]ometimes the people went into the mountain valleys to hunt deer and elk or to cut lodge-poles; but *Pa Sapa*, the Black Hills, were sacred ground, the heart of the Teton land, where people did not often venture to camp." Citing Lakota names and legends relating to the Black Hills—the Race Track, the Bear's Lodge, Buffalo Gate—Hyde sounds an elegiac tone: "A whole epoch in the life of the Tetons has been lost through the failure to record in writing at an earlier date the tale of the Sioux migration to the Black Hills and their early life in that region."[33]

Chapter 2: Contact

"There was things which he stretched, but mainly he told the truth," says the most famous boy in American literature about his creator. Huck Finn's remark about Mark Twain applies to many an early account of adventures in the Black Hills. The storyteller falls into the "traveller's habit of drawing a long bow," as a historian once observed of John Smith: "In the narration of incidents that had occurred in his own wild life, [Captain Smith] had an aptitude for being intensely interesting; and it seemed to be his theory that if the original facts were not in themselves quite so interesting as they should have been, so much the worse for the original facts."[1]

That observation often applies with force on questions involving the Black Hills. Some of the stories sound a little *too* interesting. The wary listener needs to catch nuances of tone, to watch for a telltale crack in the storyteller's deadpan face.

"Long, long ago," goes a white man's legend concocted in Deadwood during the gold rush, "when the oldest man now living had not yet been born, there came from the Land of the Morning Sun a band of white men in search of gold." They traveled for many moons over prairie and through forest until at last, from a high place, they beheld the Valley of the Beautiful River, beyond which, glistening in the sun, rose the peaks of the *Paha Sapa*. "Then were their hearts glad, for this was the land of their desire." But in the valley they came upon a village of red men stricken by disease and famine, which melted their hearts with pity. They fed and warmed the red men. A great medicine man among the whites cured his red brothers, leaving them well and strong.

The whites went on their way to the land of gold, but among the red men was one whose heart was bad, angry that his own medicine had been of no avail against the sickness. He whispered in the people's ears that if the pale faces were allowed to leave the mountains, taking gold with them, they would return in great numbers to drive the red men from their hunting grounds. So with tomahawk and knife the whites were murdered in their sleep, their bodies burned to ashes.

"Then was the Great Spirit angered," goes the legend. He sent thunder and lightning, and winds that carried the white men's ashes far and wide. The red men fled from his wrath onto the plains, henceforth forbidden to enter the *Paha Sapa*. "Never more might the Indian hunter pursue the elk or deer in their fastnesses; never again build his campfire in the beautiful parks or trap the beaver along the streams. To the place of the sinking of the waters [the eastern foothills] he might go, but no farther." The Great Spirit, his wrath appeased, sent rain to the earth, "and wherever the ashes of the pale faces had found a resting place sprang up and blossomed in beauty the wild rose."[2]

The wild rose does indeed bloom throughout the Black Hills, but this "Legend of the Roses" calls for reflection. Apparently written by a Deadwood attorney and reproduced from memory by a leading early journalist, it offers what Watson Parker has called a "semitheological background" for the fear of Black Hills thunder and lightning often attributed to the Indians by whites—the sort of legend "quickly seized upon and nurtured by white men who were eager to possess [the Hills.]"[3] Anyone who has experienced the lightning and heard thunder crackling and rumbling over the Black Hills knows why man or woman can be awestruck, but this legend is pure hokum. It sanctions the digging of gold as a perfect good and provides warrant for excluding Indians from the Black Hills. Beneath the patronizing tone is a touch of guilt.

An earlier counter-legend related by Edwin Denig was attributed to the Lakotas: The principal peak, the Hill of Thunder, was volcanic, and in 1833 was almost constantly active. On most any clear day huge volumes of smoke billowed from it, believed by Indians to be the breathing of the Big White Man buried beneath. The unnatural noises they heard were thought to be the moans of the Great White Giant, weighed down by rocks as punishment for invading their territory. He issued forth on occasion, leaving tracks in the snow twenty feet in length, but the Indians believed he was condemned to perpetual incarceration under the mountain as an example to all whites to leave the Indians in quiet possession of their hunting grounds.[4]

Here again, a legend suggests an underlying motive, but the wish-fulfillment embodied in this one predates the Gold Rush by more than twenty years—clearly a response to earlier white incursions.

The first white men believed to have seen the Black Hills were the La Vérendrye brothers, François and Joseph, in search of a land route to the Pacific. In 1742, perhaps escorted by Mandan guides, they arrived at a "Mountain of the Horse Indians," presumably Bear Butte, from which they traveled southwestward, apparently through the Black Hills.[5]

These first incursions by white explorers are more fully documented than those of previous inhabitants, though their accounts are often vague. A story of "Shining Mountains" that sparkled and glowed in the sun was told by Jonathan Carver after a long journey he claimed to have made through the West in 1766-68, a tale giving rise to the legend of a crystal mountain in frontier folklore. Carver may possibly have intended to describe the Black Hills. In 1874 Professor A. B. Donaldson, with the Custer expedition, noted that the shales on the mountains sometimes glistened like silver. A report of mysterious booming noises in the Hills was related to Lewis and Clark in 1804 by Jean Vallé, a trader-trapper who had spent the previous winter in the Black Mountains—clearly the Black Hills, from his description. Vallé found the Hills abounding in mountain sheep, with peaks he claimed could be snow-capped all summer. Other voyageurs told of "mysterious boomings and bangings." Even the presence of gold in the Black Hills, the "discovery" of which created a sensation many years later, was reported in 1804 to the lieutenant governor of Louisiana in a letter from Régis Loisel that mentions nuggets to be found in the Costa Negra.[6]

Wilson Price Hunt and the Astorians, traveling overland, passed near the Black Hills in 1811. The account later written by Washington Irving speaks of a singular "natural phenomenon" occurring in even the most serene weather: "successive reports . . . now and then heard among these mountains, resembling the discharge of several pieces of artillery," reports that remained "one of the lingering mysteries of nature." The nomadic prairie tribes, wrote Irving, considered the Black Hills "the abode of the genii or thunder-spirits who fabricate storms and tempests." With amusement Irving recounts an incident in which a greenhorn member of the party, pursued by a grizzly, passes the night in a tree, "a prey to dismal fantasies." In the end, encountering great difficulty in negotiating the canyons, most of which ended in "a wild chaos of rocks and cliffs, impossible to penetrate or avoid," the Astorians simply bypassed the uplift itself, but this account by the most celebrated

American writer of the day served to publicize the Black Hills and further invest them with mystery.[7]

The first party of whites that actually passed through the Black Hills was Jedediah Smith's in 1823, recorded by another mountain man, James Clyman. Looking back half a century later, Clyman appears to have remembered creatively. A man of thirty-one with some education, and often original spelling, Clyman had read his Shakespeare. Of the "crew" he had collected in the "grog Shops and other sinks of degredation" in St. Louis, he declined to offer a "discription," but observed that "Fallstafs Battalion was genteel in comparison."

Clyman tells of a clash along the Missouri between the Arikaras and an American regiment backed by seven or eight hundred Sioux Indians. At one point, he says, the plain covered with Indians "going in all possible directions" looked "more like a swarm [of] bees than a battle field." Relating his own narrow escape from pursuing Arikaras, Clyman launches into an account of Indians taking scalps, hacking off enemy hands and feet. Then he abruptly breaks off to say "I will not tire you with details of the savage habit of Indians to their enimies but I will merely state that it is easy to make a savage of a civilised man but impossible to make a civilised man of a savage in one Generation."

Clyman tells of a later, peaceful encounter with Sicangus and Oglalas on the Bad River, where his party traded with them for horses. At the "foot of the black Hills" he recalls the party entering "a pleasant undulating pine Region cool and refreshing," but encountering "rocky inaccessible places" and running afoul of a "grissly Baare." The grizzly attacked Jedediah Smith, taking his head in its mouth, leaving the skull bare, one ear hanging only by its "outer rim." With needle and thread Clyman says he stitched the ear back in place.

Proceeding up French Creek through a "narrow Kenyon" known today as the Gorge, Clyman reported "immence cliffs of the most pure and Beautifull black smooth and shining [slate] and perhaps five hundred to one thousand feet high." One of his companions remarked that "here or at some such place Mosses . . . must have obtaind the plates or tables on which the declogue was inscirobed." Clyman discovered "Quite a grove of Petrifid timber [of which] one stub in Perticular [was] so high that I could barely lay my hand on the top sitting in the saddle."

Here we can observe the genesis of a tall tale. Clyman's "petrified grove" was mentioned in St. Louis, in the presence of a reporter. Next morning, Clyman wrote in his journal, his "exagerated statement" came out in the newspaper saying "a petrified forest was lately dicovered whare the trees branches leaves and all were perfect and the small birds sitting on them with their mouths open singing at the time of their transformation to stone."[8]

Still another tall tale, bereft of the petrified songbirds, came early in a tradition that has flourished in the Black Hills. This yarn grew out of an explosion in 1832 at Thomas L. Sarpy's trading post at the mouth of Rapid Creek. Sarpy was evidently trading furs secured from the Black Hills and selling gunpowder by candlelight. When the post blew up, old-timers claimed "it rained bear traps for a week," a phenomenon equally as credible as the legend of a stream that ran so fast down Harney Peak that it boiled away before reaching the bottom.[9]

Tall, short, or medium, Louis Thoen's discovery of a stone on the west side of Lookout Mountain near Spearfish in 1887 has become a staple of Black Hills lore. That miners may well have visited the Black Hills in the 1830s lends a degree of plausibility to the tale. The Thoen Stone, as it is called, bore the following inscription:

> Came to these hills in 1833 seven of us DeLacompt, Ezra Kind, G. W. Wood, T. Brown, R. Kent, Wm. King, Indian Crow. All died but me Ezra Kind. Killed by Ind. beyond the high hill got our gold in 1834. [Obverse] Got all the gold we could carry our ponys all got by the Indians I have lost my gun and nothing to eat and Indians hunting me. [Reverse]

Watson Parker, who has heard many a tale of gold in the Black Hills, notes that Thoen was a stonemason and drolly adds, "Many testimonials have been obtained regarding his upright character, but no one, so far, has come forward to swear that he was without a sense of humor."[10]

While these early white adventurers were exploring, or devising tall tales, the Lakotas were expanding into wider and wider territories. Their history doesn't faithfully reflect the idyllic life depicted by George Hyde in the previous chapter. With population rapidly increasing and the buffalo herds diminished, the Lakotas kept pushing into hunting grounds occupied by other tribes. In 1846 Francis Parkman witnessed an episode in their conquest of the Medicine Bow Valley. Fresh out of Harvard Law School, the youthful Parkman "rejoiced" at the prospect of going along with a Lakota war party off to chastise the Shoshones: "I had come into the country chiefly with a view of observing the Indian character." Parkman wanted to observe savage warriors out for blood revenge. He accompanied an expedition into Crow and Shoshone territory and came away disgusted that the Lakotas were pleased merely to escape without losses. He completely misinterpreted the aim of a hunting foray into enemy territory.[11]

The Pawnees, a horticultural tribe and a power on the plains along with the Lakotas, found them cruel and ferocious enemies and called them the Tsu-ra-rat, or Throat Cutters. The Sicangu and Oglala Lakotas seemed "always [to be] around," says a chronicler of the Pawnees, "ready to pounce, raptor-like, on small groups of women in the fields and young men herding the horses." The women were often scalped and mutilated. In 1843 the Lakotas struck a devastating blow on a Pawnee village on the Loup River, killing sixty-seven and forcing the Pawnees back to the Platte. Thirty years later they surprised a hunting party on the Republican, far to the south, killing a hundred Pawnees. Their numbers drastically reduced, the Pawnees were finally driven from Nebraska not by the whites but by the Lakotas.[12]

As mid-century approached, the Crows suffered greatly from the Lakota advance into hunting grounds on the Platte and beyond. They had fought the Lakotas for more than a century. In 1822 or 1823, while Jedediah Smith's party was trading peacefully for horses with Lakotas east of the Black Hills, a Crow village near the Yellowstone had been surprised by as many as a thousand Lakotas, who destroyed hundreds of lodges and, Crow oral tradition holds, killed half the people in the village. In 1825, when the Atkinson-O'Fallon expedition arrived on the Upper Missouri, the Crows signed a treaty in the hope American friendship would provide a counterbalance.[13]

For a while the Crows held on. In 1834 they scored a major victory over a Lakota raiding party in the Bighorn Valley. In 1840 Father DeSmet found the Crows "the most indefatigable marauders of the plains," in control of country from the Black Hills to the Rockies. But soon their fortunes would turn. By 1855 the proud Crows were so reduced by epidemics and warfare that Edward Denig feared their "entire extinction." Soon the weakened Crows, along with the Arikaras and Pawnees, would join the Americans against the Lakotas.[14]

In 1876, in the run-up to American disaster on the Little Big-horn, a sizeable force of Crow warriors joined General George Crook's command on the Tongue River, ready to fight the Sioux. The Sioux had stolen their lands, Chief Old Crow told Crook—lands given the Crows by the Great Spirit. "They hunt upon our mountains. They fish in our streams. They have stolen our horses. They have murdered our squaws, our children. What white man has done these things to us?" Old Crow asks. "The Sioux have trampled upon our hearts. We shall spit upon their scalps. [Our] young warriors had come to fight. No Sioux would see their backs."[15]

A more temperate view was later voiced by Plenty Coups, the statesman-chief of the Crows, looking back from his old age. The Crows, Plenty Coups recalled, had learned from the Chickadee, "by listening—profiting from the mistakes of others." They knew the whites were strong, "without number in their own country," so the Crows helped them. As a consequence, he said, "we have held our beautiful country to this day. . . . Our lands are ours by treaty and not by chance gift."[16]

By mid-nineteenth century the destiny of the Black Hills hinged upon events in the country to the west. The annihilation of Custer and his men on the Little Bighorn, and the other bloody clashes that shocked the nation, came out of a history long under way. With the buffalo diminishing and scattered, and the Lakotas fighting other plains tribes for survival as wagon trains of whites passed through their country, something had to give. The focal point became Fort Laramie, a hundred miles southwest of the Black Hills along the Oregon Trail.

In 1846, to contend with the imminent conflict, the first Indian agent was appointed for the Upper Platte and Arkansas. Thomas Fitzpatrick was known and trusted by the Indians, who called him "Broken Hand." An Irish immigrant, he had made himself a legend throughout the West as trapper and explorer, Indian fighter, and guide, a man of great courage and skill. Fitzpatrick was "a man of broad sympathies," says his biographer, "of keen intelligence and close observation—a reading and thinking man, well schooled, and gifted with a turn for accurate and telling expression," qualities not common on the frontier.[17]

His nickname came from a rifle accident that had shattered his left wrist. "A warm hearted, gentlemanly Hibernian," an observer called him. Fitzpatrick had come to the United States at sixteen from County Cavan. "He has a spare, bony figure," a German traveler said, "a face full of expression, and white hair; his whole demeanor reveals strong passions." Fitzpatrick passionately disapproved of missionaries tampering with Indian lives. He developed a warm relationship with Father DeSmet, but the Reverend Joseph Williams called him "a wicked, worldly man . . . much opposed to missionaries going among the Indians. He has some intelligence, but is deistical in his principles."[18]

Fitzpatrick questioned whether any "immediate improvement and civilization" of the tribes was possible. That would involve a long cultural process of aid and encouragement—with punishment, rigorous and swift, for acts of violence. The first step alone would require a "long and protracted ordeal." Fitzpatrick considered the introduction of missionaries beneficial but thought they started at the wrong end, by baptizing the subject. When the white man's "medicine" failed to produce powerful results, the Indians lost faith in it. The missionaries should first address the tribes' physical needs, teaching them hygiene and industry, and then attempt to instill moral principles and explain how the Great Spirit wished his children to conduct themselves[19]

Around Fort Laramie the Lakotas had been remarkably helpful to the whites, considering what tens of thousands of emigrants had done to their domain: bringing the scourge of cholera, trampling the life-giving grass to dust on a wide swath along the Oregon Trail, destroying the game, especially the buffalo. Like locusts, the emigrants destroyed everything within reach. Still, relations with the personnel at the fort were easy and cordial. The sutler's store was the busiest place, a vital supply link on the wagon road west, but also, says Merrill Mattes, "a focal point of social intercourse for all classes of men in the melting pot of frontier society." A colonel's wife found an atmosphere where the clerks attended courteously to white and Indian alike and seemed "equally ready and capable, talking Sioux, Cheyenne, or English, just as each case came to hand." Some of the clerks married into the tribes—men like Ben Mills, whose descendants are well known today on the Pine Ridge Reservation.[20]

The Indians around the fort were more nuisance than anything. They "danced a little, stole a little, ate a great deal, and finally went on their way rejoicing," wrote an unidentified soldier in 1850 about two hundred Sioux and Cheyennes around the post. He thought the Sioux on the Platte were "the best Indians on the prairies. Look at their conduct during the past summer. Of the vast migration, which rolled through their country this year, not a person was molested, not an article stolen." Without their aid in keeping off the Pawnees, Cheyennes, and Arapahos, one of the Forty-Niners noted, "no whites could get through this country without a big army." After the 1850 migration Fitzpatrick himself reported, "I have had no reason to complain of the Indians or their conduct for the past two years; nor am I aware of any act of aggression committed by the Indians alluded to, on whites, during that time."[21]

During the 1840s the predicament of the Lakotas had grown worse and worse. In 1846 the headmen of the Oglalas and Sicangus had petitioned President Polk for help. The buffalo were leaving their hunting grounds, they complained, because of the emigrant traffic, "thereby causing us to go into the Country of our Enemies to hunt, exposing our lives daily for the necessary subsistence of our wives and Children . . . . We have all along treated the Emigrants in the most friendly manner," they reminded the President, "giving them free passage through our hunting grounds."

The reply they received sounds familiar to anyone who has dealt with large bureaucracies. Their petition was passed along to Commissioner William Medill, a political appointee from Ohio with no prior knowledge of Indian affairs. "It is the nature of the Buffalo & all other kinds of game to recede before the approach of civilization," Medill crisply informed them, "and the injury complained of, is but one of those inconveniences to which every people are subjected by the changing & constantly progressive spirit of the age."[22]

The spirit of the age was certainly progressive, sustained by the elixir of Manifest Destiny. Anglo Saxon Americans were destined to "overspread the continent," held the expansionist faith, a conviction that gathered force with the incorporation of Texas and the Southwest into the Union. By 1849, following the discovery of gold in California, the commissioner's "inconveniences" along the emigrant trail had become explosive.

Fitzpatrick was deeply troubled. He felt the Indians deserved compensation. He proposed a general treaty with all the plains Indians that would provide annual payments for the losses they suffered. Backed by David D. Mitchell, Superintendent of the western region, he sent out word summoning the Indians to a grand council for the summer of 1850. When the bill to fund the council was killed in the House of Representatives, Fitzpatrick wrote Superintendent Mitchell, reminding him how the emigration had "desolated and impoverished" the Indian country. "Under these circumstances," he implored Mitchell, "would it not be just, as well as economical policy, for the government at this time to show some little liberality, if not justice, to their passive submission?" What might be the consequences "should twenty thousand Indians well armed, well mounted, and the most warlike and expert in war of any Indians on this continent, turn out in hostile array against all American travellers through their country?"

Following this outburst, Fitzpatrick was removed from office. The Missouri congressional delegation rallied to his support, and he was reinstated in 1851, whereupon Congress authorized the funds.[23]

The "Big Talk" got under way in September at Fort Laramie, the greatest gathering of Indians ever held: Lakota, Assiniboine, Cheyenne, Arapaho, Arikara, Gros Ventre, Mandan, Shoshone, even Crow. The Comanches, Kiowas, and Apaches had refused to come, unwilling to risk their horses and mules among such notorious horse thieves as the Sioux and the Crows. Even so, ten thousand Indians assembled, the most immense force of Indians any white man had ever seen.

First came the plains tribes, late in the summer—Lakotas, Cheyennes, and Arapahos, all friendly with one another. The test would come when their enemies, the mountain tribes, appeared, especially the Shoshones, or Snakes, and the Crows. Above and below the fort the plains were covered with people, horses, and dogs, smoke curling from a thousand campfires, accompanied by a cacophony of women talking as they worked, children laughing, dogs barking.

On the first of September, Superintendent Mitchell arrived with more dragoons, making a total of two hundred and seventy troops on the scene. But a vital component was missing—a wagon train of provisions and presents that had been delayed en route, an omission that jeopardized the entire undertaking. "Without these [gifts and provisions]," wrote a reporter for the *Missouri Republican*, "no man living—not even the President of the United States—would have any influence with [the Indians], nor could he get them into council or keep them together a day." The chiefs were deeply disappointed. The only thing that saved the day was their trust in Broken Hand's promise that the goods would soon be coming. They stayed.

When word went out that the Shoshones were approaching, led by Washakie, their head chief, a friend of the whites, excitement spread through the camps. "About noon one bright day," wrote Percival Lowe, a corporal in the First Dragoons, "a long line of dust was seen from our camp, looking west towards Laramie Peak. Soon a long line of Indians came moving slowly down in battle array, arms ready for use and every man apparently expectant, the women and children and baggage bringing up the rear, well guarded." The Sioux and Cheyennes had been assured they would not be molested. "[D]own they came," wrote Corporal Lowe, "moving very slowly and cautiously, the chief alone a short distance in advance." . . . [D]ressed in their best, riding fine war horses, [they] made a grandly savage appearance."

A Lakota warrior suddenly leaped on his horse, brandishing bow and arrow, and rushed out to avenge himself on the chief who had killed his father. Instantly a French interpreter who had been watching for trouble mounted his horse and gave chase. He pulled the avenging warrior from his horse just as Washakie raised his rifle to fire. The warrior was disarmed and led back to his camp. The Shoshones stood their ground, undaunted.

Their position was strong, wrote Corporal Lowe. Every Shoshone had a good gun. Almost no Sioux had a gun. The battle would have been "the most bloody ever known among the wild tribes." Lucky for that fool Lakota, remarked the legendary scout Jim Bridger, proud of his Shoshone wards. "[M]y chief would 'er killed him quick, and then the fool Sioux would 'er got their backs up, and there wouldn't have been room to camp 'round here for dead Sioux."[24]

The entire gathering migrated thirty-six miles down the Platte to Horse Creek, where broad areas of bottom land provided good grazing for the horses, and the "Big Talk" began. The Oglalas had staged a feast the previous day for the Cheyennes and the Arapahos—and their enemies the Shoshones, a good augury. Next morning on Horse Creek the Stars and Stripes were unfurled. The cannon thundered. The tribes gathered around a circle of their lodges, leaving a third of the circle open. In the center sat Superintendent Mitchell under an arbor with Fitzpatrick and a reporter. The Indians were "decked out in all their best regalia," the reporter noted, the chiefs and warriors "dressed with punctilious attention to imposing effect." The young men, "on horse or afoot, [were arrayed in] all the foppery and display of prairie dandies," the women richly dressed as evidence of the wealth and station of their husbands and fathers.

Superintendent Mitchell opened with words of good will, offering to smoke the pipe of peace. He took a few puffs and passed the three-foot red pipestone to Fitzpatrick. As the pipe passed solemnly from chief to chief, most of them extended it to each of the four directions, then upward to the Great Spirit and down to the Bad. Most added a significant gesture, drawing the right hand along the stem from the bowl to the throat, a pledge of utmost sincerity and truthfulness.[25]

Mitchell addressed the Indians directly. The Great Father at Washington "has heard and is aware that your buffalo and game are driven off, and your grass and timber consumed by the opening of roads and the passing of emigrants through your countries. For these losses he desires to compensate you." But your condition has changed, he told them. You must abandon "your favorite amusement and pursuit," making war, and agree upon boundaries for your territories, to make war unnecessary. If they accepted his proposals in a treaty, the Great Father would give them $50,000 a year in goods and provisions for fifty years. If they should violate the treaty by making war, stealing horses, or doing other bad things, the annuity would be withheld until the wrongs were corrected. The Great Father alone would determine whether the treaty was being honored. The Indians would have to trust him.

Mitchell had previously asked that each tribe elect one chief "who shall be recognized as the head of the nation or tribe, and through whom your Great Father will transact all Government business." He wanted an answer in two days. In the tone of a stern father to a wayward son he announced, "I desire that each Nation select one or two to speak for it, that I may not have to listen to all who may desire to speak."

Hungry, the tribes kept their silence.

Presently, each tribe selected a head chief to enforce the treaty—all but the Sioux, the largest tribe on the plains. "Father," a Sioux chief told Mitchell, "we cannot make one chief." Mitchell proceeded to make his own selection, Conquering Bear, a Sicangu chief. Protesting that he would be only a "paper chief," Conquering Bear told Mitchell, "Father, I am not afraid to die, but to be chief of all the nation, I must be a *big chief,* or in a few moons I shall be sleeping on the prairie." With great reluctance, he finally accepted the role.

While the talking and dancing went on, Mitchell and Fitzpatrick proceeded to draft the treaty. Every tribe claimed more territory than other tribes would allow. The challenge of fixing boundaries was left to three men who knew the region in detail—Jim Bridger and Robert Campbell along with Fitzpatrick.

The parties "do hereby covenant and agree," read Article 1, "to abstain in future from all hostilities whatever against each other, to maintain good faith and friendship in all their mutual intercourse, and to make an effective and lasting peace." With "aforesaids" and "in consideration ofs," the treaty granted the United States the right to build roads and military posts within tribal territories. In return the government would protect the nations against white depredations. To help them adapt to an agricultural mode of living, each tribe was promised an annuity of fifty thousand dollars for fifty years. The President could withhold annuities from any tribe in violation of treaty provisions until "proper satisfaction shall have been made."

The territory assigned the Sioux—and all Sioux bands were lumped together in the greater nation, though it was really the Lakotas in question—encompassed the Black Hills and extensive surrounding areas, terminating on the south at the Platte River. The Oglalas objected to that limitation. "You have split the country," said Black Hawk, an Oglala chief, "and I do not like it. These lands once belonged to the Kiowas and the Crows, but we whipped these nations out of them, and in this we did what the white men do when they want the lands of the Indians."[26]

Superintendent Mitchell calmed them with the assurance they would be free to hunt south of the Platte as long as they were at peace. Then he read the treaty out to them, sentence by sentence. The participating chiefs "touched the pen." Not one of the Oglalas signed. Four days later, long overdue, the wagon train of gifts and provisions arrived. The cannon spoke, calling the tribes to receive their presents. First the chiefs, one by one, were called into the Superintendent's tent. Each emerged in a gorgeously colorful and epauletted uniform with shining saber and a certificate from the Great Father bearing a large seal and ribbon. Around his neck each wore a medal stamped with the likeness of President Millard Fillmore. Then, over two days, the presents were distributed to the people: tobacco, cloth, beads, knives, and blankets.

The grand council came to an end and the tribes went their separate ways. A spirit of great hope prevailed. Fitzpatrick must have felt quiet elation. Father DeSmet predicted "a new era for the Indians—an era of peace. In future, peaceable citizens may cross the desert unmolested, and the Indian will have little to dread from the bad white man, for justice will be rendered to him." Superintendent Mitchell expressed the hope in his report to the Commissioner that fifty years would tell whether the Indians could successfully adapt to agricultural pursuits. The tribes had amply demonstrated their good faith at the council, Mitchell attested, and "nothing but bad management, or some untoward misfortune, can ever break it."[27]

During the following spring the United States Senate reduced the annuity period from fifty years to ten, with an optional five additional years at the President's discretion. It fell to Fitzpatrick, old Broken Hand himself, to seek ratification of the altered treaty from the Indians who trusted him. Two and a half years later he died in a hotel on Pennsylvania Avenue, far from the scene of his triumphs.

One matter, at least, was made clear in the Fort Laramie Treaty of 1851: the Lakotas were left in quiet, uncontested possession of the Black Hills.

The era of peace foreseen by Father DeSmet ended almost as soon as the great council of 1851 broke up. The wars that followed would have profound consequences for the Black Hills. The Lakotas went back to fighting the Crows and Pawnees as busily as ever, though ultimately what took place was the clash between two expanding powers—the United States and the Lakotas and their allies. Neither had a full appreciation of the other's strength. Undefeated, the Lakotas were totally unaware of the government's ability to punish them. Washington officials had little conception of the true power of the Lakotas. To deal effectively with them the army would need highly mobile forces, commanded by officers who knew Indians. "It is want of this knowledge," Fitzpatrick informed Commissioner Medill, "that [has] been the cause of the total failure of all the expeditions made against the Indians."[28]

There was certain to be a "great struggle for ascendancy." In 1849 the government had purchased Fort Laramie from the American Fur Company as a military post near the dwindling buffalo herds, where the most formidable tribes gathered. At first the Indians appeared to welcome the soldiers, who they were told would protect them from the devastation caused by the emigrants. Fitzpatrick protested stoutly against the posting of a mere skeleton crew of infantry at the fort, which could be overrun at any moment by a swarm of warriors. To let the tribes know the power of the government, a force of three hundred mounted men was required.[29]

In the long war to follow, the figure who would come to champion the Lakotas was a rising young Oglala warrior named *Mákhpiya Lúta*—Red Cloud, who was about thirty at the time of the great council. Red Cloud was born on Blue Water Creek, a tributary of the North Platte River in western Nebraska, in May 1821. His father was Lone Man, chief of a Sicangu band called the Kuhee, or "standoffish." His mother, Walks As She Thinks, was probably a Saone, or northern Lakota. When the boy was only four, Lone Man died, a casualty of liquor supplied by American companies eager to capture their share of the fur trade. After Lone Man's death, Walks As She Thinks took her children to her people in Old Smoke's band of Saones, now living among the Oglalas.[30]

Intensely competitive, young Red Cloud was so aggressive that occasionally his maternal uncle had to scold him. He aspired to leadership but found his choices limited. He could strive to distinguish himself by the four Lakota virtues: bravery, fortitude, generosity, and wisdom. He might make himself a renowned warrior or buffalo hunter, or seek visions by which to lead the people. But lacking good connections, as the son of a Sicangu rather than an Oglala father—and worse yet, of a man who had died of drunkenness—he suffered a major disadvantage. His most promising avenue lay in the role of warrior. At sixteen he joined a retaliatory raid on the Pawnees and took his first scalp, demonstrating exceptional bravery by counting coup on three Crow warriors. He surprised a Crow sentry and made off with fifty horses. At twenty he killed Bull Bear, the domineering chief of a rival Oglala camp, which raised him in the eyes of his own people. Soon he was given a leadership role in a raid on the Pawnees in which he took an arrow below the rib cage that nearly ended his life, a wound that troubled him ever after. By thirty, with a reputation for cruelty as well as ferocity, Red Cloud had achieved the status of *blotahunka*, or war leader.

Among Lakota leaders he acquired a rare understanding of the whites through his association with white traders. Having lived much of his early life in the Platte River country, he knew his way around

Fort Laramie. The Oglalas could acquire superior trade goods at Fort Laramie, Robert Larson observes, "and yet still lead the restless life of a Plains band, being able to come and go as they pleased." Along with his qualities as a warrior and his familiarity with the whites, Red Cloud possessed unusual intelligence and charisma. "Certainly if any Lakota warrior could have perceived the ultimate threat posed by the increasing influx of whites into Sioux country by the 1840s and 1850s, it would have been Red Cloud." Now he was to face "the greatest challenge of his life: leadership against an enemy more formidable than any the Sioux had ever faced before.[31]

The long, slow-burning fuse that led to Red Cloud's War was ignited in 1854 by an absurd incident. The Indians near the fort were starving, Fitzpatrick reported, shortly before he died. "Their women are pinched with want and their children constantly crying out with hunger."[32] When a Mormon cow bolted into a Sicangu camp along the Oregon Trail near Fort Laramie, it was killed by a visiting Minnecoujou warrior, and promptly eaten. Now the familiar Broken Hand, with his calming presence, was gone. Add to that a brevet lieutenant fresh out of West Point, John Grattan, a man given to boasting that with thirty men he could "whip the combined force of all the Indians on the prairie." Though the treaty held the tribe, not the individual, responsible, Grattan volunteered to go bring in the offending warrior. The second lieutenant in command at Fort Laramie sent him out with a detachment of twenty-two men and two howitzers. In the ensuing face-off, Conquering Bear, who had so reluctantly accepted the role of head chief, was mortally wounded.

The Sicangus promptly annihilated Grattan's entire detachment.

The Grattan Massacre set off a chain of events designed to punish the Lakotas while vindicating the army. The whole affair, it was said, had been deliberately planned by the Lakotas. On the cow's demise the official account ascends to a truly comic plane: the Minnecoujou warrior first shot at a Mormon and missed, then aimed at the cow, declaring, "I have missed you; you are protected by God; but I will kill your cow."

The army was excoriated by Thomas Hart Benton, the "lion of Missouri." The Sioux had been our friends for fifty years, he told the House of Representatives. Now we had turned them against us by "sending our school-house officers and pot-house soldiers to treat the Indians as beasts and dogs." A more judicious summary by Remi Nadeau details the circumstances: a frontier army poorly schooled in the treatment of Indians; an inexperienced commanding officer; a drunken interpreter;

a trader who feared to accompany the soldiers into the Sicangu village; Grattan's lack of respect for Indians. "[E]ach of these unhappy ingredients was present," Nadeau observes, and the consequences severe: "Two generations of peace with the Plains Sioux were shattered, and a generation of hostility began."[33]

The following spring an expedition under General William C. Harney was sent out to punish those who had massacred Grattan and his men. Harney learned of a Sicangu camp along Blue Water Creek. Informed that these were the murderers, Harney unleashed a devastating attack on the peaceful village of Little Thunder, a chief who had taken the lead in dissuading the Lakotas from attacking Fort Laramie. Many women and children were among the hundred killed. The soldiers, when they realized what they had done, were shamed by it and cared tenderly for their prisoners.

Harney himself—the "Wasp," as the Indians came to call him— apparently had his eyes opened. Upon reaching Fort Laramie he learned the Grattan massacre had been forced on the Sicangus. The following spring, when he met Little Thunder at Fort Pierre, Little Thunder asked to shake hands. Harney replied that he was "sorry it fell so hard on Little Thunder," and added, "I feel like shaking hands with all the chiefs, particularly Little Thunder."

"West Point discipline made a simple debt into a crime," charged Thomas Hart Benton in the House of Representatives. "It is history!" he thundered:

> The history of our Indian intercourse! Hospitable reception, land taken, Indians killed. Is there not enough in this history to induce us to stop, and think, and try to settle with all possible gentleness, these calamitous Indian wars, of which our own dreadful misconduct has been too much the cause?[34]

If the scattered Lakota bands had been unaware of the government's power to punish them, the Sicangus had now gained a bewildering sense of that power. "Never in the memory of living men," George Hyde says, "had one of the big Sioux camps been captured by enemies, and never had they suffered such losses in a fight or seen scores of Sioux women and children carried off as captives." To lose a few ponies and three or four warriors in a fight was regarded as shocking. "[T]he loss in Little Thunder's camp was an overwhelming disaster."[35]

The young Sicangu war chief Spotted Tail had fought bravely in the assault and had been severely wounded. His wife and child had been taken captive. When Harney demanded the Lakotas surrender the warriors who had recently attacked a mail wagon, Spotted Tail was among them. Stunned by the catastrophe on the Blue Water, the chiefs in council begged him and the others to give themselves up in order to save the people. Singing their death songs, Spotted Tail and his fellow warriors came riding into Fort Laramie on fine ponies. Transported hundreds of miles to Fort Leavenworth, in an unknown country swarming with whites, they were held until granted a presidential pardon.

Spotted Tail was transformed by the ordeal. He had witnessed the number and power of the whites, to whom the attack on Little Thunder's camp was a small matter. He had seen the Kansas Indians living in houses, planting corn. Eager a year earlier to fight the Americans, he now seems to have concluded, like Plenty Coups of the Crows, that sooner or later the Sicangus would be forced to give up their wandering life and learn to live like white people.[36]

Red Cloud disagreed, as did an Oglala boy called Curly—Crazy Horse. Curly was profoundly affected by what he had witnessed. As Conquering Horse was dying after the Grattan affair, young Curly, then about thirteen, had gone out into the Nebraska sandhills in search of a vision. The killing of women and children in Little Thunder's camp the following year taught him a lesson he would never forget: white people were capable of great cruelty and not to be trusted.[37]

In the summer of 1857 a great council of the Lakotas assembled at Bear Butte. Mari Sandoz imagines how the young Curly must have experienced the gathering:

> Here the seven people of the Teton Lakotas were moving into one great circle camp that seemed wide as the horizon, their pony herds making all the higher ground dark as the *Pa Sapa*, the Black Hills that rose beyond the foothills, the warriors like a great forest, like many, many tall, straight trees standing thick. The Lakotas looked around them and saw their strength with swelling hearts. . . . With all this power they had let their women and children die before the guns of the whites in their own camps, seen their friends, the Cheyennes, killed in small bunches, because they were few and nobody helped them.

Never again! The Lakotas were "still the same as in the old days . . . . [Their chiefs] had vowed resistance to every white man who pushed in anywhere on Teton lands."[38]

Shortly thereafter, a surveying party under Lieutenant Gouverneur Kemble Warren encountered a party of Lakotas at Inyan Kara, on the western flank of the Black Hills. An old man among them told Warren the Lakotas had given up all the country they could spare to the whites; the Black Hills must be left wholly to them. Warren was "necessarily compelled to admit to myself the truth and force of [their] objections." Circumventing the range on the south, he proceeded to Bear Butte and departed.[39]

For a time the Black Hills were left in peace as the American nation drifted toward Civil War. Red Cloud's band of Bad Faces migrated north into the Powder River country between the Black Hills and the Big Horns, the best hunting area remaining, and went on fighting to drive the Crows out. In 1861-1862 Red Cloud led a victorious war party against the Crows. During the first years of the Civil War, with the whites distracted, the Lakotas lived well. Red Cloud became their leading war chief.[40]

In 1862 the relative peace of the Black Hills was threatened by two events: the discovery of gold in Montana and the uprising of the Santee Sioux in Minnesota. After scores of white settlers were massacred in Minnesota, thirty-eight Sioux were hanged on a single scaffold the day after Christmas. The events in Minnesota inflamed relations on the plains, which worsened dramatically in 1864 with the ruthless massacre of peaceful Cheyennes on Sand Creek in Colorado. The very mention of Sand Creek evokes horror to this day. The massacre brought the Cheyennes, Northern Arapahos, and Sicangus into an alliance that sent as many as a thousand warriors marauding up through Colorado into the North Platte country.

The discovery of gold in Montana led to outright war. The Bozeman Trail to western Montana traversed Lakota hunting grounds on the Powder River. To protect the gold seekers passing through Lakota lands the government began constructing forts along the trail in 1865— Fort Reno on the Powder, Forts Philip Kearny and C. F. Smith to the north and west. The Lakotas set out to close the road. Young Crazy Horse was ready to fight. Many of the most hot-blooded Oglalas were turning to Red Cloud for action. In 1866, weakened by the Civil War and military cutbacks, hoping for lasting peace, the government sent out a call for a treaty council with the Lakotas and Cheyennes.

In early spring the prospect appeared hopeful. Spotted Tail had lost Falling Leaf, his beloved daughter, who had grown close to the whites and had asked to be buried among them. In a moving scene of reconciliation, Spotted Tail brought her body in to Fort Laramie. But the government was suffering from "bureaucratic schizophrenia," as one historian put it. While the Indian Bureau was organizing a peace movement, the army was contemplating military occupation of the Bozeman Trail. For several weeks a column of troops under Colonel Henry Carrington had been moving up the Platte. Just as the treaty council was getting under way, Carrington arrived on the scene with a force of two thousand men.[41]

Red Cloud was enraged. Seeing Carrington, wrote Frances Carrington, the colonel's future wife, who was not present at the time, Red Cloud refused an introduction. Pointing to the colonel, he issued a denunciation: "The Great Father sends us presents and wants us to sell him the road, but White Chief goes with soldiers to steal the road before the Indians say Yes or No." An enlisted man's account holds that Red Cloud made a dramatic speech accusing the commissioners of treating the Indians like children and vowed that "for his part he preferred to die fighting rather than by starvation." Another tale holds that Red Cloud held up his rifle and proclaimed: "In this and the Great Spirit I trust for the right." A few of the chiefs present signed the treaty, primarily those with no stake in the Powder River country. Red Cloud refused, determined to carry on the war.[42]

The army proceeded with the construction of Forts Philip Kearny and C. F. Smith. Just before Christmas in 1866, a force of eighty men commanded by Captain W. J. Fetterman, who had boasted that with eighty men he could ride through the whole Sioux nation, was drawn into an ambush by a decoy party led by Crazy Horse and exterminated to the last man. The Fetterman Massacre was the greatest disaster the army had ever suffered in the West, though clearly it was no massacre but a battle in which the military had been outwitted and outnumbered.[43]

General William T. Sherman, the man who "marched through Georgia" during the Civil War, now commanding the Department of the Platte, issued an order. This act of war must be punished "with vindictive earnestness, until at least ten Indians were killed for every white life lost." The troops should "carry the war to the Indian camps, where the women and children are, and should inflict such punishment that even Indians would discover they can be beaten at their own game. . . . It is not necessary to find the very men who committed the acts," Sherman added, "but destroy all of the same breed.[44]

A presidential commission investigating the Fetterman Massacre found that continued war could be avoided only by ceasing to invade Indian territory, which the Supreme Court had ruled illegal. But as the emboldened Lakotas continued attacking parties of whites passing through their territory, western whites were taking matters into their own hands. In Colorado a bounty was offered for Indian scalps: twenty-five dollars for scalps "with the ears on."[45]

In 1867 Congress created a new Peace Commission to effect a broad new policy for all the western tribes. The commission reflected the usual dichotomy between advocates of peace and those who demanded punishment. The commissioners decided to negotiate two treaties, one with the southern tribes, the other with the Lakotas of the Powder River region. When the Commissioners arrived at Fort Laramie, they found only some peaceful Crows waiting. Red Cloud refused to come in. "He sent us word, however," the commissioners reported, "that his war against the whites was to save the valley of the Powder River, the only hunting ground left to his nation, from our intrusion." Red Cloud assured them that whenever the garrisons at Fort Philip Kearny and Fort C. F. Smith were withdrawn, his war would cease. The Commission adjourned and went back to Washington.

The new year, 1868, brought greater promise: Red Cloud would make peace if the government abandoned the Bozeman Trail and evacuated the forts. Stretched thin as it was in occupying the South, with the Northern Pacific Railroad soon to offer easy access to Montana, the government accepted his terms. A less conspicuous motive for the decision is noted by James C. Olson: "The mere fact that the pressures of expansion were depriving the red men of their homes and destroying their way of life weighed heavily upon the conscience of a Christian nation, and when accompanied by such outrages as the [Sand Creek] massacre, the burden became insupportable.[46]

In April the Peace Commission returned to Fort Laramie to find Red Cloud absent. The commissioners presented the proposed treaty to Spotted Tail and the other Sicangu headmen and secured their marks on the paper. Red Cloud stood by his word: only after the forts were evacuated and he and his warriors had burned them to the ground, as they did in late summer, would he come in. Early in November, after the commissioners had departed and the commission had been officially dissolved, he appeared at Fort Laramie to put his mark on the treaty.

The Treaty of 1868 remains the principal basis for the Lakota claim to the Black Hills. Ten pages in print, with seventeen articles, it recognizes the Black Hills as exclusive Sioux territory, together with extensive unceded lands. The Sioux agreed in return to cease attacks on whites and resistance to the construction of railroads. Proclaiming that war between the parties "shall forever cease," it makes specific provisions for measures to help the Indians adopt an agricultural mode of living. Red Cloud promised to live up to the treaty as long as the white man did. Whether he truly understood the document, or just what was meant by living up to it, remains open to question.

Chapter 3: The New Eldorado

Cries of pain and loss went up from prospective white settlers as soon as word of the 1868 treaty was out, long before Red Cloud came in from the Powder River. "No greater calamity could befall Dakota," declared the *Yankton Union and Dakotaian*, "than to have that portion of our Territory closed to exploration and settlement by the whites." The idea of creating two great reservations for the wild tribes was "the most foolish and puerile invention that ever emanated from the brain of a full grown man." Editorial scorn soon gave way to lamentation:

> The people of Dakota were invited here by the Government of the United States. They came here to make homes for themselves and their children and to lay the foundations of a future state. After years of toil, privation and hardship, . . . and just as they are beginning to anticipate brighter days and reap the reward of toil, this Indian Commission comes along and proposes to rob them of the fairest and wealthiest portions of their Territory, and dedicate the same to the cause of barbarism forever.

The rights of the people of Dakota, "if not guaranteed to them by the lex scripta creating the Indian Commission, are at least secured by the law of common justice and common decency."[1]

Underlying this appeal to common justice and decency is a hint of class resentment, a feeling directed against do-gooders in the East: the comfortable humanitarians behind the Peace Policy, all too happy to deny others what they already have themselves. This Garden of the

World, the unsettled expanse of the West, was it to be fenced off from those who labor and suffer privation to make homes for their families? Were the upstanding and virtuous to be cut off from the American Dream? And the *Black Hills*! The Black Hills were the very epitome of the dream!

The allure was more than gold alone. It encompassed the powerful myth of the American interior as a garden. Captain W. F. Raynolds, whose expedition had skirted the Black Hills in 1859, foresaw the area as a future home for a thriving population. Raynolds considered much of the short grass prairie between the Black Hills and the Missouri unsuitable for agriculture because of the scant rainfall, but he felt the mountains would supply ample lumber for the adjoining districts. For settlers drawn to jumping off places such as Sioux City and Yankton, the myth of the garden exerted a commanding pull. The forces which would control the future originated not in "the picturesque Wild West beyond the agricultural frontier," says Henry Nash Smith, "but in the domesticated West that lay behind it," in the "master symbol" of the garden, which embraced "a cluster of metaphors expressing fecundity, growth, increase, and blissful labor in the earth, all centering around the heroic figure of the idealized frontier farmer armed with that supreme agrarian weapon, the sacred plow." That image is an enduring force in American thought and politics, the vision of an "agricultural paradise in the West [that embodied] group memories of an earlier, a simpler and, it was believed, a happier state of society. . . ."[2]

Add to that beguiling image the lure of gold, and you can imagine the betrayal felt by those waiting to "open the Hills." And what stood in their way? Savages! Through all the West, along with land, transportation links, and protection from Indian attack, white citizens demanded removal of the Indians. Incapable of sympathy for what they considered an inferior race, most Western people saw the destruction of Indian tribes as a blessing. Indians blocked the way to Manifest Destiny. White citizens had even less regard for the Peace Policy, though in fact it had been launched by astute observers of conditions in the West, or had any notion they themselves might benefit from the policy, well applied. "A good father is not always indulgent," observed the *Cheyenne Daily Leader*, voicing the prevailing sentiment in its demand that the Great Sioux Reservation be opened to settlement. "He discriminates and sometimes finds occasion to frown at the wayward children and even to use the rod. . . . If it is necessary let the nation assert its rights and dignity at the mouth of the cannon." The frail notion common in the East that westerners would help peaceful Indians, asserts one historian, was simply nonsense. The West had no compassion for "peaceful" Indians, who at best were a nuisance or a "hindrance to progress."[3]

The attitudes and tribal organization of the Lakotas likewise hindered any peaceful resolution. If the whites with their faith in manifest destiny were ethnocentric, so too were the Sioux, asserts Royal B. Hassrick. They had such confidence in their national destiny that they ruled the heartland of the Northern Plains for nearly a century. "They made no concessions, few alliances, and many enemies. They were hated by many and feared by most, and they boasted of this reputation. . . . Their arrogance was born of successful conquest." More than aware of their great power, the Sioux were "overbearing in their vanity."

Tribal power was paramount. For the Lakotas, an enemy tribe must not only be forced into submission, but driven from the territory. The collapse of their society came from a realm they could neither foresee nor control, in the form of white conquerors "so unbelievably powerful, so overwhelming in numbers that even the Sioux's most desperate defense was of no avail."[4]

In the final phase of Lakota expansion, other tribes found that the loose structural organization of the Lakotas made them more difficult to resist. There was no unified nation to confront. Accommodation with one Lakota band might simply encourage inroads from others. No band was actually ruled by one man. Young men seeking laurels were beyond control. The Americans encountered the same difficulty with the scattered bands. In the early days, before the tide of emigration roiled relations along the Platte, white traders considered Red Cloud's Oglala bands "the best and most orderly Indians in the country." The Minnecoujous, physically distant from whites, were "always more wild than other bands," an early observer noted. The Hunkpapas, more distant yet, had become "completely hostile," and in Little Bear they had a chief who from his youth up manifested hatred for the white man, prefiguring the implacable Sitting Bull.

For five years following the Treaty of 1868 the Lakotas in and around the Black Hills enjoyed a relatively peaceful interregnum, thanks to the Army, which blocked a number of expeditions heading for the Hills, one of them a party of two hundred and fifty men. The Lakotas incorporated the region so completely they affectionately called it their Meat Pack. Perhaps because they had been a woodland people, they found the Black Hills homelike. They wintered in sheltering wooded hollows near rivers, or in the Hills themselves on bottom lands protected by bluffs or ridges, close to good sources of firewood. At times the rigors of a severe winter told. After signing the treaty, Red Cloud disappeared into the north country only to reappear at Fort Laramie in the spring with a thousand of his people, begging for food. Yet in retrospect those years would look good, if not idyllic.

In his old age Black Elk told of hunting deer with his father near Buffalo Gap. He recalled a happy summer before the big trouble came, cutting tipi poles along the streams flowing out of the Hills, fishing with Iron Bull, a boy his age. The boys always made an offering of bait to the fish: "You who are down in the water with wings of red, I offer this to you, so come hither." They would kiss the first fish they caught. If they caught a little one, they would kiss it and throw it back. To think of losing the Black Hills to the *Wasichus* made the boy sad. "It was such a good place to play and the people were always happy in that country."[6]

In February 1869 the U. S. Senate ratified the Fort Laramie Treaty. By spring 1870 Red Cloud let it be known he wanted to visit the Great White Father in Washington to talk about the treaty and maybe about going on a reservation. Though the army was skeptical, the government welcomed his visit as a way of supporting the one chief they thought could speak for all the Lakotas. "Red Cloud is undoubtedly the most celebrated warrior on the American continent," said the *New York Times*, expressing a hope common in the East. He is "a man of brains, a good ruler, an eloquent speaker, an able general and fair diplomat. The friendship of Red Cloud is of more importance than that of any other ten chiefs on the plains."

From the West came a sarcastic dissent by a citizen of Cheyenne: "Rumor has it that [Red Cloud] is to become a member of the Cabinet . . . and thus [will] have a voice in our national affairs equal to the power which he has so far exercised." The army's doubts were sounded by General Augur, commanding the Department of the Platte, in a note of caution to his superiors. Nothing could be further from the truth, he warned, than the impression common in the East that Red Cloud was head of all the hostile bands. Any chief or head man who became friendly with the whites would lose any influence he had over the "hostiles."[7]

When Red Cloud arrived in the nation's capital with his entourage on the first of June, Spotted Tail, considered by whites the leader of the "friendlies," was already there with his delegation. Red Cloud's people were introduced to Secretary of the Interior Cox and to Ely Parker, Commissioner of Indian Affairs, himself a full-blood Seneca. A sightseeing tour of the Capitol was followed by an excursion to the Navy Yard and the Arsenal. The Lakotas seemed little impressed when the fifteen inch coastal guns sent a shell ricocheting three or four miles down the Potomac. They were more excited two days later when as they were ushered into the East

Room of the White House the great chandeliers were lighted, filling the room with a blazing light. President and Mrs. Grant entered, followed by a few congressmen. The introductions were made. The British Minister made a failed attempt to converse with Red Cloud in English. Then they all moved to the State Dining Room, to tables loaded with the white man's delicacies. Over dessert of strawberries and ice cream, Spotted Tail, who liked his worldly pleasures, noted that the whites had many more good things to eat than they sent the Indians.

Next day the conference got down to business. Secretary Cox opened the session. Reviewing what his guests had witnessed in the past few days, Cox told them they now knew that the President did what he did, not because he was afraid, but because he wanted to do "what was right and good." He had recently blocked an expedition of whites into the Bighorns because he had given that country to the Sioux. The President wished to find a place where the Indians could live undisturbed by the whites. That was why he had sent "our great soldier," General Sherman, to make a treaty with them. So long as some of the Indians were at war, he could not honor Red Cloud's request for powder and lead to hunt with. When all were living at peace on the reservations, he would see what he could do. Secretary Cox concluded with a warning: "The first thing we want to say to [the Indians] is that they must keep the peace and then we will try to do for them as is right."

Solemnly Red Cloud walked to the table and shook hands with the officials. Then he sat down on the floor to give his response. "Look at me," he said through an interpreter.

> I was a warrior on this land where the sun rises, now I come from where the sun sets. Whose voice was first sounded on this land—the red people with bows and arrows. . . . [Now the whites] have surrounded me and left me nothing but an island. When we first had this land we were strong, now we are melting like snow on the hillside while you are growing like spring grass.

Then alluding to the Black Hills and the Bighorns, he announced, "I have two mountains in that country. I want Great Father to make no roads through."

The New York papers reporting on the event praised Red Cloud and found fault with the government and its policy. "The clear conception which this unlettered savage possesses of what he claims as his rights," said the *Times,* "and what he is disposed to resent in his wrong, shows very plainly the necessity for treating with the leaders of the aboriginal 'nations' on some straightforward and intelligible principle. The attempt to cajole and bamboozle them, as if they were deficient in intelligence, ought to be abandoned, no less than the policy of hunting them down like wild beasts." The *Herald* echoed the bamboozling theme, with the hope Red Cloud had convinced Secretary Cox that "palaver has very little effect on the Indian character . . . that faithlessness on our part in the matter of treaties, and gross swindling of the Indians by our agents and their tools—the contractors—are at the bottom of all this Indian trouble."

Possession of the Black Hills seems not to have been a particular concern of Red Cloud's, after his initial reference to his two mountains. With President Grant he focused on his demand that Fort Fetterman be abandoned. The thunderbolt came in his exchange with Secretary Cox on the Treaty of 1868: "This is the first time I have heard of such a treaty," Red Cloud announced. "I never heard of it and do not mean to follow it."

Cox knew that General William Dye, commander at Fort Laramie, had gone through the document point by point with Red Cloud before he put his mark on the treaty, and that when Dye had come to the sections on the reservations and farming, Red Cloud had remarked that he'd heard all he cared to know about that from others.

The commissioners would not tell a lie to save their lives, Cox assured him.

"I do not say the Commissioners lied," countered Red Cloud, "but the interpreters were wrong." He was offered a copy of the treaty to take with him, so that he could have it explained to him. "I will not take the paper with me," Red Cloud said angrily. "It is all lies."

Leaving behind him a trail of complaints and demands, Red Cloud departed Washington for a noteworthy visit to New York. As he and his delegation rode up Fifth Avenue and through Central Park, New Yorkers turned out by the thousands to ogle them, curious to see the man who had forced the government to abandon the Powder River Road. That evening the Indians were taken to the Grand Opera House to see the "Twelve Temptations." The guests, "sad to say," commented the *Times*, seemed to take "especial delight in the fantastic gambols of the semi-nude coryphées and the gorgeous display of parti-colored fusions, glittering tinsel and red fire."

The high point of Red Cloud's tour was his appearance at Cooper Institute. The great hall was packed. He was welcomed with a tumultuous ovation. When his turn came to speak, drawing his blanket around him with impressive dignity, Red Cloud spoke through an interpreter in simple, direct Lakota:

> The Great Spirit made us poor and ignorant. He made you rich and wise. . . . In 1868 men came out and brought papers. We could not read them, and they did not tell us truly what was in them. . . . When I reached Washington the Great Father explained to me what the treaty was, and showed me that the interpreters had deceived me.

Virtually every sentence was followed by applause. Red Cloud spoke more rapidly, in a higher key, voicing a different theme:

> I was brought up among the traders, and those who came out there in the early times treated me well and I had a good time with them. But, by and by, the Great Father sent out a different kind of men; men who cheated and drank whisky; men who were so bad that the Great Father could not keep them at home and so sent them out there. . . .

The many words he had sent the Great Father "were drowned on the way," Red Cloud concluded, "so I came to speak to you myself; and now I am going away to my home."

His speech brought sustained applause. It was a triumph. The *Times* moralized that Red Cloud's gestures and manner "might be imitated with advantage by civilized and highly educated pale faces."

As Red Cloud's delegation left for the West, officials in Washington felt the visit had been beneficial to all, and probably had averted a bloody war. The press was more skeptical, in the East as well as on the frontier. The *Herald* and the *Nation* predicted war; the *Yankton Union and Dakotaian* saw "a dose of terrible war" as the only solution to the Indian problem. Credible reports had the Lakotas attacking the Crows in Montana in an attempt to take over the buffalo ranges. Red Cloud himself, after returning to Fort Laramie, was said to be out working for peace, trying to enlist the Arapahos and Cheyennes in the cause, but he appeared to be losing influence. An officer of the Seventh Cavalry reported hearsay from the Assiniboines and Gros Ventres that after Red Cloud had come back from Washington with wonderful stories of what he had seen there, some of his bands had gone over to Sitting Bull: "Red Cloud saw too much. The Indians say that these things cannot be; that the white people must have put bad medicine over Red Cloud's eye to make him see everything and anything that they please."[8]

The impression that Red Cloud's head had been turned can only have been reinforced by his indifference to the extension of the Northern Pacific Railroad. Lakotas were deeply agitated by the railroad's growing presence in their region, but Red Cloud, primarily concerned about the location of his agency after a second visit to Washington he had insisted upon, declined an invitation to meet with a Lakota delegation that included Sitting Bull, the great Hunkpapa chief. Red Cloud sent them a message: "I shall not go to war any more with whites. I shall do as my Great Father says and make my people listen." He added a newly discovered faith: "Make no trouble for our Great Father. His heart is good. Be friends to him and he will provide for you."[9]

While Red Cloud was engaged in locating his agency, and wrangling over a census count of the Oglalas, Sitting Bull and his Hunkpapas resolved to halt the railroad's encroachment on their territory. Then in 1873 the Northern Pacific Railroad and the nation encountered a financial crisis that would call upon all the skills at their command.

Railroads opened the West. In 1869 the golden spike connected the coasts and made us a transcontinental power. Soon afterward, the railroads contributed to development of the Black Hills—familiar stories all, trumpeted in our histories. But what for the conquerors signaled the triumphant advance of civilization, for others meant the death of free life on the plains. And the railroad played another, less public role in the massive incursion into the Hills. If Red Cloud had been more alert and more fully informed, he would have been more concerned about the iron horse clomping its way into Lakota territory.

In July 1874 an expedition headed by George Armstrong Custer set out for the Black Hills. Advertised as strictly military, its mission was to explore routes and to locate a site for a military post. A permanent military post in the Black Hills had been proposed in 1857 by Lieutenant Warren, who considered war with the Lakotas inevitable: "Here they can assemble their largest force, and here I believe they would make a stand."

As early as 1865 the army had planned to establish a post in the Hills. In 1865-1866 the Dakota Territorial Assembly had memorialized the Secretary of War to establish a post there.[10] The Fort Laramie Treaty of 1868 declared the Black Hills and surrounding area to be set apart for the "absolute and undisturbed use" of the Sioux Nation. Article II specifies that except for "such officers, agents, and employes of the government as may be authorized to enter upon Indian reservations in discharge of duties enjoined by law," no one would ever be permitted to "pass over, settle upon, or reside" in the area. To see this expedition— ten companies of cavalry, three of infantry, a hundred Indian scouts, and a battery of Gatling guns, along with newspaper correspondents, photographers, and a band—simply as officers and agents of the government is grotesque. To dispatch such an expedition into the heart of Paha Sapa risked all-out war.

The backdrop to this drama has seldom been fully explored. It had been crafted over a period of years. Only a month earlier the eminent Bishop William Hare had written President Grant to warn that unless the expedition was stopped, the result would be war. "We are the marauders in this case," Bishop Hare wired the Secretary of the Interior. General Terry, commanding the Department of Dakota, responded. "I am unable to see that any just offense is given to the Indians by the expedition to the Hills," he assured the bishop. "Plunder is not the objective of the expedition; neither is it sent out for the purposes of ascertaining the mineral or agricultural resources of the Black Hills. It seeks neither gold, timber nor arable land," though inevitably it "found" all of these.[11]

That the expedition was not stopped, George Hyde noted decades ago, proves that "very strong influences" were backing the project. More recently, historian Richard Slotkin leveled a more targeted allegation: "The secret history of the Black Hills expedition, with its sordid commercial and bureaucratic maneuverings, was concealed behind an elaborate ideological facade, a facade erected to sway public opinion." Slotkin's charges demand attention after a sketch of the circumstances and a glance at two participants in the drama—two very different men, Charles Collins and Jay Cooke.[12]

The Grant Administration was under pressure to "open the Hills." Agitation had been building even before the Civil War. In 1861 the Black Hills Exploring and Mining Association, formed in Yankton, had enlisted more than half the town's adult males before its ambitions were hampered by the war. For the duration it was forced to content itself with requests to Congress for surveys, and with trumpeting rumors of gold in the Black Hills for the territorial governors to use in their annual addresses. In December 1865 Major General John Pope announced his intention to place a large military post at the northern base of the Black Hills early the next spring, "with a view to open that country to explorers."[13]

The appetites of would-be settlers and prospectors were whetted by Professor Ferdinand Hayden, a geologist who had accompanied Lieutenant Warren and Captain Raynolds into the Hills. Hayden said he had seen "every indication of rich gold deposits." He rhapsodized about the "Big Sheyenne, with the Black Hills clasped between its two arms or forks," the "abundant growth of young, thrifty pines" and the hills "abundantly watered by small streams of pure cold water, running through small beautiful valleys of inexhaustible fertility."[14]

By 1870 the campaign to open the gold fields was led by Charles Collins, an energetic immigrant from Ireland. Collins developed an ambitious Fenian scheme to found an Irish-American empire in Dakota Territory, a base from which patriotic Irishmen could invade Canada at such time as "England's embarrassment and Ireland's opportunity" should come. A journalist and promoter, veteran of earlier ventures in Colorado and Nevada, Collins bought the *Sioux City Weekly Times* in 1870. His enthusiasm for Black Hills gold seems to have been ignited by a conversation with Father De Smet. The Black Hills would soon be opened, Collins prophesied, and would bring riches to Sioux City.[15]

In 1872 he organized an association in Sioux City with himself as president. In his *Weekly Times* Collins broadcast his estimate that 50,000 people would enlist that year in a massive invasion of the Hills. He printed a pamphlet giving directions and the cost of outfitting a party of five. Participants were advised to come well-armed, one rifle and one revolver per man. "Ho! for the Black Hills!" read the headlines. "Off to the 'New Eldorado!'" Those who joined the expedition, Collins guaranteed, would enjoy freedom from care and responsibility. They could expect "a good time during the whole trip," a sort of low cost excursion for the weary business or professional man.

Alas, the expedition was blocked by official proclamation: any violation of the Treaty of 1868 would be prevented—by force, if necessary! Collins grumbled that thirty-eight thousand men had been forced to abandon the enterprise, a figure he later admitted was "purely mythical." The actual number was two. Collins blamed the "Indian Ring," an unholy alliance of Indian agents, missionaries, and traders determined to maintain their profitable monopoly of supplying goods to the Indians.[16]

The resourceful Collins had still another rabbit in his hat: a "stumpage corporation." The "corporation" would pay the Lakotas a royalty for cutting timber in the Black Hills, under cover of which it would survey the Hills for minerals. A gold strike was sure to follow, generating demand for seizure of the Hills, at which point "favored friends of the administration" would capitalize on their inside information to "secure the choicest tracts in the Hills." It was a scheme worthy of its time, the Gilded Age. But the amateurish populist efforts of Charles Collins fell short, soon to be reinforced by a truly potent force, a crowd of masters of the arts of lobbying—the railroads.[17]

Jay Cooke has rarely, if ever, been directly linked to the Custer expedition. One of the titans of the triumphant industrial order following the Civil War, he receives only passing mention in *The New Enclopedia of the American West*. Cooke deserves a more honored place: his dealings triggered the Panic of 1873.

In *The Rise of American Civilization*, Charles and Mary Beard offer some perspective on powerful capitalists such as Cooke. "To draw the American scene as it unfolded between 1865 and the end of the Century without these dominant figures looming in the foreground," they aver, "is to make a shadow picture; to put in the presidents and the leading senators—to say nothing of transitory politicians of minor rank—and leave out such prime actors in the drama is to show scant respect for the substance of life."[18] Angry farmers came to call these dominant figures who made their fortunes in the railroad business the "Robber Barons," though like Sitting Bull and his Lakotas they would not have recognized the name of Jay Cooke.

Cooke's biography is subtitled *Financier of the Civil War*, and phantasmagorical as it may seem that any one man could finance a war, the label fits. Before turning to railroads, Cooke had marketed the huge foreign loans that financed the war for the Union. By 1873 his main enterprise was the Northern Pacific Railroad.

Cooke was a successful financier in Philadelphia, a self-made man who began as a clerk in Sandusky, Ohio. A strict Episcopalian, he taught a Sunday school class and contributed a tenth of his profits to charity. "We must all get down at the feet of Jesus," Cooke said, "and be taught by no one but Himself." As a boy he wished for no schooling but trade, having concluded early that money was "chiefly the object for which all men contend." Speaking of Philadelphia, he wrote in a letter, "I see the same all-pervading, all-engrossing anxiety to grow rich. This is the only thing for which men live here." His biographer had nothing but admiration for a life "lived without guile . . . a career so open and good and honest," with "nothing to conceal. . . . [Jay Cooke] lighted his own way through mists and shadows and helped thousands of his fellows to find the sunshine."[19]

Sometimes he also worked in the dark.

The construction of the transcontinental railroads in little more than one generation was a major human achievement. Their financing employed devices that might have been invented by Rube Goldberg. By a mathematics of magic, says Richard Slotkin, promoters convinced political sponsors and the public that their methods could generate "a literally infinite supply of wealth from the finite heritage of Frontier land." The western railroads had essentially become land companies. Congress granted them millions of acres along the proposed rights-of-way in return for their promises to build. The railroads then had to develop town sites

and farm lands to turn a profit and as collateral to secure the necessary
mortgage loans in Europe.[20]

The Northern Pacific Railroad was granted 47,000,000 acres, an
expanse thirty times the size of the Black Hills, on its promise to build a
line from Duluth to Puget Sound. As Congress debated the railroad bills,
the lobbyists and agents of the Northern Pacific followed the proceedings
so closely that a correspondent for the *New York World* pictured them as
"looking down on the scene like beasts of prey."[21]

When construction got under way in 1870, the directors confronted an urgent problem: to increase security, and thereby increase the
appeal to prospective settlers, the Great Reservation of the Lakotas must
be pushed back from the right-of-way. A Black Hills gold rush, by generating added demand, would be of immense help.

When Jay Cooke, the man who had financed a war, signed on to
sell the Northern Pacific's securities, success seemed assured. Cooke
began a systematic campaign to promote the railroad's holdings as the
new "garden of the West." Borrowing heavily from the mystical view of
William Gilpin, the first governor of Colorado Territory, that it was the
"untransacted destiny of the American people to subdue the continent,"
Cooke developed a propaganda so florid that the district came to be
derided as "Jay Cooke's Banana Belt."

Prospective investors were informed that Duluth was the "Zenith
City of the Unsalted Seas." A Kentucky Congressman, J. Proctor Knott,
rose in the House of Representatives to lift his voice in satirical praise.
Duluth, he warbled, the name for which his soul "had panted for years as
the hart panteth for the fresh water brooks. The symmetry and perfection
of our planetary system would be incomplete without it." Duluth's latitude
was precisely half-way between those of Paris and Venice, "so that
gentlemen who have inhaled the exhilarating airs of the one, or basked in
the golden sunlight of the other, may see at a glance that Duluth must be
a place of untold delights," nothing less than a "terrestrial paradise fanned
by the balmy zephyrs of an eternal spring, clothed in the gorgeous sheen
of ever-blooming flowers and vocal with the silvery melody of nature's
choicest songsters. . . ."

Widely disseminated, Knott's hymn brought a great nationwide
roar of laughter.[22]

So confident was Cooke that Sioux title to the Black Hills would
be extinguished that his first promotional pamphlet claimed the government had already made the decision to do so. Lobbying government officials, he saw nothing wrong with bypassing established channels. In 1870
he wrote General W. S. Hancock, commander of the military district

through which the Northern Pacific would pass, ostensibly to learn the general's views on the likelihood of conflict with the Indians if the line should be built near or through their reservation. In such a case, Hancock replied, war was indeed likely. However, the general assured Cooke, if the Northern Pacific required protection for its surveys, "It will be our duty as well as our pleasure to give all assistance possible."[23]

The participants in such intimate exchanges masked the reality of their actions from themselves, alleges Richard Slotkin. Grouping Cooke with Hancock, Commissioner of Indian Affairs Walker, and President Grant, Slotkin compares them with Charles Collins, "a shameless rascal" who boasted, after the fact, of circumventing the law. These eminent men, by contrast, "preferred to see themselves as the agents of a genuine moral and progressive enterprise," Slotkin asserts, "compelled by circumstances to get their hands a bit dirty (and of course to take a reasonable profit from the exchange), but not fundamentally corrupt." Cooke's propaganda, he says, "linked railroad agrarianism to the larger theme of the racial struggle between savages and Anglo-Saxons for control of the future." To reap the profit of a bribe from "an enterprise of such symbolic appeal," Slotkin observes, "must have been all but irresistible: the perfect combination of vile lucre and moral uplift."[24]

A more straightforward approach was taken in 1872 by Judge W. W. Brookings. On the movement to organize expeditions to the Black Hills, Brookings acknowledged that the motive was to develop Dakota, but he added a precaution: "Don't let us Humbug the people, let us work honestly." The Black Hills held other sources of wealth besides gold. The lumber was needed to build cities and towns, and pine was abundant. "Let us not deceive the public," Brookings urged, but state the case so as to induce the Government to remove the obstacles in the way of an "immediate exploration of the Black Hills."[25]

The Northern Pacific reached Bismarck in June 1873. There it stopped, bankrupt. The officials managing the railroad, who did not live in the region it served, had other concerns and little stake, financially or otherwise, in the railroad's success. They spent recklessly. Their accounting methods were poor, or worse. Without consulting Cooke, they entered into construction contracts before he had sold the bonds to fund them. Having invested next to nothing themselves, they had little to fear. The one who stood to lose was the most inventive banker of his era—Jay Cooke. On September 18, 1873, in less than an hour, the whole edifice of his "seemingly impregnable" house came crashing down. "No one could have been more surprised," wrote the *Philadelphia Inquirer*, "if snow had fallen amid the sunshine of a summer noon."[26]

The ensuing panic plunged the nation into a severe depression, halted the Northern Pacific Railroad, and intensified demand for a new gold strike—where but in the Black Hills?

In the throes of a deep nationwide depression, the Custer expedition started for the Black Hills. The military authorization from General Sheridan to General Terry is devious in what it does *not* say. Terry was directed to send a column of ten companies of the Seventh Cavalry under the command of Lieutenant Colonel G. A. Custer "to examine the country in and about the North Fork of the Sheyenne, shown on the maps as the Belle Fourche: also, the country south of it in the vicinity of Bear Butte, especially South and West of Bear Butte, commonly designated as the Black Hills on the map." Custer was to determine the longitude and latitude of Bear Butte and "any other well-marked feature in the Black Hills which would serve as a good point of reference for that unknown section of country."

"[A]nother triumph of official indefiniteness," write Herbert Krause and Gary D. Olson: the "unique spell of the Black Hills tucked away in two off-hand expressions." Nothing to excite a public mired in a depression, "certainly no mention of even a hen's tooth of possibility of looking for gold, . . . no hint of newspaper correspondents, of geological experts, of experienced miners accompanying the column; nor was an inkling given that the guides would be Arikara Indians, hiding ancient vengeance in their sheathed hunting knives."[27]

The expedition was necessary, Sheridan explained, because the Lakotas were not living up to their agreements, though their agents unanimously reported that the tribes were behaving well. Sheridan himself had reported in 1873 that the "condition of Indian affairs in the Department of Dakota had been remarkably quiet." In reality, Stephen Ambrose suggests, every level of American society had some interest in opening the Black Hills to prospecting. Railroad men, especially backers of the Northern Pacific, wanted the hostiles subdued. Businessmen, farmers, and laborers wanted Black Hills gold coined and put into circulation. The army wanted revenge. President Grant wanted to show that the government could take decisive action. Moreover, American pride simply could not accept that this "vast enclave" of territory should be permanently excluded from an expanding nation.[28]

On July 2, 1874 the expedition left Fort Abraham Lincoln, near Bismarck—four long lines of white-crowned wagons flanked by a row of cavalry to either side, guidons flying. Dressed in buckskin, Custer himself led the formation on Dandy, his prancing bay, followed by sixteen musicians on white horses playing "The Girl I Left Behind Me." Once out of sight of Fort Lincoln, says Donald Jackson, the bandsmen "tossed their instruments into a wagon," the scouts moved into the lead, and "Custer's hounds dashed to and fro, flushing birds out of coulees and dodging clumps of prickly pear."[29]

Accompanying Custer as acting aide was the President's son, Frederick Grant, in a jaunty straw hat. Twenty-four, a second lieutenant of cavalry three years out of West Point, Grant held the brevet rank of lieutenant colonel. Two of Custer's younger brothers came along: Thomas, commanding Company L, and Boston, the frail brother who had come west to spend the summer—a guide, though he knew nothing of the West and sometimes became lost himself.

Opinions of Custer showed the usual division. The twenty-three-year-old star reporter for the *Chicago Inter-Ocean*, William Eleroy Curtis, found him not the "big-whiskered, swearing, ranting, drinking trooper" he had expected, but a great and noble man, "a slender, quiet gentleman with a face as fair as a girl's, and manners as gentle and courtly as the traditional prince." Private Theodore Ewert, a twenty-seven-year-old cavalryman who had once been an officer, confided to his journal that his commander was a "restless spirit" seeking fresh laurels in the Black Hills, "no matter at what cost of labor, trouble, or life." The colonel's honor and that of his country, in Ewert's view, "weighed lightly in the scale against the 'glorious?' name of 'Geo. A. Custer.'" For its part, Ewert wrote, the United States Government "forgot its honor, forgot the sacred treaty in force between itself and the Dakota Sioux, forgot its integrity, and ordered the organization of an Expedition for the invasion of the Black Hills."[30]

For two weeks the expedition moved west and south, a thousand men and more than a hundred wagons, with three hundred beef cattle trailing along behind. Custer had little fear of hostile Indians. Before the expedition left, he reported to General Terry, he had sent "pacific messages to all the tribes infesting the region." If the Lakotas meant war, he assured Terry, "they [would] be the party to fire the first shot."[31]

On into southeastern Montana the expedition went, then south into northeastern Wyoming, three hundred miles over virtually treeless plains. As they came within sight of their destination, the men's excitement is not hard to imagine. They were embarked on the expedition cited by the *Army and Navy Journal* as promising to clear up "the only mysterious spot of any size" left in the United States. What might they find there? Then to mystery, add the lure of the forbidden. And the Black Hills! A recent editorial in the *Bismarck Tribune* crooned they held the promise of nuggets of "pure gold as large as walnuts." Even the reporters were becoming excited. They "have enjoyed themselves hugely," wrote one reporter about his fellows, and "as newspapermen love excitement as a duck loves water, they are reasonably happy."[32]

"The Black Hills look beautiful in the distance," wrote correspondent Fred Power on July 18 from their camp on the Belle Fourche River, north of the range. "We are at present resting under the shade of large pines," he noted in his diary, the first timber they had seen since the Missouri. After days of nothing but horses for shade, another correspondent expressed delight at "the prospect of having a real, live tree—a tree that would not tread on you just as you had dropped to sleep."

Every night the men had witnessed a bright comet in the sky. "[T]he sun moon & stars take their natural course here as elsewhere," Power observed, "and even the comet gladdens us by making its nightly appearance." A spectacular lightning storm one night had lighted tents half a mile away. George Bird Grinnell, the expedition's paleontologist, had found a large leg bone that Custer believed had belonged to an animal larger than an elephant. The geologist, Professor Winchell, found the soil to be "good, very good." Power himself thought the scarcity of rain would keep the country from ever being of much use, though the picturesque valley in which they were camped looked to him like a place where a white man could live contentedly. Of a fresh Indian grave they had passed, Power ventured, "His spirit is wandering over the [B]lack Hills—the Happy hunting ground of the Sioux."[33]

The expedition threaded its way south between the Bear Lodge Mountains to the west and the Black Hills in search of an opening through which they might find their way into the mountains. One officer found a tin cup marked "William Robertson," a man identified as of mixed blood. "So far," Power confided to his diary, "we have not found the wonderful gold producing country." Upon reaching the vicinity of Inyan Kara Mountain, the expedition buried two soldiers, one who had died of disease, one shot by a companion. Powers thought the playing of "Taps" the most impressive he'd ever heard.[34]

They stayed over a day at Inyan Kara. Custer climbed the mountain, where he had his engineer chisel a monument on the summit: *"'74 Custer."* On July 24 they found an opening into the Hills. Journeying east over rough terrain, they came upon a beautiful valley profuse with flowers and strawberries, with "a stream as cool as ice running through it," wrote Power, "& disappearing in the ground." Nathan Knappen of the *Bismarck Tribune* called it "one of the most beautiful spots on God's green earth," remarking, "No wonder Indians regard this as the home of the Great Spirit . . . and guard it with jealous care." Samuel Barrows of the *New York Tribune* was ecstatic: "An Eden in the Clouds—how shall I describe it!"

Custer designated the spot Floral Valley. "[H]ardboiled troopers fell in love with it," says Donald Jackson. "Teamsters picked blossoms to decorate the harnesses of their mules; infantrymen plumed their hats; young officers slipped petals into their notebooks to take to their wives." The expedition's botanist collected fifty-two varieties of flowers from within the bounds of the camp. Except for butterflies, they found hardly an insect. The valley was photographed in black and white by William Illingworth, the expedition photographer. Illingworth's photos, taken under the most difficult conditions, would prove to be an invaluable record of the Black Hills before development.[35]

In his dispatch to the *St. Paul Daily Press*, Power records a legend of this stream: "Its source is in a beautiful cave, supplied with all of the luxuries of life, both artificial and natural, fruits of all kinds from every clime, wine the finest, foreign and domestic." It was endowed with fountains of champagne, walls of purest gold, floors of pearl. Those "fortunate enough to enter this paradise are so enchanted that they desire to spend the rest of their lives there, and after life take it for their heaven." Power's diary attributes the legend to Professor Donaldson, the expedition botanist, who "of course" got it from the Santee Sioux scouts. "The stream is swallowed by a snake of immense size," Power adds, "and he remains under ground in another cave."[36]

On July 26 the expedition made its only direct contact with Indians. As they had moved on up Floral Valley the previous day, entering South Dakota for the first time, they had encountered well-worn trails left by travois poles. Crossing a divide at about 6800 feet, the column two miles long in single file weaved its way between high limestone cliffs. Captured by Illingworth in a photo from above, the column of white-topped wagons resembles a snake entering Castle Creek Valley. When the expedition came upon a smoldering fire where a party had camped, Custer sent Bloody Knife with a few scouts to reconnoiter. One of the scouts soon returned: Indians ahead!

"Anticipating some fun," Power and three other reporters joined Custer in the advance. When they sighted five lodges a couple of miles ahead, "our hearts beat faster than usual," Powell confided to his diary, but from a hill commanding a view of the camp they realized to their sorrow that the encampment contained only the five lodges. "I must confess that the encampment look[ed] beautiful, as we saw it through our glasses," Power wrote in his dispatch, picturing the scene with empathy:

the newly tanned buckskins covering the lodge poles, as white as an officer's tent, the "squaws seated on the ground cutting up deer meat, others eating and some beading moccasins, the young Indians lying around in every attitude enjoying their freedom in the sunshine, [even] the dogs lying in the shade of a teepee . . . happy; but that happiness was soon to be broken in upon . . . ."

The encampment proved to be a Lakota hunting party from the Red Cloud and Spotted Tail agencies. They had been in the Hills for several months and had no idea troops were in the area. The Arikara scouts were eager to ride in and scalp the entire party in revenge for a Lakota raid on one of their villages, an attack in which Bloody Knife's son had been killed. Among the Lakotas in the hunting party was a daughter of Red Cloud himself—Plenty Horses, or Libbie Slow Bear. "A not uncomely squaw," correspondent Samuel Barrows described her. "Her teepee was the cleanest and neatest of the five; . . . The family effects, such as were not needed for immediate use, were packed up in clean skins tied with thongs and disposed around the tent."[37]

A lovely scene, with only words to capture it or the encounter to follow, because Illingworth was not there to record it. Custer needed information. His maps were no longer adequate, and his guides knew next to nothing about the Black Hills. Restraining the Arikaras, who had stripped and painted themselves for war, he offered the Lakotas his protection. In response to a plea from Plenty Horses, he had them supplied with coffee, sugar, and tobacco. When their chief arrived— One Stab, or Stabber, an old man in a breech clout and weather-beaten shirt and hat but with an air of authority, as chief of eighty lodges—he smoked a peace pipe with Custer while they discussed the topography of the Hills.

In the ensuing confusion the Lakotas slipped away, one of them possibly hit by the only shot fired, from the musket of a Santee scout. One Stab remained behind, either as guest or captive. Custer wrote, surely tongue in cheek, "I have effected arrangements by which the Chief One Stab remains with us as a guide." According to correspondent Curtis, One Stab was told he would be held hostage until the expedition was out of the Hills, and that he must show them a good road. The Arikara scouts maintained that One Stab was hobbled and picketed to a stake.

One myth about the Black Hills had been shattered, says Donald Jackson: "the place was not teeming with hostiles. So Custer turned to another legend and pursued it as vigorously as he had ever pursued a band of warriors. He began to look for gold."[38]

After a day's layover and a night cold enough to produce frost, the expedition pressed on, led by One Stab—"Genl Custers prisoner" [sic], Power calls him. On Reynolds Prairie they found a stack of elk horns five or six feet high. Camping amid an abundance of flowers at a site now occupied by Deerfield Lake, they enjoyed strawberries and fresh fish from Castle Creek. Next day they departed reluctantly, veering south along an Indian trail, leaving the wagon train to catch up. On the second day, writes Power, they discovered "a beautiful valley surrounded by grand hills whose heads had withstood the storms of many a winter & [been] watered by [s]treams whose waters have flowed since the flood . . . . A perfect fairy land in summer."[39]

Custer, riding ahead, had been first to find the valley, which is now occupied by the western portion of the town that bears his name. "After much entreaty," Professor Donaldson observed wryly, "his modesty as far gave way as reluctantly to consent to the request of the topographical engineer that the name be Custer Park."[40]

One of the miners promptly went down to French Creek. His pan turned up a few grains of "color," nothing to create much excitement. As Custer went off the following day to climb Harney Peak, the miners went on panning. The enlisted men played a game of baseball. That evening, in Custer's absence, the officers staged a spirited champagne supper, complete with a barber shop quartet singing "If I Had but Thousand a Year" and other selections. Whiskey flowed, along with champagne. "Wish I had a pretty girl & good floor," Power confesses to his diary, "but I have not." Lieutenant Hodgson, he observes, "found some difficulty in crossing the creek." The whole party was "pretty well hobbled."

Given her husband's repeated assurances, Elizabeth Custer might have been troubled by the festivities. In a letter only two weeks earlier, Custer had written her, "I am more than ever convinced of the influences a commanding officer exercises for good or ill. There has not been a single card party, not a single drunken officer, since we left Ft. Lincoln."[41]

Custer returned well after midnight. Next day, the wagon train having caught up, the expedition moved three miles down French Creek and set up permanent camp, where it remained for five days. The miners, both experienced men, got seriously to work. Horatio Ross had run a productive gold mine in Colorado. William McKay was a member of the Dakota territorial legislature. They were not officially attached to the command; that would have been awkward. They were just "with" Custer.

Half a century later, one of the teamsters said that Custer had financed them himself.

Ross and McKay found excellent colors in loose soil along the creek, though Ross doubted the gold would yield more than $50 or $75 a day. Almost everybody went prospecting, even Aunt Sally, the black cook—Sarah Campbell, who called herself "the only white woman that ever saw the Black Hills."[42]

Correspondent Power saw little reason for excitement. After praising the beauties of Custer Park, he notes in his diary, "Gold has been found in quantities, also silver." At the end of his dispatch of August 2, he adds an afterthought: "Oh! I forgot to say gold has been discovered." His only comments about the mission of Charley Reynolds have to do with the letters Reynolds was carrying on his "lonely trip to Laramie."[43]

Reynolds' dash to the nearest telegraph station brought the news to the world: gold in the Black Hills! Custer's initial notice was rather muted. "I have upon my table," he wrote, "40 or 50 small particles of pure gold, in size about that of a small pin-head. Most of it was obtained today from a single pan of earth." Pending further investigation into the richness of the deposits, no opinion should yet be formed. Custer extolled the grazing qualities of the Black Hills as equal to the Blue Grass region of Kentucky, adding a note of enticement: "I know of no portion of our country where nature has done so much to prepare homes for husbandmen and left so little for them to do as here."

The truly masterful touch appeared in his field report of August 15 from Bear Butte. In a single phrase Custer managed to combine the allure of gold with agrarian promise: "The miners report that they found gold among the roots of the grass." Gold in the roots of the grass: the image that was to become the leitmotif of the Black Hills gold rush.[44]

There was joy in Bismarck. "Count me in for the Black Hills," echoed the *Tribune* on August 12 In response to a special dispatch of August 3 from its correspondent, the *Tribune* quoted popular exclamations: "How do you like it? Glorious, isn't it?" Fortunes were about to be made and lost, and Bismarck, the nearest rail connection to "this new Eldorado," would be the town to "gather the gold." Those who had been despondent for weeks, what with grasshoppers, drought, and "the universal dullness, brightened up and were themselves again, and a better feeling prevails in town than has been felt since the panic last fall, when the bottom fell out of everything that had Northern Pacific in it."[45]

The *Yankton Press and Dakotaian* was even more jubilant:

STRUCK IT AT LAST!
Rich Mine of Gold and Silver
Reported Found by Custer
PREPARE FOR LIVELY TIMES!
Gold Expected to Fall 10 per Cent—
Spades and Picks Rising.—The
National Debt to be Paid
When Custer Returns.

The *New York Tribune* sounded a note of caution: the region belonged to the Sioux, and the value of the gold fields had yet to be determined. The *Chicago Inter-Ocean* devoted the entire front page to the news on August 27: "Gold! The Land of Promise—Stirring News from the Black Hills." The headline was followed by eleven subheads and a breathless, folksy account by William Eleroy Curtis dated August 7: "They call it a TEN DOLLAR DIGGIN'S, and all the camp is aglow with the gold fever. . . . From the grass roots down it was 'pay dirt.'" The same edition reprinted a claim drawn up by twenty-one men of the expedition, posted at the site, headed "District No. 1, Custer Park Mining Company."[46]

To many, the solution to the nation's crisis was simple. The *Inter-Ocean* quoted a miner, Captain Russell: "Money is scarce, and the country needs gold." To Russell the sequence could not have been more obvious. "There was a crisis in 1848-49; California was opened and helped us out. There was a crisis in 1857; in 1858 Colorado was opened and helped us out. There was a crisis in 1873, from the effects of which we have not yet recovered; the Black Hills will be opened and pull us through."[47]

The *Tribune* warned of manipulations behind the scenes: "Speculators in St. Paul and Bismarck in the interest of the Northern Pacific Railroad, are actively engaged in fomenting the gold fever," claiming gold had been found in "unlimited quantities." In truth, "all the gold actually discovered thus far, could be put in a thimble." But the *New York World*, reversing its earlier opposition to the Northern Pacific as a useless extravagance, now declared that the line's recovery, and railroad building in general, would realize everything its friends had hoped for: help end the depression and prove a "mighty instrument" in finding a "final and peaceable solution of the Indian question."[48]

For the men of the expedition, what followed was anticlimactic. It was time to go home. Custer sent two companies southeast with pack mules, but the detachment, most likely blocked by French Creek Gorge, failed to reach the Cheyenne River. Custer himself led a battalion south and southwest, almost to the Cheyenne, where he dispatched Charley Reynolds to Fort Laramie with word of the gold discovery.

On August 6 the expedition broke camp, retracing its journey for a day before branching off to the northeast. Near the Belle Fourche River four Cheyenne warriors informed them that Sitting Bull and five thousand warriors were planning to intercept them near the Little Missouri. The war party never materialized, but the rumor was wired to General Sheridan as fact and swiftly broadcast to alarm the nation.

The expedition left Bear Butte on August 16. They had killed a thousand big-game animals. The most notable was the huge grizzly that fell to Custer with help from Captain Ludlow, and most likely dispatched by Bloody Knife with a blade.[49] They needed thirteen balls to kill the old fellow. Some eight hundred pounds, the immense bear sprawls in the foreground of an Illingworth photograph that has been widely published. Custer presides over it in triumph.

In his notebook Power penciled an elegy that resembles William Faulkner's description of the death of "Old Ben" in his novella *The Bear*. Old Ben took fifty-two pieces of lead, "buckshot rifle and ball," before falling to a knife. Faulkner likens the bear in death to a piece of statuary as it surges erect, a fierce dog at its throat, a man astride its back probing with a knife—Faulkner's monument to the passing of the wilderness. "It didn't collapse, crumple," he writes. "It fell all of a piece, as a tree falls, so that all three of them, man dog and bear, seemed to bounce once." Of this solitary old Black Hills grizzly, Power notes simply, "[I]t backed up to a large tree & stood on its hind feet and took the shots manfully."[50]

So ended one phase of the Black Hills story, and of the life of the Plains Indians. Another was about to begin.

PART TWO

Chapter 4: *The Rush to Gold and Grass*

While Custer's expedition was camped along French Creek near the head of Stockade Lake, a second party led by the Reverend Samuel Hinman set out to explore the Hills. The Hinman commission had been charged with locating a site for a new agency for Red Cloud and Spotted Tail. The commission's aim, Hinman reported, was "if possible to find some place where water should be abundant and good and where there would be sufficient timber to afford lumber for building and wood for fuel."[1]

An Episcopal missionary born in Connecticut, Hinman had become fluent in the Santee dialect of the Sioux tongue. He performed the first Christian marriage conducted entirely in Santee and later published *The Book of Common Prayer* in Santee and English. At Custer's request he had recruited thirty Santee scouts for the Custer expedition and escorted them to Fort Lincoln before departing on his own mission.

Accompanied by two companies of cavalry, the Hinman expedition left Cheyenne on July 28, 1874. Unlike Custer, they planned to enter the Black Hills from the south. Hinman was warned not to proceed by Spotted Tail and Two Strike, who were already disturbed by Custer's expedition, but he persuaded the chiefs that his exploration might serve to discredit the widespread rumors of wealth in the Hills. At length, Spotted Tail condoned a brief tour, for observation only.

Entering through Buffalo Gap, Hinman's party penetrated the Hills to a site on French Creek within ten miles of Custer's permanent camp. They found no gold or precious metals. "The Black Hills we found to be a bleak, and except for its abundant growth of hard pines, a forbidding and sterile mountain," Kinman reported, "and only a garden spot when compared to, and contrasted with, the bad and utter desolation that surround[s] it." For agricultural or stockraising purposes, the region was worthless. Perhaps out of a desire to forestall exploration, he depicted the area as unfit for even an Indian agency. "[T]o open the country would be a mistaken kindness to the whites and a great uncalled for wrong for the Indians."[2]

The Hinman report was largely ignored by the press. Not so, the report of Professor Newton Winchell, official geologist of the Custer expedition. The miners did indeed report finding gold and silver, wrote Winchell, "though I saw none of the gold nor did I see any auriferous quartz. I have taken the gold reports with a large grain of allowance."[3]

No gold? A large grain of allowance?

Custer could hardly let such a notion stand. "Why Professor Winchell saw no gold," he rejoined, "was simply due to the fact that he neglected to look for it." A college professor could of course be written off as "addlepated and absentminded," suggests Donald Jackson, but the same could hardly be said of Fred Grant, "a friend of Custer's, a hearty drinker, an easygoing young fellow that everyone liked, and the son of a president besides—and he had seen no gold." Grant confided to his journal, "I don't believe any gold was found at all." The *New York Times* pointedly observed that such information as it received from the West about gold was invariably accompanied by effusive praise of Bismarck and the Northern Pacific Railroad.[4]

Custer declared he would follow orders to keep miners out of the Black Hills, but he let it be known that for "military reasons" he favored extinguishment of Sioux title. At the same time he detailed the Northern Pacific's facilities for transporting miners to Dakota Territory. The chief military reason he gave for extinguishing Sioux title was that the Black Hills served, in Richard Slotkin's words, as "the nexus of a secret communications network, linking the disaffected tribes as they conspire for a grand race war," a sort of "backroom to which [the Indians] escape after committing depredations."[5]

From Bismarck the *New York World's* correspondent elaborated on this allegation. Custer had found that the Indians guarded the Hills jealously not out of any special value they held for the red man, but as "a sort of covered way, a natural underground, or elevated railway" through which to maintain "undiscovered communication . . . between the hostile camps in the Powder River and Yellowstone country and the agency Indians located on the Missouri River." The best way to break up this alliance, ventured the *World*, would be to occupy the Black Hills, "peopling it with thrifty industrous settlers."[6]

Then came a thunderbolt from on high: settlers would not be permitted to enter the Black Hills in violation of the Fort Laramie Treaty of 1868! General Sheridan issued the order in a telegraph to General Terry that was made public right on the heels of the Custer expedition: "Should the companies now organizing at Sioux City and Yankton trespass on the Sioux Indian Reservation, you are hereby directed to use the force at your command to burn the wagon trains, destroy the outfits and arrest the leaders, confining them at the nearest military post in the Indian country." If any of them should reach the interior, Terry was to dispatch cavalry to remove them. If Congress should open the country by extinguishing the treaty rights of the Indians, Sheridan would of course give "cordial support" to settlement of the Black Hills.[7]

Other officials pointed to difficulties. With the buffalo declining, Colonel Ludlow observed in his report as topographer of the Custer expedition, the Sioux looked forward to settling in and around the Black Hills as their permanent home, "there awaiting the gradual extinction which is their fate." For the next half century the best use of the Hills would probably be as "the permanent reservation of the Sioux, where they could be taught occupations of a pastoral character."[8]

Commissioner of Indian Affairs Edward P. Smith, another Connecticut missionary, who had been an Indian agent, agreed with Ludlow, but added an "if": if there were no gold in the Black Hills and the Indians could be left undisturbed, "this region, naturally suited to agriculture and herding, is the one of all others within the boundaries of the Sioux reservation best adapted to their immediate and paramount necessities." Smith injected a rare moral consideration: "[I]f for the want of another such country, [the Sioux] are obliged to begin civilization under increased disabilities, humanity as well as equity demands that such disability shall be compensated by increased aid from the Government." That the Sioux made "little if any use of the Black Hills has no bearing upon the question of what is a fair equivalent" for the loss of these lands. "They are children," Smith added in a note of paternalistic concern, "utterly unable" to envision their own future. But their ignorance "makes the stronger appeal to our sense of what is right and fair."[9]

Considerations of "right and fair" became lost in the circumstances. "It's the same old story," General Sherman remarked in St. Louis, "the story of Adam and Eve and the forbidden fruit." The English journalist Edwin A. Curley asked why the Custer expedition had been permitted to begin with, then allowed to be promoted so as to excite the thirst for riches and the love of adventure. "Is it not true that in practical effect the officers of the government were sent to pluck the forbidden fruit, and to show it to the people, saying, 'This is most excellent food?'"[10]

A tall square of heavy timbers, newly reconstructed at the head of Stockade Lake near the site of Custer's permanent camp, stands today as a monument to the Gordon party. The Collins-Russell party, as it was initially known, left Sioux City barely a month after Custer's return to Fort Lincoln. The party was organized by Thomas Russell and the unwearying Charles Collins. Collins opened an office in Chicago to attract recruits. When their activities caught the eye of General Sheridan, the general issued another order against trespass. Russell and Collins returned to Sioux City, closed the Chicago office, and published a dispatch declaring the expedition abandoned for the present.

"This dispatch was merely a blind to put the military authorities off their guard," wrote Annie Tallent in her celebrated eyewitness account published a quarter century later, *The Black Hills, or Last Hunting Grounds of the Dakotahs*. Secrecy was necessary because "the movement was in direct violation of the orders of the United States government . . . ." Most any day toward the end of September 1874, she noted, "small groups of determined looking men" could be seen on the streets or in the hotel lobbies of Sioux City—a common enough occurrence at the time except that in this case "whenever closely approached they would immediately disperse," which could arouse suspicions of "some dark conspiracy."[11]

The party set out on October 6th, twenty-eight strong, including Tallent, the only woman, along with her nine-year-old son, Robert. She lamented that only twenty-six men "had the hardihood to defy the authorities and undertake the perilous journey." The language in which her narrative is couched speaks for itself:

> Thenceforth the beautiful pine-clad Black Hills were no longer to echo the shrill war-whoop of the Sioux, nor the turf of the fair, smiling valleys lying between, respond to their stealthy tread. . . . The gold-ribbed Black Hills were to be snatched from the grasp of savages, to whom they were no longer profitable even as a hunting ground, and given over to the thrift and enterprise of the hardy pioneer . . . .

Read a few pages of this and you understand Virginia Driving Hawk Sneve's scorn of Tallent's book, in her introduction to the second edition brought out in 1974: a "malicious, bigoted treatment of the Dakota or

Sioux Indians [that] would best serve mankind if it were burned rather than reprinted . . . to perpetrate a distorted, untrue portrait of the American Indian."[12]

For contemporary Americans a more profitable use for Tallent's *The Black Hills* might be as a text, a revelation of the dominant outlook of her pioneer generation, adorned with references to savages skulking about, squaws and papooses, glittering gewgaws, the blood of innocent women and children—all the ethnocentric trappings of a righteousness that never questions itself.

Tallent all but boasts that the expedition was beyond the pale of the law. As they journeyed westward, crossing the Niobrara River near present-day Valentine, they feared the authorities more than the Indians. When one member of the party, Ephraim Witcher, contracted an acute case of homesickness and announced he was going back to civilization, a council was speedily assembled. Much as the leading Pilgrims aboard the Mayflower, before landing at Plymouth, formed a compact among themselves by which to maintain order, the leaders of the Gordon party gathered on the eve of Witcher's departure to resolve that "no member of the expedition shall be permitted to return to civilization which we all voluntarily left," and that any such attempt "shall be deemed treasonable to the expedition." The offender would be disarmed and placed under guard "until the dangerous inclination subsides." Grumbling, Witcher remained with the party.

Great excitement occurred when they came upon a herd of Indian ponies along the Cheyenne River. The men grabbed their Winchesters, sequestering Tallent out of sight in a covered wagon, for "the presence of a woman might lead the Indians to suspect that the party contemplated a longer stay within their domain than would be agreeable to them." The Indians proved to be not the "fierce and bloodthirsty Sioux" but a band of Cheyennes who, though friendly, were "like all their race, the most inveterate of beggars." Given food and tobacco, they left peacefully.

The expedition set foot on Black Hills soil on December 9th, near Sturgis, where they encountered Custer's trail. As they followed it southward, Tallent experienced "a profound solitude, with peace, like a guardian angel, reigning over the whole wide expanse." Never having experienced mountains, awed by the landscape and the primeval silence, she felt inclined to "fall prostrate at the footstool of the Great Unseen." On December 23rd the party arrived at the site on French Creek where the present stockade stands. Some of the "boys" immediately rushed to the stream. "Eureka! They had found particles of gold in the bottom of each gold pan . . . . [T]here was great rejoicing in our camp on French Creek that winter's night." Next day was wash day, for "although branded as outlaws, we were not barbarians," and the following day was Christmas.

In his history of Plymouth Plantation, William Bradford relates that when the Pilgrims touched land on Cape Cod in 1620 "they fell upon their knees and blessed the God of Heaven who had brought them over the vast and furious ocean." Bradford then makes a "pause" to contemplate the mighty ocean, now "a main bar and gulf to separate them from all the civil parts of the world." Surrounded by a "hideous and desolate wilderness, full of wild beasts and wild men," he asks, "What could now sustain them but the Spirit of God and His grace?" Tallent, looking back on that Christmas morning on French Creek, recalls her thoughts at how far they were from home: "Completely cut off from the whole Christian world with its precious privileges; no Merry Christmas greeting from the loved ones away back toward the rising sun; no sweet chimes of Christmas bells [or] grand organ notes . . . among the mountain fastnesses; no church privileges—but, wait—was not the whole visible expanse a church, grander by far than any cathedral ever built by human hands?" She finds a sermon in the beautiful quartz scattered on the hillsides, moral lessons in tree and bush, song in the "mournful cadences of the wind." In the "awful silence that brooded over each hill, valley and beautiful glade" she feels the power to "lift the thoughts Heavenward . . . ."

Constructing the stockade required two weeks. Within the walls seven cabins were built, "comfortless homes" for a "trying time." Early in February, John Gordon and Ephraim Witcher set out for Sioux City to mount another expedition, "steal a march on the government," and return with reinforcements and supplies. In March four members of the party made their way to Fort Laramie. These pioneers of 1874, Tallent vows, "were neither fillibusters, freebooters, nor pirates, but peaceable, law-abiding citizens of the United States—however, 'with keen eyes to the main chance.'"

More than one military unit failed in the attempt to reach the Gordon party. On December 26 a detachment led by Captain Guy Henry was dispatched from a camp at Red Cloud Agency to find and disperse the miners reported to be in the Black Hills. Caught in a blizzard, the men suffered amputation of frozen ears, fingers, and toes, and discovered not a single miner. In March a detachment under Captain John Mix was dispatched to arrest the Gordon party. To show him the way to their camp, Mix commandeered two of its four members who had made it to Fort Laramie. He followed the trail of the Hinman commission through Buffalo

Gap. On April 5th his troops established Camp Success where Hinman had camped on French Creek, eight miles from the Gordon Stockade. Mix found the stockade itself formidable, ten feet high and "well adapted for defence except against artillery."[113]

Given two days to collect its stock and effects, the party was escorted out of the Black Hills. A skilled horsewoman, Tallent says she had been expected to ride a "prancing, dancing steed." Instead she was given "an old, scarred mule," its head bowed with the weight of its years. "Jupiter, Olympus," she cried, "you don't expect me to ride that beast to camp, a distance of twelve miles, do you?" When the procession paused at the Red Cloud Agency, she found herself, "the only innocent member of the party," surrounded by a dozen of the "most diabolical looking specimens of the human form" she had ever seen, perplexed to have been taken for the "arch-trespasser of the party."

Another element came into play, of course: the sight of a white woman. When Thomas Fitzpatrick led a party of missionaries across the Rockies in 1836, the wives of the missionaries attracted keen attention at rendezvous—the first white women the Indians had ever seen. "The two ladies were gazed upon with wonder and astonishment," said one of the trappers. "Our females," noted a husband of one woman, "found it quite difficult to get along for the multitudes that pressed around to shake them by the hand, both men and women." Some of the Indian women could only be satisfied by saluting the white women with a kiss, though they were "very orderly."[14]

Were it not for the presence of troops, Tallent felt certain, "I would have been speedily disposed of then and there, and my scalp would have graced the belt of one of those inhuman savages." She maintained that Captain Mix told them their party had been "in far greater peril than we dreamed of," that he had ordered forced marches in order to reach them before they were "massacred by the incensed savages." Captain Mix tells a very different story: "During our entire trip we were offered no molestation whatever from the Indians. All those seen at the agencies on our return, expressed great and complete satisfaction as the result of our scout, whose direction and destination, unseen by us, they had closely watched."[15]

A fair equivalent for the loss: this notion introduced by the Commissioner of Indian Affairs was to become the government's catch-phrase in its response to demands to open the Hills to settlement. The assumption that white settlement was inevitable, sooner or later, went virtually unchallenged. As illegal sallies into the Black Hills continued and the clamor to extinguish Sioux title intensified, the question became what are the Hills worth? What would the government acquire in return for a prospective purchase in dollars? Did they possess gold in paying quantities? On that, testimony was divided. What about other sources of wealth? Just what were the Black Hills *worth*?

"To settle this question satisfactorily," wrote Secretary of the Interior Delano to the Secretary of War in the spring of 1875, "the Department has decided, under the advice of the President, to send a competent Geologist to explore that region."[16]

A scientific expedition was dispatched to determine what the Black Hills had to offer. It was an optimal moment. The Hills bore almost no footprints, no marks of human passage. Fire had cleansed them for millennia, pushing the timber back to make way for grassland. The Indians had left hardly a scratch. The Custer expedition had cut a lazy eight through them, leaving a gash but few permanent scars. The Black Hills were pristine.

The expedition left Fort Laramie on May 25. Heading a party of seventeen as chief geologist was Professor Walter P. Jenney of the Columbia School of Mines, with Henry Newton as assistant geologist. The topographer was Dr. Valentine T. McGillycuddy. Commanding the military escort—for Custer's presence would further antagonize the Lakotas—was Lieutenant Colonel Richard I. Dodge, a seasoned officer who had spent most of his career in the West. Dodge commanded an escort of six companies of cavalry and two of infantry, with a supply train of seventy-one wagons and more than a hundred beef cattle. Five correspondents for major newspapers tagged along.

Serious and purposeful enterprise though it was, the Jenney-Dodge expedition had its comic elements from the start. A few days into the march one of the "privates" turned out to be the legendary Jane Dalton, also known as Martha Canary, outfitted as a trooper. When approached by the officer of the day, one Von Leutwitz, she drew herself up and saluted smartly. His return salute evoked bursts of laughter. The "damn little German," as she called him, demanded to know what was so funny.

"Don't you know the lady who saluted you?" he was told. "It's Calamity Jane."

Von Leutwitz was not amused. He reported her presence to Colonel Dodge, who, struggling to suppress a smile, ordered her from camp. Next morning Calamity hitched a ride with the wagon train and went on with the journey, a ritual repeated daily. The correspondent for the *Chicago Inter-Ocean*, observing her costume, informed his readers that "it does not appear to be the custom here for ladies to ride as they do further east." This "Calamity" had the reputation of being "a better horseback rider mule and bull whacker, . . . and a more unctious coiner of English, and not the Queen's pure, either, than any (other) man in the command."[17]

The expedition headed north for the Black Hills. For his guide Dodge had hired Joe Merivale, the man recommended to him as the best in the War Department. The most detailed commentary on the enterprise, and certainly the most candid, is found in Dodge's private journals, recently published. A reader well versed in Shakespeare, Scott, and Dickens, Richard Irving Dodge was a grandnephew of Washington Irving with a literary flair of his own. His journal records that on the second day out, at Meridale's suggestion, the command took a short cut through deep sand that made "abominable" traveling. They had to backtrack two and a half miles. "My faith in Merivale is gone," Dodge wrote in his journal, "& I must myself play guide." A longtime resident of the Fort Laramie area, the genial Merivale in fact knew next to nothing about the country in question. He had promised "a nize easy slope to the foothills." Instead they encountered a steep precipice rising five hundred feet. For a moment Merivale looked worried. "Jese Christ," he exclaimed, "how this damn country he change [sic] since I was here last!"[18]

The plains crossed by the expedition were not easy traveling. Only in name are the plains plain, Dodge observed in his book *The Black Hills*. "The lack of trees exposes them peculiarly to the action of the elements, and nowhere can one find more irregularity of surface, more abrupt ascents and precipitous descents, more broken, jagged, and apparently impassable country than on the plains."[19]

On the following day, having abandoned his faith in Meridale, Dodge followed the trail left by Captain Mix on his way to extract the Gordon party. Traversing some difficult ravines, the expedition struck the remnants of a trail left most likely by Lieutenant Warren in 1856. They proceeded north along an old Indian trail, a fine road, and passed over long divides separating tributaries of the Niobrara. On one height suddenly they came upon a "steep pitch" from which Dodge beheld "one of the most splendid views I have seen. The whole valley of 'Old Woman' Creek spread out at our feet bounded by steep crags, high rounded hills covered with pine, & in the distance the haven of our hopes 'The Black Hills[.]' The country is most lovely," he noted in his journal, in marked contrast to Reverend Hinman, "& I don't blame the Indians for wishing to hold on to it." Once the expedition made camp, nevertheless, he intensified vigilance to protect the stock from theft: "We are in the home of the Red Man, & just where we came into the valley passed the camp of a war party of about 100 strong bound west, . . . probably about three days old."

Dodge needed all his diplomatic skills in dealing with the chief geologist. Jenney was intent upon establishing points along the 104th meridian, the line between Sioux treaty lands and Wyoming Territory. "The astronomer has most carefully rated and adjusted his instruments," he had assured the commissioner, and barring some accident "will be able to determine the meridian very accurately." The topographer and the astronomer objected. They had no orders to "run the west line of Dacotah," they told Dodge, and lacked the instruments to do so. Marches and countermarches in search of the meridian threatened to exhaust the expedition's resources, yet in the beginning Dodge went out of his way to accommodate the young geologist.

Jenney seems to have become a riddle to Dodge. The colonel himself became known among the younger officers as "Richard the First," a play on *I,* his middle initial, that may also suggest an authoritative bearing. The *Chicago Tribune* portrayed him as a man "born in North Carolina, of a good old stock, . . . full six feet in his stockings, his powerful frame surmounted by a fine Grecian profile . . . a fine type of the rapidly-passing-away Southern gentleman and soldier." Jenney paid tribute to Dodge as a "splendidly qualified" officer who did everything possible to facilitate the explorations. For his part Dodge, upon meeting Jenney, thought him a very good man, though apparently "rather timid and fearful of his knowledge of things."[20]

Three weeks earlier, on his way to Fort Laramie, Dodge had met a Lakota delegation headed for Washington, one that included Red Cloud and Spotted Tail. The chiefs warned him he might have to fight the northern tribes now in the Black Hills. Dodge seems not to have felt particularly threatened. On May 31st, camped on the Cheyenne, he notes simply, "The Indians have just found us out. Two Smokes were sent up today on edge of Black Hills. I hope some of them will come in tomorw." Two days later he notes that some of the men claim to have seen Indians. "All have orders to treat them kindly & bring them into Camp if possible." He fears loss of the beef herd. "They know we are here & their failing to come in is a rather bad sign. They will get our stock if possible."

The expedition is now "just at the door of the great unknown— the Black Hills," he writes on June 1. Superlative hunting: four elk, three deer, and a brown bear. "So the camp is full of meat, & we rejoice in fatness." Camped in a grove of cottonwood trees whose tops have been cut off each year as winter feed for Indian ponies, Dodge observes an Indian grave in the branches of one tree "which I am sorry to say, was rifled by the Doctors of the Expedition (there are two (2) military and several civil Doctors) & the head & all curious articles carried off. Dr. McGillicuddy of the scientific got the lower jaw, which he proposes to take home as a present for a dear friend to be used as a pen holder." Dodge's terse comment on the incident is drawn from *Hamlet*, where the prince has just held in his hands the skull of Yorick, his merry boyhood companion: "To what base uses may we come at last."[21]

In his private journals Dodge often manifests a respect for his subject that can be missing from his book *The Black Hills*, where he tailors his depictions to his prospective readers, as in this passage: "Far out of the ordinary lines of plains travel, surrounded on all sides by the arid wastes of the 'Bad Lands,' by bands of hostile and treacherous savages, the 'Black Hills' loomed up in silent majesty, mysterious, unknown." The language can go stale and trite: "Though many had, afar off, gazed in wistful wonder at the long black Mass, no white man had ever penetrated their recesses, or bared the secrets hidden in their dark bosoms."[22]

The journals give succinct appraisals of other members of the expedition. Merivale is "no sort of a guide." The reporter for the *New York Herald*, Reuben Davenport, writes well but is "green as a gourd, as credulous as a ninny." Some of the young officers are "stuffing him with the most incredible stories," scaring him half to death with hints that the hooting of an owl means an Indian attack on the morrow. As his defense, Davenport plans to hoist his "*Herald* Flag" over his tent to assure the Indians he's a noncombatant. Dodge cautions him that he's being "imposed upon by these youngsters" and advises him to "beware of publishing any stories or rumors coming from them." The *Inter-Ocean* man, Thomas MacMillan, is of an "entirely different stamp very gentlemanly, hard to stuff, & with excellent good sense." McGillycuddy is "smart and bright, well up in his business as a professional map maker, but runs too much to fancy, & pretty."

Dodge considers Jenney an aspiring man from whom he can expect only hostility when Jenney writes his report. To put this boyish young man in charge of such an expedition leads Dodge to suspect a "job" of some kind. A professional soldier who would never voice such a suspicion publicly, he writes, "My opinion is that the report to be made in regard to Gold has been decided upon already at Washington & that the sending him out is the merest blind."

On June 2 Dodge's patience with Jenney gave out. Dragging the expedition around in order to locate the 104th meridian imperiled their mission. Soon after crossing Beaver Creek they struck "the great North and South Indian Trail" from the White River agencies to the Powder River country. Astronomical calculations placed them in Dakota, several miles too far east, though they were actually still in Wyoming. Jenney wants to go "westing," Dodge says, at wit's end. "We have been piddling along a few miles a day hoping to suit all his ideas." Jenney "still has the boyish hope of getting everything just as he desires." Dodge presented him with a choice: "either abandon good wood, water & grass, & mountain work for 104 or abandon 104 for these." If they continued in the present fashion, their rations would give out.

"He saw it all," Dodge notes with relief, "& tomorw we strike straight for the mountains for what appears to be a pass, & is practicable for horsemen." A good day's march brought them to a beautiful spot on a branch of Beaver Creek, where they established Camp Jenney and would stay for several days. Dodge ordered construction of a storehouse and stockade. Jenney returned from a brief exploration, delighted. He found the Black Hills "an Earthly Paradise," Dodge writes, "the most lovely streams, the most beautiful timber, the finest game."

Two boys had come along on the expedition. One was Dodge's son Fred, sixteen, who had lived most of his life in New York with his mother. Fred was "naturally very timid, having been brought up entirely by women." When Jenney's party caught a beaver, Dodge took his son to see the creature, and actually handle it. Released to the stream, the poor beast "gave us a fine specimen of his skill in diving & soon disappeared."

On the eve of their departure from Camp Jenney, Dodge had two callers. The first was Jenney, "morbidly anxious lest some one should be ahead of him in reporting Gold." To Jenney, secrecy was critical; he simply had to make the first discovery and the first report. Then came Davenport, the gullible *Herald* reporter, seeking Dodge's help in finding a reliable man to carry a dispatch to Fort Laramie: "I can afford to pay more than any body else, and I think I will go to Jenney's man and see if I can't get him to go back on Jenney, for money." Dodge told Davenport "they were all Kilkenney Cats & might use each other up, or 'beat' & bribe as suited them. But I rejoice that I am a soldier," he confides to his journal, "if success in civil life depends on such small dirty practices that Jenney & the Herald man, seem disposed to put in operation against each other."

The first evening out, on a branch of Red Water Creek, a tremendous thunderstorm stampeded the cattle. It was raining hard, "as dark as Erebus." The quartermaster went out after them, but not the colonel: "I wouldn't go out tonight for all the Texas cattle in the country." Next day, pausing to drink from a stream of delicious water, the advance party had a nip of whiskey, toasting their success up to this point, and climbed to the summit of a divide that gave them a splendid view of the northern rim of the Hills. A bank of dense clouds was moving their way from the east and northeast. Before noon the expedition was overtaken by hail and snow.

At midday they went into camp where Custer had camped the previous summer. From Custer's map Dodge determined they were at the head of Floral Valley. But "alas for the 'floral' part of it": the trees were just budding, and only the hardiest flowers were in bloom. Unless the country had mineral wealth, it was "worth but little. Two months of summer & ten of winter is not a good climate for settlers. . . . Wood and water excellent — No grass."

Following Custer's trail up Floral Valley, Dodge noted the remains of last year's Indian camps—temporary encampments devoted to harvesting spruce for lodge poles. A succession of springs made an awful bog of the road. "Bog bog, all the time 16 mules on a team, & as many men as could get hold prying & lifting the bed out of the mud." Waiting for the wagons to get through, Dodge led a party to the top of a high bare hill, Prospect Peak. The view was more than simply magnificent: "We seemed to be fixed in the center of a circle formed of huge hills and mountains."

On June 12 they struck gold, "undeniable unmistakeable. It is only a little 'show' but it is gold." The grass in the valley was splendid, unsurpassed as grazing country. Dodge passed lightly over the gold, with a forecast: "In ten years the Black Hills will be the home of a numerous & thriving population, & all the Administrations & Interior Departments cant [sic] stop it. It is not an Indian Country," he insisted. "They can live in it for only a small portion of the year and being Plains Indians they do not like to go into a country where they cannot ride everywhere they wish to go. They use it as a nursery for game, & a fine one it is." Himself an avid hunter, Dodge surmises that it "must be a magnificent [hunting] ground in the fall and winter. The whole country is covered with dropped horns, elk & deer."

The more he saw of the Black Hills, the more credit Dodge gave Custer, whose map he found remarkably correct and helpful. Failing to locate a less boggy route, he settled upon Custer's road south, traversing the soggiest places by corduroy—logs laid crosswise. On June 14th the expedition struck the valley of French Creek, open glades amid timbered hills, and followed it to the Gordon Stockade, which was situated in a lovely park: "At irregular intervals huge rocks thrust their heads through the green turf, & clustered about each such group, as chicks about the mother hen . . . group[s] of pines towering to the skies."

While looking for a site for his camp, Dodge spied a man dashing into a narrow gorge: "the inevitable miner." Preferring to avoid contact, assuming that his role in escorting a scientific mission exempted him from the order to arrest them, and lacking the forces to carry it out, Dodge sent his adjutant to investigate. When the adjutant was slow to return, Dodge himself rode into a little ravine to find his adjutant congregating with six miners.

"How do you do, Colonel," one of them startled him by saying. The man had often seen Dodge in Kansas, during an assignment at Fort Larned. Dodge asked if the men knew they had no business here.

"We do," the fellow said.

"Well I dont [sic] intend to arrest you," Dodge told him.

"Thank you. I am very glad to hear it."

The man informed Dodge there were more than twenty miners on the creek, with plans to build a flume. They had met the day before to resolve conflicting claims. Dodge decided to let it go it at that. He took away some gold he himself had seen panned out, to send to General Crook. Jenney would go wild, Dodge knew, when he learned the troops here had panned fifty times more gold on that day alone than he had found on the entire trip.

"Jenney is 'scooped[,]'" Dodge wrote on June 16. And indeed Jenney was so disgusted the soldiers had found gold before he did that Dodge felt sorry for him. "But he is a 'royal' ass," Dodge swore in his journal. Some of Jenney's party had found gold several days earlier, but Jenney had bound them to secrecy. "The ass! ass! ass!"

Dodge's telegram to General Crook was widely reprinted in newspapers: "Harney's Peak, June 17.—Gold has been found in paying quantities on French Creek. Custer's report has been confirmed in every particular. The command is well and in fine condition."

Jenney's telegram to the commissioner on the same date announced his discovery of gold in small quantities on Castle Creek. On French Creek the prospects for gold were disappointing. "The prospect at present is not such as to warrant extended mining operations." Nonetheless, Jenney acknowledged in his final report that the whole valley of

French Creek, for almost six miles, was full of prospecting pits. Camp Harney, the camp was named, in honor of the old Indian fighter.[23]

Once the presence of gold had been confirmed, the journalists lost interest. They filed fewer and fewer stories. Some left, others simply stopped writing as attention shifted to research and exploration. The expedition left Camp Harney on July 19 to explore the Northern Hills. Jenney, citing the absence of recent trails and other signs, concluded that the Indians seldom visited the interior, though they often camped in the foothills where streams broke through the hogback ridge onto the plains and game was most abundant. He found the native flora mixed: plants peculiar to the Mississippi Valley side by side with those found in the Rocky Mountains. On July 31 he affirmed a judgment voiced earlier by Dodge. "It was truly said of [the Hills] that there was gold in the very roots of the grass," Jenney wrote, "but it is not the gold of the gravel bars or quartz ledges, not the gold of the miner or geologist but the future solid wealth of the Black Hills that is to be sought in the luxuriant growth of fine grasses that everywhere spreads over this beautiful country."[24]

The illegal presence of miners remained a dilemma for the government. Since the presence of gold had been announced, Jenney estimated, the number of miners in the Hills—"pilgrims," he called them— had grown from twenty or so to more than a thousand, perhaps as many as fifteen hundred. They kept pouring into the Hills from all directions. If ejected by the military, they simply returned. One man told Dodge he had been captured and sent out four times. "I give the troops more trouble in catching me each time," he told Dodge, "and I guess I can stand it as long as they can."[25]

Dodge's sympathies were with the miners. His feelings about Indians ranged from sympathetic understanding to indifference, from admiration to incomprehension and downright revulsion. The present circumstance brought out his most intemperate feelings. "This portion of the country has not an Indian trail," he wrote General Crook on June 16, "and Custer was never more right than when he said they held on to it from a dog-in-the-manger spirit." Dodge believed the Indians were put up to it by agents hoping to manipulate the millions paid by the government if the Indians only made enough of a "row." The Black Hills "would furnish cattle butter & cheeze for a nation," he asserted in his letter to Crook. "The absurdity of turning over such a country to miserable nomads is too manifest for discussion."[26]

The scientists went on exploring and mapping. McGillycuddy could find "no order or system whatever to the water courses and ridges," which made it impossible to form an idea of the drainage without following each stream from its head to its exit from the the Hills. Jenney reported that virtually all the streams sank into their beds and vanished when they reached the foothills, a tendency he had observed of the Cheyenne River. Thunderstorms were frequent, leaving trees all over the Hills marked by lightning strikes. From a mountain near Harney Peak one afternoon, Dodge saw five separate thunderstorms occurring simultaneously in different parts of the Hills. Lightning struck three members of his party, seriously injuring two, killing a horse. One of the injured was Andrew Burt, the eleven-year-old son of an officer, struck on the cheek. The charge passed out at the ball of his foot, Dodge noted, "boring a hole in the shoe-sole as clean and round as if made by a bullet." Unconscious for more than an hour, the boy survived. "God was good to us and spared our dear boy," wrote his mother, "but with one eye paralyzed beyond redemption."[27]

In July the expedition, now on Rapid Creek, received a visit by a delegation from the commission assigned to negotiate the purchase of the Black Hills, a group that included Reverend Hinman. Dodge had only scorn for Hinman, "one of the Preacher scoundrels who cloak their stealings with their religion," he scoffed in his journal. "I would not trust him an inch, just from his face, which is secret and crafty — never looks square." Red Dog, a Lakota from the Spotted Tail agency who was with Hinman, demanded to know why the soldiers were so friendly with the miners, since the question of whose territory it was had yet to be settled.

"This is a matter for the chiefs above me," Dodge replied.

General Crook came through a week later in a reconnaissance of the Hills. Crook had new orders to expel unauthorized persons, but he'd heard complaints from the miners that every summer the Indians were violating the treaty hundreds of times, raiding the settlers, stealing their horses. Crook felt the miners' side of the story should be heard. Advising them to leave peacefully, he issued an order to that effect but also, with Dodge's support, invited them to hold a meeting to secure their rights, if and when the Hills were opened. When such a meeting took place after his departure, the *Chicago Tribune* reported that Dodge was given "three hearty cheers" and Crook "three cheers and a tiger."[28]

On October 13, after four and a half months of exploration, the Jenney-Dodge expedition arrived back at Fort Laramie. Its findings, together with Dodge's journals and book, give us the most complete picture we have of the Black Hills before whites had left a major foot-print, though Indians had left many signs of fire used to manage the landscape. McGillycuddy's map, given the difficulties involved, is surprisingly accurate. Dodge's journals offer abundant detail on the wildlife.

The whole affair, Dodge wrote General Crook in a letter that reflected the beauty of the Hills while minimizing the difficulties, was "a delightful pic nic (without the ladies)." His report called it "the most delightful summer of my life." The hunting had been splendid, though as an ardent fisherman he was disappointed to find no trout native to the streams. In retrospect, a greater disappointment might well have been that an expedition mounted to survey the Black Hills and gauge their value had so little impact on the immediate outcome. Negotiations for the sale of the Hills had been broken off before the command returned to Fort Laramie.[29]

Gold among the roots of the grass!

The phrase resounded among prospectors itching to "open the Hills." During the spring following the Custer expedition, hundreds schemed to find avenues to the gold. The army undertook to stop them, a difficult if not impossible task. Its only real success lay in escorting the Gordon party to Fort Laramie. A scant ten days later, Gordon himself, who with Ephraim Witcher had gone back to Sioux City to launch a second expedition, set out once more, this time with a hundred and seventy-four men, two women, and twenty-nine wagons. Intercepted by troops on the Niobrara, they refused to turn back. The army burned their wagons. Gordon was arrested, tried in Omaha, and released. Witcher joined Charles Collins and went to Chicago to raise a third expedition. After bilking hundreds of adventurers of five dollars apiece, they absconded with the take. Meanwhile, other prospectors kept coming.[30]

During the spring and summer of 1875, when the Lakotas needed unity as never before in defense of the Black Hills, their most influential champion, Red Cloud, was embroiled in a feud with his agent. Red Cloud had crossed swords with his agents from the outset. When he had agreed to go on the reservation in 1870, he had made clear he wanted Ben Mills, a white man married to a woman of his own band, as his agent. The request was denied by the Board of Indian Commissioners: Mills, with his Oglala wife and his children of mixed blood, was "too nearly on a social level with the Indians [to] do any serious work for [their] salvation." Under the terms of the Peace Policy, agents for the various reservations were parceled out to the major religious denominations—Episcopalians, Methodists, Presbyterians, Catholics. The agent appointed for the Red Cloud Agency, John W. Wham, had nothing but trouble with the chief, as did his successor, Dr. J. W. Daniels, another Episcopal appointee. In the summer of 1875, with the fate of the Black Hills in the balance, Red

Cloud was concentrating on his struggle with a third agent, Dr. J. J. Saville, still another Episcopal appointee.[31]

Red Cloud had protested against the Custer incursion the previous summer, but six weeks into the expedition, almost as an afterthought. Now in May of 1875 he managed a third invitation to Washington, where he and Spotted Tail wrangled with government officials for three weeks to little effect. Ben Mills had died. On his choice of agent Red Cloud now wanted not a western man, but a wealthy man from the East: "These western men fill their pockets, and when they are full, they fill their hats; and then they say, 'goodby,' and go away." On the paramount question of the Black Hills, Spotted Tail told Secretary of the Interior Delano it wasn't worth talking about because the Lakotas would demand a very high price. For his part, Red Cloud was engaged in a desperate struggle to maintain his leadership among his people, "a struggle," notes James C. Olson, "that involved not only his own role but a whole way of life."[32]

On June 18, as the Jenney-Dodge expedition was reporting gold in paying quantities from its camp on French Creek, Secretary Delano appointed a commission to treat with the Sioux for "relinquishment" of the Black Hills. The commission was headed by Senator William B. Allison of Iowa, whose principal qualification was his close friendship with President Grant. It began preparations for a "grand council" to secure mining rights to the Black Hills and outright purchase of the Bighorns in Wyoming. For the Sioux the outlook was by no means encouraging, wrote the Commissioner of Indian Affairs in his charge to the commission: "They cannot live by the chase; they cannot be supported in idleness by the Government. They must begin at once to learn to live by herding or by agriculture, or both."

In a major shift of official policy the commissioners were no longer to deal with the Sioux as a foreign nation, but as dependents. The commissioners would be negotiating with "ignorant and almost helpless people." They must keep in mind they were to represent the interests of the Indians as well as those of the government. They were to assure the Indians that the government's sole desire in negotiations was to maintain the peace, and that no property or rights would be taken from them without returning a "fair equivalent."[33]

Prospectors were swarming into the Black Hills, as many as a thousand by mid-summer. General Crook reported finding at least twelve hundred. In August, as the miners on French Creek were laying out plans for the town of Custer, Spotted Tail made his own journey into the Hills to assess their value. While Red Cloud remained at his agency, squabbling with his agent, Spotted Tail persuaded his agent to accompany him and some of the minor chiefs on a visit that became an almost official affair. Spotted Tail gained a fuller sense of the value of the gold. He also found Colonel Dodge's troops mingling on friendly terms with the miners they were supposed to remove.[34]

When the grand council assembled in September, the Sioux were split between a minority determined never to part with the Black Hills and a majority, including Red Cloud and Spotted Tail, who were willing to sell at the right price. Cheyenne and Arapaho representatives attended as well. Crazy Horse indicated he might come in, but never did. Sitting Bull vowed that while any game remained in his country, he would never talk to the white man.

An acrimonious quarrel between Red Cloud and Spotted Tail over the meeting place delayed the proceedings. When the first formal session opened on September 20, eight miles east of his agency, Red Cloud boycotted the meeting. The price demanded, as Spotted Tail had predicted, turned out to be high. In their report the commissioners lamented that some of the agents and other officials had given the Indians an exalted sense of the value of the Black Hills, encouraging them to demand thirty to fifty million dollars. The commission's report observed only that all the tribes were "in bad spirit" on September 23. The historical accounts describe the meeting as tempestuous.

Some five to twenty thousand Indians had gathered on the plain surrounding the commissioners tent. On hand, in case of trouble, were a hundred and twenty cavalrymen. After an hour of talk among the chiefs seated directly in front of the commissioners, a warrior from Crazy Horse's camp, Little Big Man, suddenly came riding into the circle naked, brandishing a Winchester. He announced he had come to kill the white men who wanted to take his land. Lakota soldiers disarmed him and led him away, but still the commissioners were the target of insulting yells and gestures. Warriors were riding up and down in little dashes, some of them calling *Hoka hey*! The interpreter warned that all hell was about to break loose.

At this point, Young Man Afraid of His Horse led his Lakota soldiers in a charge past the tent and took up a position screening the troopers and commissioners from the Indians. Young Man Afraid rode into the center of the circle and shouted at the Indians to go back to their lodges and not to come back until their heads had cooled! They all knew Young Man Afraid was not to be trifled with; he would kill the first man who opposed him. Slowly, band by band, the warriors left the circle, and the commissioners, escorted by cavalry went back to Red Cloud Agency "in a very thoughtful frame of mind."[35]

Seeing the futility of attempting negotiations in the presence of thousands of Indians, the commission invited twenty of the leading chiefs to their quarters at Red Cloud Agency. For two days the chiefs presented their complaints and demands. They would not sell the Bighorns. In exchange for the Black Hills they had come to agreement that their people should be taken care of for seven generations.

"There have been six nations raised," said Red Cloud, "and I am the seventh, and I want seven generations ahead to be fed."

Spotted Tail raised the ante: "As long as we live on this earth, we will expect pay." The money should be left with the President "forever." Spotted Tail wanted to live on the interest. Good cattle, guns, ammunition, clothes, "until the land falls to pieces . . . ."

"The Black Hills are the house of gold for our Indians," said Little Bear. "If a man owns anything, of course he wants to make something out of it to get rich on." "I have a right to payment for the Black Hills as well as the Ogalallas," put in Black Coal, an Arapaho. Little Wolf, a Cheyenne, added, "My people own an interest in these hills that you men speak of buying . . . . We want to be made rich too."

The most extravagant demands were raised by Red Cloud. He wanted Texas steers for seven generations. He wanted "flour and coffee, sugar and tea, and bacon, the very best kind," together with tobacco, soap and salt, "and pepper, for the old people." For every family he wanted a wagon and a span of horses, working cattle, a sow and a boar, a cow and a bull and more. He wanted some white men's houses and furniture, and a sawmill. He would sell only the Black Hills inside the racetrack. "Maybe you white people think that I ask too much from the Government, but I think those hills extend clear to the sky—maybe they go above the sky, and that is the reason I ask for so much."[36]

At Spotted Tail's request, the commissioners put their offer in writing. Expressing the desire to live in "perpetual peace and unity" with the Sioux, and to deal with them "in all things liberally, fairly, and justly," the commission submitted six propositions, recognizing the tribe's right "to accept any one or reject all of them." For $100,000 a year the government offered to purchase the license to mine, "and also as incidental thereto the right to grow stock and to cultivate the soil," *or* to buy the Black Hills outright for $6,000,000—the exact amount specified by Spotted Tail before negotiations began. The government proposed to buy the Bighorns, a suggestion that had been refused from the outset, and would designate three routes to the Black Hills. Any agreement would be binding only upon approval by Congress and by three-fourths of all adult males of the Sioux Nation, a provision of the 1868 Treaty.

On September 29 the conference ended, with no prospect of success. "The Indians, in their present temper," the official report concluded, "would not agree to any terms that ought to be proposed by the Government," nor would any such agreement be sanctioned by three-fourths of the adult Sioux males. The commissioners voiced a belief echoing what Captain Clark had said about the Lakotas along the Missouri: "We do not believe their temper or spirit can or will be changed until they are made to feel the power as well as the magnanimity of the Government."

Unanimously the commission recommended that Congress settle the law for itself and notify the Sioux Nation of its determination—as a "finality." Deep frustration emanates from the official report: "[N]o progress whatever has been made toward civilization or self-support" at the agencies during the past six years. "[T]he Indians have done absolutely nothing but eat, drink, smoke, and sleep, except indulging each day in the healthful exercise of horseback riding . . . ." They exalted the value of the gold but would not make the effort to acquire it. "Their leading chiefs ask $70,000,000 for the Hills in the morning," said the report, though the Indians probably meant $7,000,000, "and in the evening beg a shirt or a blanket!"

Notwithstanding "serious doubts" that there was enough gold in the Black Hills to make mining profitable, the commission had made its proposition "most liberal," to test the possibility. The appropriations made by Congress during the last two years were no longer required under the 1868 Treaty; they had been made "on the theory that either starvation or a war" would result if they were not made.

For all its vexations, the Allison Commission acknowledged the justice of Sioux claims. Its report ends on that note: "This sacrifice [of territory and game for subsistence] has brought to them destitution and beggary; to our nation wealth and power, and with these an obligation to make good to them, in some way, the loss by which we have so largely gained."[37]

Unaware that negotiations had been broken off, Colonel Dodge went on exploring the Hills, enjoying the most delightful summer of his life. He was proud of the map his surveyors were completing: "as perfect a map," he wrote General Crook on September 4, "as can be made without surveyors compass & chain." No part of the wilderness was as well known as the Black Hills now were. The miners on French Creek had left "in excellent humor, & were much gratified at your courteous & considerate treatment."[38]

Crook's gentleness and sympathy with the miners conflict with Sheridan's orders, but in reality the army could no more stop thousands of gold-hungry men from streaming into the Hills than Red Cloud and Spotted Tail could control the actions of young warriors hot to join the hostile tribes in the north. With no military post in the Hills, the miners slipped through, minnows through a seine. Dozens were arrested and escorted out, only to be released. Others hid in the mountains, like those who camped high on the side of Harney Peak, whose slate-roofed cabin was found only in the 1930s by the Civilian Conservation Corps.[39]

As it became clear that those miners caught and ejected were not being prosecuted, the numbers increased. In the fall of 1875 a temporary post was established in Custer under command of the assiduous Captain Edwin Pollock, who arrested scores of miners and confined them in a notorious "bull-pen." Sent under guard to Fort Laramie, offenders were invariably released. Compounding Pollock's difficulties, many of his meagerly paid soldiers deserted to go after gold.

With thousands of miners prospecting in the Hills, the northern tribes were attracting warriors from the agencies. On October 1 Agent Saville reported many Oglalas heading north from the Red Cloud Agency. A U.S. Indian inspector sent out to reconnoiter confirmed the War Department's worst fears and proposed a winter attack on the northern tribes, to "whip them into subjection."[40]

On November 3 President Grant held a secret meeting with Generals Sheridan and Crook and his top officials. The Allison Commission had failed, leaving the government to confront a crucial question: how to crack down on the defiant bands without appearing to violate the Treaty of 1868. Grant made two major decisions: while overtly maintaining its prohibition against mining in the Black Hills, the government would simply stop enforcing it, and would compel the northern tribes to leave their unceded lands and settle at one of the agencies. These policies were not made public. Minimizing acquisition of the Black Hills as a motive, the government justified it as a response to Lakota depredations on the Upper Yellowstone and raids on the Crows and the Arikaras. Both provocations were presented as violations of the 1868 Treaty and would be used, Robert W. Larson observes, to "legit-imize a war against a people who, in the case of the northern tribes, had never subscribed to this oft-ignored treaty in the first place."[41]

Two weeks after the secret meeting in Washington, Captain Pollock led his troops out of the Black Hills. On December 6 Commissioner of Indian Affairs Smith directed his agents to send runners out to the camps scattered throughout the unceded territory with a merciless ultimatum: return to their agencies by January 31 or be considered hostile. Sitting Bull's Hunkpapas on the Yellowstone and the Minicoujous and San Arcs along the Tongue apparently received the word with disbelief, unaware that troops would be sent to force their return. For many bands, compliance within two months was impossible in the harsh winter, which may have been its intent, and operating with a different concept of time the Indians simply may not have attached great importance to a precise deadline. When none of them appeared on January 31, their fate was turned over to the military.

The gold rush gathered momentum as the Southern Hills enjoyed a mild winter. Custer, the "Mother City of the Black Hills," swelled to a population of a thousand. Crook Street, the wide main thoroughfare was laid out in February. In March a thousand dollars in gold dust was carried from Custer to Cheyenne. In a mass meeting, the miners set up a provisional government and formed the "Custer Minute Men," a company of militia for defense against rising Indian hostility. Then as spring temperatures warmed, the move to the Northern Hills began. Deadwood was laid out on April 25. The history of Custer, explains Watson Parker, replicates the story of most Black Hills towns: "a brief, tempestuous early rush, followed by migration to richer, farther gold fields. Then, sporadic returns to open up new prospects, followed by another depression when the new discoveries proved fruitless."[42]

Miners of course wanted beef. In the spring of 1876 the first herd of cattle was brought in from Wyoming Territory. During the previous winter, surreptitiously, W. L. Kuykendall had led a party of thirty-five into the Hills. Three weeks later he returned to Cheyenne, convinced the Black Hills offered rich possibilities for stock raising and farming along with mining. In Spearfish Valley ranchers were energetically confirming the predictions of Custer and Jenney encapsulated in California Joe's widely quoted observation: "[T]here's gold from the grass roots down, but there's more gold from the grass roots up."[43]

Chapter 5: War

Wounded Knee. The name resounds in the consciousness of those who know what happened in 1890 on a little stream in South Dakota. It echoes with tones of anger, sadness, and doom, more sharply edged in English than in the softer Lakota, *Cankpe Opi Wakpala*, though in either tongue the wounds go deep. The massacre at Wounded Knee sprang not from any single source, but from many. The failure of the northern tribes to report to their agencies by January 31, 1876, as Commissioner of Indian Affairs Smith had ordered, gave General Phil Sheridan an opening to launch a favorite tactic—a surprise winter campaign against the Lakotas.

Sheridan commanded the Division of the Missouri, a vast area containing most of the country's Indian population. He had found a key to success in war: ravage the enemy's homeland, destroying his will to resist, "for the loss of property weighs heavy with the most of mankind; heavier often, than the sacrifices made on the field of battle." Sheridan had once advised Count Otto von Bismarck that people must suffer so terribly they can only long for peace: "The people must be left nothing but their eyes to weep with over the war."[1]

Dispatched by Sheridan to hunt down the northern bands, General George Crook left Fort Fetterman in March, in temperatures reaching forty or fifty below zero. On March 17, 1876, confident he had discovered Crazy Horse's camp along the Powder River, Colonel Joseph J. Reynolds made a dawn attack in deep snow on a village of Northern Cheyennes. His troops captured the pony herd and burned the village, but the Cheyennes recaptured the ponies that same night, and the attack brought unforeseen consequences. The dazed survivors sought refuge in Crazy Horse's camp downriver. Their tale of soldiers burning the village, leaving the poorly clad refugees to freeze to death in the open, moved Crazy Horse, Sitting Bull, and the Cheyenne leaders to a strong vow of unity. They would stay together as long as it took, and they would fight.[2]

The great herds of buffalo that had sustained the Plains Indians were being exterminated with astonishing rapidity. The splendid beasts had once been so numerous that in 1541 one of Coronado's men could only compare them with the fish of the sea. In 1863 a single herd in motion had been estimated as a mass five miles wide and twelve long. By 1870 their numbers had been reduced from perhaps thirty million in all of North America to four million south of the Platte, a million and a half north of it. Professional hunters were slaughtering them for their tongues and hides, while Indians joined the hunt as a means of gaining access to the goods of the white economy. By summer's end 1873, thousands of square miles on the Southern Plains were littered with decaying carcasses, rendering the air "pestilential and offensive to the last degree," as a traveler said. Two years later the southern herds had been all but exterminated.[3]

Sheridan applauded this annihilation, the first step in a total war on the Indians. He praised the hunters. "These hunters have done in the last two years," he declared, "and will do more in the next years, to settle the vexed Indian question, than the entire regular army has done in the last thirty years. They are destroying the Indians' commissary," preparing the way for the "festive cowboy, who follows the hunter as the second forerunner of civilization."[4]

The pace of events quickened early in May when the new agent at Red Cloud Agency charged Crook with conducting an inept winter campaign. Incensed by the charge, Crook paid a visit to the agency, convinced that agency Indians were helping the hostiles. Ordinarily Crook was a reticent man, but on this occasion his warm remarks to Red Cloud, who had shown ambivalence in the present crisis, triggered the chief's most aggressive response since 1868. The Lakotas were ready for action, Red Cloud warned Crook. "They are not afraid of the soldiers or of their chief." Every lodge would send its young men, "and they will all say of the Great Father's dogs, 'Let them come!'"[5]

Events were building toward the catastrophe that still reverberates in American mythology. Through the late spring an immense village of Lakotas and Northern Cheyennes was following the dwindling buffalo herds westward—six tribal circles, with the Hunkpapas protecting the rear. On May 28 a lieutenant returning from the Powder River sighted seven or eight hundred warriors heading north from the agencies to join Crazy Horse and Sitting Bull. Colonel Wesley Merritt estimated that as many as two thousand Indians had left the Red Cloud Agency in the preceding three weeks.

On June 17, 1876, Crook's camp on the Rosebud suffered a surprise attack by Lakota and Northern Cheyenne warriors who fought with unprecedented ferocity. They left Crook's forces effectively out of commission for most of the summer. During the following week the village along the Little Bighorn doubled in size to seven thousand, with at least eighteen hundred warriors. On June 25, 1876, as every schoolchild must know, George Armstrong Custer and the Seventh Cavalry stumbled upon this sprawling encampment, where Custer and five companies were exterminated to the last man.

Apprised of the catastrophe while celebrating the centennial of its birth, the outraged American nation reacted swiftly. *Settle the Indian question once and for all!* The army's humiliation must be avenged. Indian agents were placed under military control. Congress established a commission under George W. Manypenny, a former Commissioner of Indian Affairs, with a clear mandate: secure the surrender of all Indian claims to the Black Hills.

The Manypenny Commission convened in September at Red Cloud Agency. This council bore scant resemblance to the failed Allison Commission a year earlier. The commissioners offered no propositions to be accepted or rejected. They had been sent out to deliver an ultimatum: no further rations would be supplied the Indians unless they relinquished claim to the Black Hills and the unceded lands to the west. In effect, sell or starve.

The conference began well enough. "We are glad to see you," Red Cloud told the commissioners. "You have come to save us from death." Manypenny set forth the conditions established by Congress, which included the demand for three wagon roads across their drastically reduced reservation and the onerous requirement that unless they removed to Indian Territory in Oklahoma the Lakotas must go to the hated Missouri River. The latter condition enraged Sitting Bull—the Oglala chief by that name, not the intransigent Hunkpapa but a chief known as a friend of the white man. Denouncing the proposed document as foolishness, he proclaimed that the Indians wanted to stay where they were, then ordered the Lakotas to leave the conference, which they did.[6]

The next day, protesting, most of the headmen present signed the agreement. One chief refused. Another covered his eyes with his blanket in a fitting symbol and made his mark blindly. The speeches of most indicated they either failed to understand the terms of the agreement or had no intention of abiding by it. Young Man Afraid protested that it would take him "a long time to learn to labor." He expected the President to feed him for at least a hundred years. Red Cloud agreed to let some of his young men go to Oklahoma to look over the Indian Territory, but he grimly informed the commissioners that if his people moved to the Missouri River country they would be destroyed: "There are a great many bad men there and bad whiskey; therefore I don't want to go there."

Eager to collect the "*x*'s" of the chiefs and clear out, the commissioners apparently made no attempt to correct the misunderstandings evident in what the chiefs had said. In hasty visits to the other agencies they collected signatures, ignoring Article 12 of the 1868 Treaty, which required approval of three-fourths of all the adult males. "We finished our labors in the Indian country," they reported, "with our hearts full of gratitude to God, who had guarded and protected us, and had directed our labors to a successful issue." One splinter of conscience found its way into their official conclusion: "The Indians trusted us. . . . If we sow broken faith, injustice, and wrong, we shall reap in the future as we have reaped in the past, a harvest of sorrow and blood."

The Black Hills question was settled at last—on paper.[7]

Among the chiefs who hadn't attended the council, who had signed nothing, were Crazy Horse and Sitting Bull. While the Many-penny commissioners were engaged with the agency chiefs, the hostiles in the Yellowstone country had been keeping Generals Terry and Crook and Colonel Miles occupied. When Indian raids on settlements in the Northern Hills intensified, Crook was ordered to the Black Hills with his Big Horn and Yellowstone Expedition in what became known as the "Starvation March."

Crook's force of over two thousand men, having exhausted its rations, was reduced to killing its own horses for food. Attacked by Indians they believed to be led by Crazy Horse, harassed along the way by rifle fire from nearby bluffs, the troops reached the Belle Fourche River in mid-September, jubilant to be met by fifty head of cattle and a wagon train of foodstuffs sent out to them by the grateful inhabitants of Crook City and Deadwood.[8]

Crook himself went to Camp Robinson in October to direct the disarmament and dismounting of warriors at the Red Cloud Agency. When Red Cloud refused to move his band as directed, Crook sent eight companies to bring him in, a force accompanied by forty-two Pawnee scouts. Surprised at dawn, Red Cloud's warriors were disarmed of their few weapons. Their ponies were taken and, in the bitterest of insults, a mount was awarded to each of their Pawnee enemies. The Lakotas were then forced to march all night into Camp Robinson.

Red Cloud's bitterness was compounded. He had refused to let Crook enlist warriors from his band for use as scouts against their own people, a strategy Crook had employed against Geronimo. Crook now humiliated Red Cloud in front of his peers by deposing him as chief of the Oglalas, recognizing Spotted Tail as leader of the Red Cloud Agency as well as his own. The ignominy bit deep. In the eyes of Indians, no chief was appointed by any white man. Red Cloud was inclined to blame the Great White Father: "What have I done that I should receive such treatment from him whom I thought a friend?"[9]

Simultaneously in Montana, Colonel Nelson A. Miles was conferring with Sitting Bull face to face, under a flag of truce. In his memoirs Miles described Sitting Bull on first meeting as determined and forceful, "a strong, hardy, sturdy looking man . . . well-built, with strongly-marked features," courteous in the beginning but "evidently void of any genuine respect for the white race." For two days the two sparred verbally. According to the chief's nephew White Bull, the first day ended amicably. Miles agreed to accompany Sitting Bull to the Black Hills, where the chief would winter after completing a buffalo hunt. Next day the talks shattered. White Bull later gave a verbatim account from memory of much of the argument. Miles demanded that Sitting Bull and the Hunkpapas go to their agencies; Sitting Bull demanded the whites get out of his country.[10]

More than talk would be required, Miles decided. Breaking off negotiations, he launched an attack in a running battle that continued for two days. His outnumbered infantry drove Sitting Bull's people out of their camps and pushed them north across the Yellowstone. In their flight the Hunkpapas were forced to abandon huge quantities of meat and equipment. In November blizzards with temperatures so low the mercury froze in the thermometers, Miles pressed his advantage, pursuing Sitting Bull back and forth across Montana with a force of less than five hundred men.

Sheridan's strategy appeared to be working. For three years, with the Northern Pacific stalled at Bismarck, Sitting Bull's Hunkpapas had enjoyed a reprieve from the advance of the Iron Horse. Now at the mercy of a harsh early winter, his forces were dispersed and on the run, pursued by troops warmly dressed and well fed. Crook, meanwhile, was building up a force that included four hundred Indian allies to go after Crazy Horse.

On November 25 this force under Colonel Ranald Mackenzie attacked a large Northern Cheyenne camp in the Bighorns, burning the village. The Cheyennes lost many dead, along with food and shelter and seven hundred ponies. Eleven babies froze to death in their mothers'arms. After three weeks of terrible suffering, the Cheyennes found refuge with Crazy Horse on the upper Tongue River.[11]

With the arrival of the refugees, peace sentiment gained in the Crazy Horse camp. A delegation of five Minnecoujou chiefs was sent to open talks with Miles. As the delegation approached Miles' cantonment at the mouth of the Tongue, it passed by his camp of Crow scouts. The Crows attacked, killing the five Minnecoujous. Angrily Miles dismounted the Crows and sent their ponies to the Lakotas as an apology, but the damage was done. A prospective peace expired with the death of its emissaries.[12]

Raiders from Crazy Horse's camp began harassing Miles' cantonment. The day after Christmas they ran off the beef herd. Convinced that only an immediate campaign could end the hostilities, Miles led his weary infantry up the valley of the Tongue in pursuit of a decoy party sent out from the Crazy Horse camp. In a snowstorm on the morning of January 8, 1877, in subzero temperatures, Crazy Horse attacked Miles' command with a force of five hundred Lakota and Cheyenne warriors. At mid-day the snowstorm turned to blizzard, lending an "inexpressible weirdness to the scene," Miles later wrote. The Indians withdrew. Miles pursued them up the valley for several miles, beyond their now deserted camp.

Casualties were light on both sides, but the Battle of Wolf Mountain energized Miles. To him it demonstrated "we could move in any part of the country in the midst of winter, and hunt the enemy down in their camps wherever they might take refuge." The Indians were bitterly demoralized. A Crazy Horse camp had been struck! Maybe the soldiers could not be beaten. Sitting Bull visited the camp—*the mighty Sitting Bull*—to announce that he was calling off the war. He would take his Hunkpapas to live in the country of the "Great Mother," Queen Victoria —Canada.

Early in May, he was to do just that.[13]

On February 28, 1877, the Manypenny agreement was ratified by Congress. In a single act, the Black Hills were wrenched from the Sioux essentially by moving the western boundary of the Great Sioux Reservation from the 104th meridian to the 103rd, excluding their *Paha Sapa*. In the Black Hills communities, celebrations began. Indian depredations in and around the Hills might continue, but under U.S. law the white inhabitants were now legal residents.[14]

General Crook, convinced he had acted wisely in disarming the Oglalas and taking their ponies, continued to enlist Indian scouts into military service. For a young Lakota male bereft of horse and gun, the allure was powerful. Warrior status was exalted. "As a soldier," Crook noted in his autobiography, "the Indian wears the uniform, draws the pay and rations, and is in all respects on equal footing with the white man." Four hundred warriors enrolled at Red Cloud alone, a hundred at Spotted Tail.[15]

With Sitting Bull and his Hunkpapas heading for refuge in Canada, on the other side of the "Holy Road," the army's main objective became Crazy Horse. Only when this great warrior was subdued would the war on the Sioux end. There might be other battles and skirmishes, and raids by small renegade groups, but the one serious threat to white occupation of the Black Hills was now Crazy Horse.

In January, Crook sent out a party to persuade him to come in. Finally, with his people exhausted and hungry, Crazy Horse gave in to save them. He consented to join his Oglala relatives at Red Cloud. His uncle, the respected Spotted Tail, went looking for him. Crazy Horse's father assured Spotted Tail that his son would bring his people in when the weather improved. In the end Crook dispatched Red Cloud to secure the surrender. When Red Cloud made rendezvous with him on April 27, Crazy Horse spread his blanket on the ground for Red Cloud to sit on and, to indicate he was surrendering to the older warrior, gave him his shirt.[16]

Ten days later, as Sitting Bull was crossing into Canada, Crazy Horse, undefeated in battle, met Lieutenant Philo Clark, a specialist in sign language, on a flat two miles north of Camp Robinson. Crazy Horse extended his left hand to Clark, explaining, "Friend, I shake with this hand because my heart is on this side; I want this peace to last forever."[17]

In a column two miles long, flanked by He Dog and Little Big Man, followed by his warriors and then by the women and children, Crazy Horse led the way into Camp Robinson. A slight figure of less than medium height, he wore only a buckskin shirt, a single hawk's feather in his hair. By one account the chiefs, when they came within sight of the camp, began to sing. The warriors took it up, then the women and children, and as the procession passed between the thousands of agency Indians lining the route, the onlookers too began singing and cheering. "By God," said an army officer, "this is a triumphal march, not a surrender."[18]

Much of what followed is enveloped in confusion. The great moral authority Crazy Horse carried with him provoked jealousy in other Lakota leaders. "Among a broken people," Larry McMurtry has written, "an unbroken man can only rarely be tolerated—he becomes a too-painful reminder of what the people as a whole had once been." Jealousy, factionalism, even hatred poison the atmosphere; gossip and rumor become lethal weapons. Crazy Horse surrendered nine hundred people, two thousand horses and mules, and one hundred and seventeen guns. That much is clear. But we have more verifiable facts about Alexander the Great, who lived more than two thousand years earlier, than we have about this young Lakota warrior. Inevitably we are caught up in "an exercise in assumption, conjecture, and surmise."[19]

One fact little known to date is that soon after his surrender, Crazy Horse and many of his leading warriors were enlisted into the army's Indian Scout Service. Crazy Horse enlisted as Sergeant, reenlisting on July 1 as First Sergeant of Company "E."[20]

First Sergeant or not, Crazy Horse inspired fear as well as respect. The young Lakota men at Red Cloud Agency were more likely to follow his lead than anyone else's. The first generation forbidden to establish their bravery as warriors in the traditional way, they looked to Crazy Horse as their hero, a symbol of resistance. But the tangled jealousies of older leaders such as Red Cloud and Spotted Tail left Crazy Horse vulnerable to the bitter factionalism at the agencies. When as a *blotahunka*, or war leader, Crazy Horse refused to assume the role of *itancan* by endorsing government receipts to receive rations for his camp, many of his followers abandoned him for other leaders.[21]

When the Nez Percés began their remarkable flight to Canada, holding off or defeating every army unit they came up against while moving camps of women, children, and old people more than a thousand miles, Lieutenant Clark decided First Sergeant Crazy Horse would be useful against them as a scout. The great warrior had given up his gun and promised not to fight; now he was asked to take it up again. At this juncture, a fatal mistranslation took place. If the whites insisted, Crazy Horse finally agreed, he would go fight until the last Nez Percé was killed. But a mixed-blood scout who had been his friend, Frank Grouard, told the whites Crazy Horse had vowed to fight until the last white man was killed. Grouard may have lied out of jealousy, or perhaps to twit the whites, or to shock them. He may have been drunk. In any case, the remark heightened fears among white authorities.[22]

Events took on the fatality of Greek drama. On August 31, evidently convinced Crook's real target was Sitting Bull, Crazy Horse threatened to take his people and head north. Crook had planned ultimately to imprison Crazy Horse in a prison cell in Florida or on the Dry Tortugas. Now he ordered him arrested. Crazy Horse fled to the Spotted Tail Agency, but Spotted Tail himself, a stern uncle, and probably jealous, went along to help escort his nephew back to Camp Robinson. When Crazy Horse caught sight of the tiny guardhouse cell to which he was being led, he broke for the door.

Multitudes of Lakotas witnessed what happened; many versions have been offered. Years earlier Crazy Horse had dreamed that he would be hurt only if one of his own people held his arms to keep him from fighting. In the account most often repeated, Crazy Horse drew a knife from under his blanket. Little Big Man—his old friend, now an Indian policeman—seized him by the arms. In the confusion and clamor, as yells of "Stab the son-of-a-bitch!" and "Shoot him!" rose from those among his own people who wanted him dead, a nervous private stabbed Crazy Horse with a bayonet.

When the troops undertook to move him to the guardhouse, Touch the Clouds stepped in, an imposing figure almost seven feet tall. Crazy Horse, he said, was a chief. He could not be put in the guardhouse. Crazy Horse was taken to the adjutant's office and by his own wish laid on the floor.

"Son, I am here," his father said.

"Father," Crazy Horse could only say, "it is not good for the people to depend on me any longer—I am bad hurt."

When Touch the Clouds saw that Crazy Horse had died, he pulled the blanket over him: "This is the lodge of Crazy Horse."

The news set off a wailing and howling in the night, especially among the women, who remembered his charity. There remained, says McMurtry, "the terrible, pitiable, Lear-like grief" of Crazy Horse's parents, who wandered the premises for three days until given their son's body to place on a burial scaffold outside the fort. Later they took his body on a travois and slipped away to bury him. No one knows with certainty where his bones lie. It may be near the little prairie creek called Wounded Knee.[23]

While the Lakotas were shunted from place to place in the late seventies, with Crazy Horse dead and Sitting Bull exiled to Canada, prospectors were scarring the face of *Paha Sapa*. The prospecting, of course, came at a price. In the summer and fall of 1876, while Crook and Terry were out combing the Powder River and Yellowstone regions for hostiles, small Lakota bands mounted raids on settlements in the Northern

Hills. An early settler and editor, Richard B. Hughes, later wrote that General Crook was no doubt in "entire sympathy" with the settlers, but fully occupied elsewhere. In any case, the Black Hills remained Sioux territory: "We were trespassing and must be so regarded." Hughes thought it a source of wonder that more whites were not killed. He credited peace chiefs like Spotted Tail and Old Man Afraid of His Horses. "Where here and there a lone prospector or traveler was cut off, it was the act of turbulent young warriors acting in small parties, who could not be held in check by the chiefs or older members of the tribe."[24]

Some forty settlers were killed in 1876, among them Deadwood's first clergyman, Henry W. ("Preacher") Smith. Scores of miners fled to the greater safety of Rapid City. In February 1877 a series of raids struck the isolated settlers and stock along the Redwater River and False Bottom Creek. Local officials telegraphed Crook and Sheridan for relief, and a company of infantry commanded by Second Lieutenant Joseph F. Cummings was dispatched from Camp Robinson. When the company arrived at the mouth of False Bottom Creek, the ensuing action, one writer observed, "had all the makings of a good John Ford movie or Charles King novel." A detachment pursuing a dozen Indians encamped along Crow Creek engaged the raiders in "quite a lively brush," trailing the stolen livestock as far as the Bear Lodge Mountains before turning back. Recovering some of the livestock, they drove it through a heavy snowstorm to Spearfish. More or less a chase with a few minor skirmishes, the Crow Creek fight nevertheless heartened local ranchers and settlers. Newspapers as far from the scene as the *Army and Navy Journal* heralded it as a victory. Cummings was cited for "evin[cing] high qualities of energy, skill and courage."[25]

Some casualties fell short of heroism. In Deadwood a trooper was shot in the foot by a drunken citizen. Another was cut in the face with a knife. Ten soldiers deserted, seven of them while the command was camped in the proximity of gold, confirming the wisdom of Captain Raynolds, two decades earlier, in moving his command along before any of his men could be converted into miners.

In July, Frank Wagnes and his pregnant wife and her brother were killed by Indians just north of Bear Butte. Shortly thereafter, reports said every ranch along the Redwater and Spearfish Creek valleys was "devastated." A sizable war party attacked a supply wagon for the survey team working on the Dakota-Wyoming boundary. In a dispiriting aside, the command sent to rescue the settlers in the northern Hills lost seventeen mules to horse thieves, who stole indiscriminately from both whites and Indians. General Crook voiced a suspicion the thieves were "sustained and supported by many people in the Black Hills."[26]

The miners did find a measure of gold, though most would have done well to heed the view of Colonel Dodge: "Of each twenty men who will rush to the Black Hills as miners, nineteen would have been better off if they had remained at home." Such a statement "will deter no man from going," Dodge wrote, "as the American people are so constituted that each man expects himself to be the twentieth."

The fascination in the search for gold, Dodge observed, is not to be accounted for. Each new arrival, whether novice or veteran, brings a "feverish hope" that in a day or two he will find a pot-hole that will make his fortune. Launching into it with force and determination, the typical miner soon finds his muscles tired and his will weakening, then sits by, disappointed, to watch some newcomer open his claim. The previous summer Dodge had seen ten men idle on French and Spring Creek for every one working. "It has passed into a proverb that 'placer' mining [panning from streams] is the poor man's diggings, while 'quartz' mining is only for the rich."[27]

The wisdom of that proverb was soon manifested in the Black Hills gold rush.

Custer, the "Mother City of the Black Hills," had been founded on August 10, 1875, with the encouragement of General Crook. In a proclamation, Crook called for a mass meeting to draft "proper resolutions to secure to each [miner], when the country shall have been opened, the benefit of his discovery and the labor he has already expended." Given the name Custer City, the town was laid out on French Creek near the site where gold had been discovered. The miners made provision for the distribution of lots, the naming of streets, the recording of deeds, and the election of thirteen officers. Departing the Hills next day, they left seven men behind, with Crook's approval, to protect their interests. One of those remaining, Thomas Hooper, later a judge of the Black Hills Superior Court, surveyed the town site with a pocket compass and a picket rope, recording the plat on a piece of birch bark.[28]

Before long, prospectors were filtering back. The town's first bar opened for business November 1, 1875. In December came a general store. Through a mild winter, the population grew rapidly. Men streamed in from played-out fields in Montana and Colorado. In April a citizen heading from the Hills to Cheyenne claimed to have passed fourteen hundred men on the trail to Custer. One man wrote his wife from Cheyenne, notes Watson Parker, to inform her he was "leaving here today for the Black Hills or death. . . . I will lose my life or find out what there is in the Black Hills or die, you bet."

One estimate had six to ten thousand men coming into the area in the first three months of 1876. At least twenty persons in town were referred to simply as "females," whose presence no doubt helped to swell the number of business establishments. In February the main avenue, Crook Street, was laid out two hundred feet wide to allow a bull team to turn around in the middle of the business district. A provisional government was established in March, with a mayor, town marshal, and judges.[29]

In April a correspondent for the *New York Times* was amazed to find, so far from civilization, "a metropolis, with its Mayor and Councilmen, courts, policemen, pawnbrokers, coroners, and its Custer, Crook, and Harney avenues." The *Black Hills Weekly Pioneer*, first newspaper in the Hills, printed a single issue in May. Then its publishers reloaded their equipment and headed for Deadwood, where the action had suddenly gone.

Amid the many flimsy structures serving as shelter, Custer's rapid growth soon took its first casualty. A roof fell in on a boy and killed him. The town had neither Bible nor preacher, nor even a cemetery, but the death of Charley Holt brought out a poet laureate, Jack Crawford, "Captain Jack" of the Minute Men, who voiced a lament:

> *Comrades here in golden land*
> *Will drop a silent tear*
> *For those poor Charley left behind—*
> *A sister or mother dear.*[30]

Maybe Captain Jack should instead have favored the citizens with an elegy for their town, which was already showing signs of decline. Custer's woes went beyond the growing Indian hostility that gave rise to the Minute Men. The heavy foraging of horses and cattle was reducing a beautiful valley to gravel and mud. With the great demand for wood, the timberline shrank back to the adjoining hills. Placer mining at best was difficult enough, and French Creek at this point was narrow, with a shallow grade, insufficient to serve the sluices and rockers required.

As mining faded through the spring, Custer dwindled from a major supply base for the northern settlements to a town that derived its income more from "fleecing" the miners than from supplying them. In early summer, word of the rich strikes in Deadwood Gulch all but emptied the place overnight. From a boom town of six thousand, the population fell to fourteen. What with fourteen hundred abandoned buildings, one citizen remarked, that left an even hundred for each inhabitant.[31]

The second town of any size was Hill City, on Spring Creek. A sawmill and a load of mining tools were shipped in, and by January 22, 1876 the town could boast thirty houses. By the end of February, after Bismarck investors took an interest and town government was established, that number increased to two hundred and fifty. Then by mid-April, with the fear of Indian hostilities and the news from Deadwood Gulch, Hill City lost two hundred houses. The population was soon down to one man and a dog.[32]

Hopeful beginnings in the area went the same way—Sheridan, Pactola, Palmer Gulch, Hayward. None could withstand the lure of reports from Deadwood, given the hard work demanded wherever a man happened to find himself. No one really knew what the Deadwood strikes would produce, but as one observer says, "It made no difference; the luck you were going to get was always better than the luck you had." As typical of the way the Hills were settled, Watson Parker cites the example of John R. Brennan. Brennan joined a party that found rich placer deposits in Palmer Gulch, on Spring Creek downstream from Hill City. After ruining two axes trying to carve out a ditch to drain the groundwater flooding the bedrock, the miners quit, one after another. One morning Brennan himself climbed out of the ditch, threw down his shovel, and swore off mining for life. He left to become a founder of Rapid City.[33]

While the trouble that led to the death of Crazy Horse was fermenting at Red Cloud Agency, Sitting Bull and his Hunkpapas resumed their old free life hunting buffalo in Saskatchewan, on the other side of the line. They enjoyed Canadian protection in return for obedience to Canadian law, a law enforced by the very thin red line of the Mounties. Major James M. Walsh, commander of Fort Walsh, administered the same lecture to Sitting Bull he'd given the chiefs representing thousands of Lakotas who had fled to Canada in the past few months. This "tough Irishman," says Wallace Stegner, with only twelve men, "rode through a fringe of warriors some of who carried carbines wrenched from the hands of Custer's dying cavalrymen, past a horse herd many of whose horses and mules wore the United States Army brand, among lodges where American scalps still hung drying in the smoke . . . ." He met with five chiefs and their "surly warriors [and] told them how they would behave if they wanted to stay in the Great Mother's country." Sitting Bull gave Walsh the same answer the others had given: the Hunkpapas wanted to stay. They would keep the peace.[34]

For decades U.S. officials dealing with Indians had often found themselves undercut by feuding between civil and military authorities, or by broken promises, often promises made by them in good faith but nullified by their superiors. One inevitable result: the "forked tongue." The encounter between Sitting Bull and Major Walsh, however, developed into mutual trust and genuine friendship. For the first time, Sitting Bull came to know white officials he found trustworthy. Few as they were, the Mounties developed extraordinary influence over the Lakota chiefs. One historian attributes their influence to the range of qualities that guided them, applied to simple rules easily understood: "fairness, justice, firmness, courage, tolerance, kindness, honesty, and, of great consequence in light of the record of U.S. officials, a resolve to make good on all promises."[35]

In the fall of 1877 General Terry was dispatched to Fort Walsh to meet with Sitting Bull to inform him that the Great Father wanted peace. His people would be well treated if they surrendered and returned to live at their agencies. Sitting Bull at first refused; the Americans always lied. But Major Walsh persuaded him to meet with Terry, and on October 17 the two met in council, face to face.

Terry opened the meeting badly, without the customary pipe ceremony. He simply stood up and began to speak. The Lakotas, he informed the assembled chiefs, could return to their country and their friends, but only if they gave up their arms and ponies and began a new mode of life. When Terry sat down, the chiefs smoked their pipes in a long silence. At length Sitting Bull rose. He spoke of the history of bad treatment that had driven his people to seek refuge with the Great Mother. They would remain where they were. They wanted to hear no more lies.

"Don't you say two more words," he told Terry. "Go back home where you came from."

Terry may have been stung by the rebuff, but in fact neither he nor the U.S. government really wanted Sitting Bull back. Terry was only making a show of good faith for the Canadians. To the Lakota chiefs, however, the American general had been dealt a defeat so humiliating he would have to take his own life. A pictograph prepared by the Minnecoujous portrayed Terry on the edge of a newly dug grave, about to shoot himself. The only record from an Indian perspective of a significant council with white officials, attests Robert M. Utley, the pictograph found its way up the line to General Sheridan, accompanied by papers attempting to interpret its meaning. Showing his "usual insight" into the minds of his Lakota adversaries, Utley notes tartly, Sheridan endorsed the papers with a dismissive statement: "I attach no more interest to these than the drawings on a slate of a boy 12 years old."[36]

Meanwhile, far to the south, Red Cloud and Spotted Tail were gathering their people to move their agencies to the hated Missouri, where Red Cloud feared they would be destroyed by unscrupulous white men and whiskey. The new President, Rutherford B. Hayes, had promised them that after wintering on the Missouri they could go to permanent reservations of their own choosing. On October 26, eight thousand people, including two thousand northern Indians, left Red Cloud Agency. When they reached the White River, the northern Indians broke off and headed for their relatives in the land of the Great Mother.[37]

Deadwood Gulch, all this while, was roaring along. By the time news of the disaster on the Little Bighorn arrived in mid-summer, the town of Deadwood may have been jammed by more than twenty-five thousand inhabitants, though as one wrote to a Chicago relative, "You can't count people who are living in layers." It was a wild, still lawless place. Piled virtually on top of each other in the narrow canyon, men sometimes settled their arguments with six-shooters. Yet even before Wild Bill Hickok drew his "dead man's hand" of aces and eights on August 2, events were laying the foundation for a more enduring community.[38]

Among the throngs who poured into Deadwood Gulch were two French Canadians from Minnesota, Fred and Moses Manuel, experienced "lode men," veterans of earlier mining ventures who knew deep-rock, or quartz, mining. They hoped to locate a "homestake," a find rich enough to sustain them for good. Finding nothing in Custer or Hill City, they moved on to try their luck at Deadwood. On April 8, 1876, with the slopes still blanketed in snow, Moses was poking around in a little draw. Through running water from the snowmelt, he sighted some exposed quartz.

"Hank," he told a partner, "this is surely a homestake."

They called it the Homestake Mine. It turned out to be the richest lode in the country, maybe the hemisphere. The following winter they took out $5,000 worth of gold. In the summer of 1877 they sold it for $70,000 to a syndicate headed by George Hearst.

Father of William Randolph Hearst, the newspaper magnate, George Hearst was the son of a wealthy Missouri farmer with an estate of nineteen slaves and interests in lead and copper mines. In 1850 George Hearst had joined the California gold rush. After nine years of struggle he made a small fortune on the Comstock lode and formed a partnership to invest in mining shares. In San Francisco one morning he picked up a newspaper and learned of Custer's discovery of gold in the Black Hills. Hearst had already received reports of copper around Butte City. He might just have his engineer swing by and look at both sites. A skeptical partner argued that Custer had found only placer gold, gold that has been washed out into streams.

"Placer gold has to come from some source," Hearst said. "We'll look at it."[39]

The Manuel brothers lacked the capital to exploit their claim fully. They had driven only a small discovery shaft and done some work on an open cut. No one knew the true value of their find, and as the saying went, Black Hills gold was like water at the bottom of a deep well: "To get it out you've got to prime the pump." The Hearst syndicate had the wherewithal, and the willingness to risk it. The Homestake Mining Company was incorporated in November 1877 and began operations the following July. The foundation of the Hearst fortune, Homestake gold enabled Hearst to buy into Anaconda copper, acquire the San Simeon ranch on the California coast, and secure a seat in the United States Senate.[40]

Other mining ventures in the Black Hills were less fortunate. Rockerville, a waterless find of placer gold, took its name from the water-saving rockers used to separate gold from gravel. Until a seventeen-mile flume from Spring Creek was completed in 1880, water had to be hauled into the arid gulch by horse-drawn wagon. Among the roaringest of mining camps, Rockerville had a population of almost a thousand and was raking in huge sums from investors in New York and San Francisco.

The writer Ambrose Bierce was brought in as local manager. Bierce expected to gain a bonanza himself. He mastered any number of difficulties, but he could not overcome the meddling of less informed superiors. Rockerville took out some $500,000 in gold before expiring, but the experience left its mark on "bitter Bierce," as he was to become known. The Rockerville interlude was one of those "cloudy episodes [he] never referred to," one of his biographers notes. He went on to work for Willliam Randolph Hearst on the *San Francisco Examiner*. Bierce crafted an acerbic definition for his *Devil's Dictionary*: "Gold, n. A yellow metal greatly prized for its convenience in the various kinds of robbery known as trade. The word was formerly spelled 'God'—the *l* was insert-ed to distinguish it from the name of another and inferior deity."[41]

Circumstances were mercilessly closing in on the Lakotas. With the establishment of Fort Meade near Sturgis in 1878, white settlers got the military post in the Hills they had long demanded. Simultaneously the Oglalas were settled on their permanent reservation, in the wide valley of White Clay Creek. Though it lacked a ridge and its pines were hidden in the ravines, the government named it Pine Ridge to minimize its identification with Red Cloud himself.[42]

As white cattlemen developed their herds in and around the Hills, harvesting the gold "from the grass roots up" that had sustained the buffalo, the Lakota bands in Saskatchewan found themselves in great difficulty. The defiant Sitting Bull served as a magnet for discontented Indians from the agencies. His camps now had some eight hundred lodges, mostly Hunkpapas, with contingents of Minicoujous and Sans Arcs and forty-five lodges of Nez Percés who had escaped into Canada—as many as five thousand mouths to feed. Their demand for buffalo soon incurred the hostility of other tribes, especially the powerful Blackfeet, traditional enemies.

During the winter of 1877-1878, prairie fires swept the range of the Northern Blackfeet, pushing the buffalo closer to the Lakota bands. White hunters in Montana were relentlessly slaughtering the northern herds. When Lakota hunting parties ventured in desperation across the line, the U.S. Army drove them back. Sitting Bull denounced Red Cloud and Spotted Tail in a newspaper interview as "rascals" who had "sold our country without the full consent of our people." Even his nemesis the Northern Pacific Railroad, stalled at Bismarck since the panic of 1873, began stirring with the country's renewed business expansion.[43]

By the spring of 1881, hunger seized the reins. The Lakotas had been received kindly in the Great Mother's country, but they had never been truly welcome; they brought nothing but trouble. The resentment of the Canadian tribes left them vulnerable and fearful. Sitting Bull's people were on the verge of starvation, and the Redcoats were pressing him to return to his homeland. They were kind men, just men. They had plenty of food. Why did they refuse to share, as Lakotas would do? Sitting Bull wondered. And despite many assurances, he feared for his life if he went back. He could not believe the Americans wouldn't hang him for killing Custer.

On April 28, ignoring pleas from Running Antelope, Gall, and others to come in and join them at Standing Rock, he took thirty-eight lodges and bolted to the north to see Major Walsh. During his absence his eldest daughter eloped and left in the exodus to the south. Hunger finally brought him in—in 1881, the peak year in the slaughter of the northern buffalo herds. The officer who accompanied him into Fort Buford asserted that "nothing but nakedness and starvation has driven this man to submission, and that not on his own account but for the sake of his children, of whom he is very fond."[44]

The procession entering Fort Buford on July 19 was anything but triumphal: forty-four men, a hundred and forty-three women and children, fourteen gaunt ponies. A casual onlooker might have seen in Sitting Bull only a man in "a threadbare and dirty calico shirt and plain black leggings," as a biographer pictures him, "with an equally threadbare and dirty blanket draped loosely about his waist," outward signs of the poverty exacted of him by the Lakota virtue of generosity.

Next morning, apparently too dazed to take in the full meaning of the occasion, the great chief surrendered his Winchester. He signaled his son Crow Foot to pick it up from the floor between his feet and hand it to the post commander: "I surrender this rifle to you through my young son, whom I now desire to teach in this manner that he has become a friend of the Americans." Sitting Bull wanted his son to learn the habits of the whites, to be educated like them. He wished to be remembered as "the last man of my tribe to surrender my rifle."

Realizing soon that he no longer controlled his destiny, he composed a song:

> *A warrior*
> *I have been*
> *Now*
> *It is all over*
> *A hard time*
> *I have.*[45]

Loss of the Black Hills simply desolated the Lakotas. Excluded from their homeland and refuge, their source of spiritual renewal, their very identity, they were also denied access to a reserve storehouse to be drawn on in times of want. The Black Hills were "just like a food pack," said Standing Bear, who as a boy of fifteen had heard Sitting Bull use the phrase. They were "full of fish, animals and lots of water. Indians would rove all around, but when they were in need of something, they could just go in there and get it."[46]

The buffalo, the source and center of Lakota life, were all but gone. The government instigated a new policy that divided the people, breaking tribal lands into separate little squares they were expected to farm, a life alien to warriors of the plains. Whites might like to "dig in the ground for food," Sitting Bull informed a journalist, but the practice was unworthy of a Lakota: "The life of white men is slavery. They are prisoners in towns or farms."[47]

All the same, soon after his nineteen months' confinement as a prisoner of war, Sitting Bull's agent had him hoeing away at a plot of ground. The great chief did surprisingly well at it during the next few years at Standing Rock, but when Buffalo Bill invited him to join his Wild West Show, he accepted. During the summer of 1885 he toured more than a dozen cities in the U.S. and Canada with the show, making a huge success. Sitting Bull apparently enjoyed it, but two years later, invited to go along to England for Queen Victoria's Jubilee, he declined. He was needed where he was; there was "more talk of taking our lands."[48]

The General Allotment Act of 1887 was pushed through Congress by humanitarians in the East who saw communal landholding as an obstacle to civilization. Sponsored by Senator Henry L. Dawes of Massachusetts, the act broke up tribal lands, giving each head of family an allotment of one hundred and sixty acres. The rest was left for settlers. Unlocking the "surplus," promoters called it. The Sioux Act that followed in 1888 proposed to carve out six reservations and put the rest of the Great Sioux Reservation—some nine million acres—up for sale at fifty cents an acre. Before it could take effect, three-fourths of the adult males would have to sign.

The proposal evoked a paralyzing fear of the incomprehensible. Principal and interest? Invisible lines? Acres? What were acres? Many people feared that once they signed, their rations would be cut off. Sitting Bull and other "non-progressives" mounted strong resistance, aggravating the bitter factionalism within the tribe.

General Crook was sent out with the commission designated to secure the plan's approval. Crook advised the Lakotas to look to their future: "It strikes me that you are in the position of a person who had his effects in the bed of a dry stream when there was a flood coming down, and instead of finding fault with the Creator for sending it down, you should try and save what you can." Indeed, a flood soon came down. Congress cut the subsistence appropriation by a hundred thousand dollars, and the beef issue at Pine Ridge was reduced by a million pounds. People were going to starve. On February 10, 1890, with three-fourths of the necessary signatures in hand, President Harrison opened the ceded territory to settlement.[49]

Rumors of a Messiah in the far west had been circulating since the summer of 1889. Christ was coming again, to help the Indians. God had appeared to the Crows. Jesus, wearing a crown of thorns, had appeared to an Arapaho hunting party. God had manifested himself to the Utes, warning them to beware of whites. When the "sun died" in far Nevada, a Paiute shaman had gone up to heaven and been given a great vision.[50]

The belief in a redeemer, wrote the anthropologist James Mooney in his monumental study of the Ghost Dance, has its origin in "a hope and longing common to all humanity." How natural for a race "crushed and groaning beneath an alien yoke" to hope for a redeemer who will drive out the usurper and win back what the people have lost: "The hope becomes a faith and the faith becomes the creed of priests and prophets, until the hero is a god and the dream a religion, looking to some great miracle of nature for its culmination and accomplishment."[51]

Everything cried out for a messiah. The land agreement had shaken the Lakotas more violently than anything in their history. The reduced beef ration condemned them to hunger. Then severe drought drained them of hope.

The drought was widespread. For white settlers in eastern South Dakota as well, a bumper wheat crop in 1888 was followed by crop failure in 1889. Among Lakota farmers, abundant spring rains in 1890 stirred new hope, but searing July winds whipped the prairie, scorching oats, wheat, even the range grass. "The pitiful little gardens curled up and died in the persistent hot winds," noted an observer crossing the Dakota reservations. "Even young men displayed gaunt limbs and lackluster faces. Old folks lost their hold on life, and heart-broken mothers mourned the last of a series of dead babies."[52]

In northeastern South Dakota the hottest July on record, followed by a late summer without rain, utterly devastated the wheat crop. An Aberdeen bank was forced to close because of uncollectible loans to bankrupt farmers. Times were so hard that when an Indiana senator argued that additional rations for the starving Indians would make more sense than issuing munitions to the states, a North Dakota senator wondered aloud that the "white people in that region did not themselves go on the war path, because they were hungry."[53]

Settlers by the score were abandoning homesteads and moving on, but the Lakotas, confined to their reservations, had no place to go. "The hot winds that withered the corn stalks," says Robert Utley, "nourished the seed of the Ghost Dance religion." If Congress had restored the rations, fulfilling the promises made by the Crook Commission, the Ghost Dance might have quietly run its course among the Lakotas, as it did in other tribes. Congress had more important items on the agenda.[54]

The Ghost Dance "craze," as it became known to whites, was a new Indian religion bearing a strong resemblance to Christianity. As it spread across the West it took on different shadings among the various tribes. The differences of interpretation, as James Mooney noted in the 1890s, resembled those we find in Christianity, with its hundreds of sects and numberless shades of individual opinion. The new faith held out a promise that the time would come "when the whole Indian race, living and dead, will be reunited upon a regenerated earth, to live a life of aboriginal happiness, forever free from death, disease, and misery."[55]

The Ghost Dance stirred fear in whites partly because of the form it took among the Lakotas, who had fresh cause for grief and anger. In March 1890 a Lakota delegation returned from a visit to Wovoka, the Paiute shaman, in Nevada. Among them was Kicking Bear, a warrior and medicine man married to the niece of Big Foot, the Minnecoujou chief. Sitting Bull invited Kicking Bear to the Standing Rock Reservation.

"My brothers," Kicking Bear told the Hunkpapas, "I bring you word from your fathers the ghosts, that they are now marching to join you, led by the Messiah who came once to live on earth with the white man, but was cast out and killed by them." He quoted Wovoka: "The earth is getting old, and I will make it new for my chosen people, the Indians, who are to inhabit it, and among them will be all those ancestors who have died. . . ." The Messiah would cover the earth with new soil five times as deep as the height of a man, and the whites would be buried beneath it. "The new lands will be covered with sweet-grass and running water and trees, and herds of buffalo and ponies will stray over it, that my red children may eat and drink, hunt and rejoice."[56]

The gospel actually propounded by Wovoka makes no reference to any burial of the whites. James Mooney went to Nevada himself in 1891 and won the confidence of Wovoka. Mooney relates how when the "sun died"—most likely the total eclipse of January 1, 1889—Wovoka said he fell asleep and was transported to the "other world." There he saw God and all the people who had died long ago, all happy and forever young, in a land full of game, engaged in their old-time sports and occupations.

After Wovoka had been shown everything, God told him to go back and tell his people "they must be good and love one another, have no quarreling, and live in peace with the whites; that they must work, and not lie or steal; that they must put away all the old practices that savored of war . . . ." If they obeyed his instructions faithfully they would "at last be reunited with their friends in this other world, where there would be no more death or sickness or old age." To achieve such happiness, they would need to dance for five consecutive days.[57]

Having won the confidence of Cheyenne and Arapaho adherents of the Ghost Dance, Mooney was visited by Black Short Nose, a Cheyenne who wanted the whites to know the ghost dancers were not hostile. Black Short Nose gave Mooney the "messiah letter" not intended for whites—

the official statement of doctrine from Wovoka himself. Urging his followers to dance for five days every six weeks, Wovoka issued a series of commandments:

> You must not hurt anybody or do harm to anyone.
> You must not fight.
> Do right always.
> Do not refuse to work for the whites . . . .
> Do not make any trouble for them until you leave them.
> Do not tell lies.

This messiah letter, Mooney points out, contains the elements of every organized religion: a system of ethics, of mythology, and of ritual observance. In forbidding warriors to make war, Wovoka's doctrine calls for "such a revolution as comes but once in the life of a race."[58]

Blind to its Christian elements, the Bureau of Indian Affairs set out to abolish the Ghost Dance as a barbaric ritual. The Standing Rock agent denounced it as "demoralizing, indecent and disgusting." Among the Lakotas the dance itself was a Paiute round dance to which they added elements of their own. Stepping to the left, the participants circled a pole, or sacred tree. On the Pine Ridge Reservation the women danced in loose cotton robes. The men wore cotton shirts, most of which were painted blue around the neck, sprinkled with such things as moon and stars, especially with painted eagles. Of the many plains tribes embracing the Ghost Dance, only the Lakotas believed the shirts to be bullet-proof, an assertion that seems to have been made after soldiers arrived on the scene.[59]

Historians are in virtual agreement the ghost dancers were not planning any general uprising, but as summer passed into fall, recalled Ed Lemmon, the legendary "boss cowboy" whose town took his name, the whole area was becoming "unsettled and uneasy. The whites were afraid of the Indians, who were coming in from the whole northwest; and the Indians were afraid of what the whites might be planning to do to them." Home Guards had been organized and armed against perceived danger, though Lemmon himself remembered the Indians as merely hungry, not hostile at all, but desperate for more rations. Many were educated and knew only too well the power of government troops.[60]

A sweeping range of forces converged to turn hardship into catastrophe. Skulduggery seems to have abounded. White witnesses reported that renegades were raiding and looting ranches, blaming their depredations on the ghost dancers. One old-time cowboy, Robert Davis, blamed big cattle operators for the "Indian Scare of 1890." Davis thought the cattlemen, upset by the increasing numbers of settlers moving in to break up prime rangeland, were trying to scare the settlers out.[61]

Early in October the spoils system that staffed the agencies coughed up a new agent for Pine Ridge, Daniel F. Royer. A small town physician and druggist who knew nothing about Indians, Royer soon became known among them as "Young Man Afraid of Indians." Faced with recalcitrance and increasing boldness from the dancers and unable to develop any authority over them, Royer soon began calling for troops.[62]

"Indian troubles" made exciting newspaper copy. In early November reports had Kicking Bear converting the mighty Sitting Bull to the Ghost Dance. Ninety miles to the east, in Aberdeen, a headline triggered an all-out Indian scare: "bellicose" Indians from Standing Rock poised to descend on Fort Abraham Lincoln! One Aberdeen editor complained that sensational stories were harming the community by driving out settlers. Another considered the scare ridiculous: the "red men" themselves were frightened by the reports of fear among the settlers, "knowing that if the whites were thoroughly aroused they would annihilate every tribe."[63]

On November 11, ration day at Pine Ridge, two hundred ghost dancers surrounded the agency police, threatening to kill them and burn the agency. Only the intervention of American Horse averted bloodshed. Stop and think, he told the dancers. Are you going to kill these men of your own race? These helpless white men? "Your country is surrounded with a network of railroads; thousands of white soldiers will be here within three days. . . . Think, my brothers! This is a child's madness."

"We need protection and we need it now," Royer wired the Acting Commissioner on November 15. Indians, "wild and crazy," were dancing in the snow. Sure enough, American Horse was right: the railroads delivered. At dawn on November 20, troops arrived at Pine Ridge and Rosebud. For the first time since 1876, the Lakotas confronted soldiers.[64]

The confrontation at Pine Ridge opened vistas of possibility for the newspapers. With little or nothing to report, something had to be imagined. A reporter for the *Omaha Bee* discovered a Pine Ridge that "seethed with impending violence and conflict." The Indian camps encircling the agency became "hostile forces holding the agency in a state of siege." In nearby Chadron, both newpapers assailed the Omaha reporters for their sensationalism. Citizens of Chadron circulated a petition demanding the Omaha papers stop printing such unbelievable, provocative stories.

The *Omaha Bee*'s "siege" of Pine Ridge was lampooned by the editor of the *Chadron Advocate*: "[Determined] to cut our way through the hostile lines and relieve the hard-pressed garrison and war correspondents [we were soon] clattering through an Indian village with dogs barking and the sound of children's voices and the hum of squaws as they busied themselves with primitive housekeeping . . . ." Luckily the "editorial relief force, unchallenged by the pickets of the Ninth Cavalry, went on into the agency square," where a lone Indian policeman gave them scarcely a glance. "[Thus the] siege of Pine Ridge was raised."[65]

"The people here are making money out of the presence of the soldiery," observed an Omaha reporter. He pointed to the infusion of cash the Indian troubles were contributing to the local economy. One miller in nearby Rushville boasted that he had contracted for 68,000 pounds of flour for the troops. The Omaha reporter was soon ousted from the reservation for his attacks on Agent Royer. "Mr. Royer may succeed in aggravating these Indians into some kind of warlike demonstration," he observed in his final story on December 1, "but it will be fighting against their will. They are not fools, and do not desire to make a winter fight with no forage in sight."[66]

Photographers found an even livelier market for pictures—those pictures that supply indelible images today. Working strictly for profit, the independents learned to produce pictures to satisfy the purchaser. "In the world of photography of the American Indian," John E. Carter reflects, "fact became subordinate to stereotype." The result sometimes was outright fraud, as in the portrait of a Kiowa man identified by a Chadron photographer as Young Man Afraid of His Horses.[67]

There were credible reports of belligerence among the ghost dancers in remote areas. In a letter to General Miles on November 26, Arthur C. Mellette, the first governor of South Dakota, relates an experience of a "very cool courageous" rancher, James ("Scotty") Philip, the man who has been credited with saving the buffalo. Twenty of Philip's cattle had been killed in the past few days. He reported that he had never been afraid of Indians before, but that now, along with everybody who had been among Indians for any length of time, he thought there would be an uprising very soon. Philip had recently talked with a small band of Lakotas he knew well, who were now "surly and defiant," armed with Winchesters. "One said he had seen the time when he used to beat out the brains of children and drink women's blood, and that the time was coming when he would do it again." Philip was "raising horses for Indians to ride," he said, and the country was just as good now as in buffalo days because there were plenty of cattle in it.[68]

The evidence suggests that the balance of atrocities was heavily weighted on the side of the whites. The most notorious killer was Riley Miller. An expert marksman who had been imprisoned at Andersonville during the Civil War and had escaped more dead than alive, Miller had learned to kill for pleasure—anything moving, especially Indians. He and a friend stripped and scalped their corpses, organizing a ghoulish collection of fresh Indian artifacts for the 1893 World's Columbian Exposition in Chicago. Its main attraction: a dried Indian baby.[69]

Implicated in these horrors were even such men as John R. Brennan, a founder of Rapid City, who was reported to have "secured" the scalp of Dead Arm, a baptized Christian, at the Cole ranch. "They are keeping the body at the ranch," Brennan wrote in a note to the *Rapid City Journal*, "so that all the neighbors and Indian fighters can gaze on a good Indian."[70]

Governor Mellette himself encouraged the newly formed Home Guard to stir up the Lakotas and provoke an uprising. In a dispatch to the Guard's commander, Mellette expressed pleasure at the killing of three Indians by "our men," with no loss to the whites, but he counseled, "Be discreet in killing the Indians."[71]

No less well known a figure than Frederick Remington partici-pated in the climactic events. Yale-educated, a friend of Teddy Roose-velt, the illustrator whose work fostered the stereotype of the good cowboy fighting the treacherous and savage Indian, Remington went along on reconnaissance missions into the Badlands. For readers of *Harper's Weekly* he pictured the Badlands near the Stronghold, where the Ghost Dancers were conducting ceremonies, as "full of savage Sioux." The Badlands, said Remington, were a "place for stratagem and murder, with nothing to witness its mysteries but the cold blue winter sky."

The killing of Sitting Bull by the Indian police on December 16 set off a fresh chain of events. Enterprising photographers discovered a bonanza in the unfolding tragedy. Some responses of the time are only now beginning to surface. For readers today the most shocking note may be the view expressed by L. Frank Baum, author of *The Wonderful Wizard of Oz*, a view he never renounced. Lamenting Sitting Bull's death, Baum recalled the "proud spirit of the original owners of these vast prairies" and the "selfishness, falsehood and treachery" marking the white man's dealings with them. The author of America's most beloved fairy tale then offered a solution—total annihilation.

"The nobility of the Redskin is extinguished," Baum said, "and what few are left are a pack of whining curs who lick the hand that smites them." By law of conquest and by "justice of civilization" the whites had become "masters of the American continent," and the safety of the frontier settlers would best be secured by annihilating the few remaining Indians. "Their glory has fled, their manhood effaced; better that they should die than live the miserable wretches that they are." So a romanticized view of the Indians now served to justify their extinction.[72]

An oral traditional story of the Lakotas recalls an obscure episode that took place a few days before Sitting Bull's death: the virtual annihilation of a peaceful hunting party of fifty, mostly women, sent into non-Indian territory by Chief Big Foot. The *Omaha Bee* announced that a party of armed cowboys would leave Buffalo Gap the next day to kill any "hostiles" they found. Their purpose: "to defend the outlying ranches and to punish the depredating Sioux." A young Minnecoujou woman, White Eyes, survived the ambush. Wounded in the thigh, she walked for three weeks to warn Big Foot the whites wanted to kill them all. When she arrived at Wounded Knee Creek, she wept at what her eyes beheld: a bonfire, with soldiers and Indian scouts walking around. "Everything looked burnt up and there were dead people on the ground."[73]

Confusion shrouds much of what happened at Wounded Knee, though certain facts are clear. Frightened homesteaders, their fear intensified by rumors, left their isolated homesteads to seek refuge in towns. When Big Foot's band of Minnecoujous learned Sitting Bull had been killed, they fled toward Pine Ridge, two hundred miles to the south. Intercepted by the Seventh Cavalry, they surrendered at Wounded Knee Creek.

Four Hotchkiss guns were positioned on the hill overlooking the camp—cannons firing up to fifty explosive shells a minute. On the morning of December 29 the soldiers were ordered to disarm the Minnecoujous. A shot was fired, by whom remains uncertain. Hand-to-hand fighting erupted. The Hotchkiss guns opened up. Their shrapnel cut down men, women, and children, even soldiers. The Army lost twenty-five dead, the Indians a hundred and fifty or more, perhaps as many as three hundred, including Big Foot himself. Some of the women and children were apparently hunted down as they fled, their bodies found as much as three miles from the scene.

On New Year's Day a long pit was dug on the hill where the Hotchkiss guns had stood. The most widely published photo of that occasion shows the frozen bodies of a hundred and forty-six humans layered in like cordwood, "a thing to melt the heart of a man, if it was of stone," said a member of the burial party, "to see those little children, with their bodies shot to pieces, thrown naked into the pit."[74]

Technically, Robert Utley suggests, it may not have been a massacre like Sand Creek, a deliberate and indiscriminate slaughter. "[O]vercharged emotions touched off a bloodbath that neither side intended or foresaw," says Utley. "Nor was it indiscriminate; the troops tried to spare women and children, and did spare many, but they were mixed up with the men and often impossible to identify in the smoke and confusion." Whatever the term, Wounded Knee burns in the national conscience as a *massacre*.[75]

Several days later a baby girl was found alive, shielded beneath the body of her dead mother. Her frostbitten head was covered by a cap decorated with stars and stripes—red, white, and blue. The girl became known as *Zintkala Nuni*, the Lost Bird. In 1991, a full century later, in a profoundly spiritual ceremony, the Lost Bird's remains were brought from a California cemetery and buried alongside those of her relatives, next to the mass grave on top of the hill from which the Hotchkiss guns had spoken.[76]

PART THREE

Chapter 6: Preservation or Plunder?

While conflict had been building into tragedy on the plains to the east, the Black Hills were undergoing radical changes. The most dramatic stemmed from the gold rush, which was ravaging the landscape. Utility became the sole measure, and any doubts that might surface about taking Lakota territory could easily be dismissed: the Indians, after all, were not *using* it. "Bitter" Bierce was not far off the mark in suggesting an *l* had been inserted into the word "God" to distinguish the new deity from the one supplanted.

Scarring the earth was of no concern. Nothing escaped the transforming hand of the white man, lamented Luther Standing Bear, looking back half a century later. Before the whites came, he said, nature was by no means a wilderness: "Earth was bountiful and we were surrounded with the blessings of the Great Mystery." But the white man, distancing himself from nature and assuming a lofty place in the scheme of things, had lost reverence and understanding. Where the Indian sought harmony with his surroundings, said Standing Bear, the white man sought only dominance.[1] Oversimplified, yes, but compare the photo of Custer's column entering Castle Creek Valley, a thousand men and wagons in a serpent-like procession, with the image of the peaceful encampment they came upon—five lodges of Lakota hunters, leaving few marks on the landscape.

The action centered in Deadwood, where by the summer of 1876 some 25,000 people were jammed into a long gulch. Sunday was the big day. Men came pouring into town from every camp, says Joseph Cash. Gold dust was the universal currency. "Street preachers competed with gamblers for space in the street, while free-lancing ladies-of-an-evening elbowed them both out of the way in the race for customers." Chinese collected and dispensed laundry; the mail was distributed; ox teams and cattle herds, "trail-driven from as far as Texas, moved through the streets. The atmosphere was lusty and exciting."[2]

In the beginning, legally, these frontiersmen were trespassers bound only by their own rules. For their motto, wrote a French nobleman in 1883, they took "self-reliance and a big revolver." Poverty was no disgrace in Deadwood, observed Baron Edmond de Mandat-Grancey. Prolonged it might be, but only transitory, for a man poor today was sure to be rich tomorrow. De Mandat-Grancey described the Fourth of July celebrations with Gallic irony. He was so astounded by the ceremonial oration of Judge Daniel McLaughlin, the mayor, that he took it down word for word.

The judge attributed American prosperity to the guidance of Divine Providence and to the circumstance that labor "among us has always been honourable, that every one was ready to sacrifice his life and his fortune to defend the life and fortune of his brethren," a view somewhat at odds with the visible evidence; "that, when poor, we were frugal, pure-living, and laborious, and having become rich, we have not given way to the allurements of luxury, but, in retaining all the virtues of our poverty, we have employed the acquired riches simply in the development of civilization in the immense continent that has fallen to us as an inheritance."

The peroration reads like a parody of the frontier origin myth once defined by Patricia Nelson Limerick. In New York or Washington, such words would not have surprised de Mandat-Grancey. In Deadwood, he found them astonishing.[3]

Poverty there was, in abundance. Colonel Dodge's saying proved out: placer mining was the "poor man's diggings"; quartz mining was reserved for the rich. Most placer miners gained little more than a subsistence. "Two-Bit Gulch" was named for the value of a day's earnings there. The Homestake Mining Corporation, by contrast, returned the immense wealth undergirding the Hearst fortune. Incorporated in California in November 1877, the Homestake paid its first dividends fourteen months later and was listed on the New York Stock Exchange. Before long it was producing more than a million dollars in gold annually.[4]

The landscape soon showed the effects. Seemingly inexhaustible pine forests were stripped to supply wood for construction and fuel and for shoring up mine tunnels. Congress facilitated the process in 1878 by passing the Free Timber Act, which authorized miners to take "any timber or trees growing or being on the public [mineral lands]," subject to regulations prescribed by the Secretary of the Interior, which were seldom enforced. Often only half of each tree was used, with the rest left to rot. Soon the hillsides within a radius of eight miles from Deadwood were virtually barren of trees. Symptomatic of the governing values, descriptions of the mining boom made no mention of the degradation prevailing at century's end, which was not acknowledged until 1948.[5]

The truth about Deadwood can be difficult to discern. In a history of the place flavored by humor and self-directed irony, Watson Parker confesses to building at times upon "old, well-worn, and familiar falsehoods," lies and misconceptions that have been taken to heart and cherished by Deadwood's citizens, and thus more important in shaping the town's history than "truer and more sober truths" would have been. Local history became the handmaiden of advertising.[6]

For almost fifteen years Deadwood was a stagecoach town with its own "stagecoach aristocracy," those who arrived before the railroads. A lively collection of young men, with few women or even middle-aged men, the town was preserved for a time from the aging effects of the railroad. Bill Cody quipped that unlike most towns "Deadwood was young so long that it will never quite forget its youth."

A surprising number of its early arrivals, as many as forty per cent, were foreign-born. The Chinese had their own section of Mount Moriah Cemetery, as did the Jews. The substantial contributions of its Jewish merchants to Deadwood's early life have seldom been fully recognized. Less heralded yet have been the itinerant Jewish peddlers, those hardy little men who carried hundred-pound packs over the mountains on what was known as the "Jew Peddler Trail."[7]

In nearby Lead—pronounced "leed," a synonym for lode—an ethnically diverse community grew up around the Homestake Mine. More than half of Lead's citizens were foreign-born, many of them "Cousin Jacks" or "Cousin Jennies," veterans of the tin mines of Cornwall. Though miners were often killed or injured in the work, sometimes crushed beneath falling rock, the inquests rarely found the management responsible. It was always the miners at fault, or the Almighty.

With its abundant reserves of capital, the Homestake gradually bought out smaller companies until it acquired a near monopoly. By 1883 the mine had burrowed deep enough under the town to precipitate a cave-in. Part of the town dropped into the two-hundred-foot level, leaving much of the business district perched on the edge of a precipice. The entire district had to be moved.[8]

   Despite such episodes, the Homestake provided stable employ-
ment, enabling Lead to overtake the more populous Deadwood—2,581
citizens by 1890, as against Deadwood's dwindling 2,366.

   On the plain to the southeast, Rapid City had made a precarious
beginning. Seven men had laid out the town as a gateway to the Hills on
February 25, 1876. Among its founders was John R. Brennan, who had
given up on mining at Palmer Gulch. Six blocks were divided into lots,
but after nine men in the vicinity were killed by Indians that spring, and
four more in August, most of the town's two hundred citizens fled to Fort
Pierre. The nineteen men and one woman who stayed built themselves a
log fortification thirty feet by thirty, huddling inside for several weeks
and venturing out only when assured by new arrivals that the Indians
were no longer hostile. By December a scant three families remained.
All the same, by 1883 enough lots had been platted to cover six square
miles: "plenty of room on every side for additions," the *Journal* editor
cheerfully noted, "when they become necessary."
   In 1885 the Black Hills National Bank of Rapid City received a
federal charter. The arrival of the railroad in 1886 brought a period of
prosperity. A broom factory produced nine hundred brooms a week. One
of the more successful industries was the manufacture of brick. The School
of Mines opened its doors in 1887 on ten acres east of town, with four
faculty members and twenty students. After South Dakota gained its
statehood in 1889, two enterprising breweries were stymied by Prohibition.[9]

   Along the southern fringe of the Hills a community was forming
around an abundant natural source—thermal springs. Mentioned by
Colonel Dodge in 1876, and evidently called Minnekahta, or Warm
Water, in the Lakota tongue, the springs issued in great volume at a
temperature of seventy-four degrees Fahrenheit. Mineral waters were
the preferred treatment for tuberculosis, which was then widespread,
and Hot Springs promised to develop into a prospering health spa. For
centuries the warm springs had been used by the Indians. In more recent
times the Lakotas had dislodged the Cheyennes in a legendary
engagement on Battle Mountain east of town. A traditional story related
by Annie Tallent holds that for more than two hundred years various
tribes had used the waters to counter epidemics that threatened to wipe
them out. One legend recalls a beautiful Sioux princess, "the envy of
all the dusky maidens," who, thwarted in love, "threw herself headlong
from towering cliffs and was dashed to fragments on the rocks below."

Eventually, says Tallent, the springs were "usurped" by the "avaricious Cheyennes" until they were defeated at Battle Mountain by the "valorous Sioux," who held the springs until they in turn were driven out by the "superior valor of the pioneers."[10]

In June 1879 the geologist Walter Jenney set out to locate the thermal springs discovered during the 1875 expedition. A young man who accompanied Jenney asserted later that he, William Thornby, chopped off the top of a cedar tree, blazed it on both sides, and wrote "I claim this spring." Alerted by Thornby's claim published in the *Black Hills Pioneer*, five men joined to form the Hot Springs Town-Site Company in 1881, with the aim of developing a health resort. When the peripatetic Baron de Mandat-Grancey came through in 1883, he found two establishments in place.

Hot Springs was named county seat of the newly established Fall River County in 1883, a choice contested by rival Oelrichs. When the Black Hills Methodist Mission came looking for a site for its college in 1887, Hot Springs edged out Custer and Spring Valley. "Hot Springs got there with the Longest Pole," chortled the *Star*'s editor, "and Took the Persimmon." After the Fremont, Elkhorn and Missouri Valley Railroad extended a branch line to Hot Springs in 1890 from its main line at Buffalo Gap, the town's future seemed assured.[11]

The same could not be said for its neighbor eight miles to the south. Cascade had a warm spring of its own that produced two thousand gallons of warm water a minute. Passing through in 1883, de Mandat-Grancey found the beginnings of a town moving along at a lively pace— store, post office, and stagecoach station, with bar and hotel adjoining. The three avenues laid out included an Avenue of Grancey running along the "river." Doctors "the most qualified" recommended the water, advised de Mandat-Grancey, who ventured that a moralist might attribute the "extraordinary suavity of disposition" of the inhabitants to the water's beneficent effects: not a single assassination had yet taken place!

In 1888 a syndicate founded Cascade officially as a resort town, laying out thirty-six city blocks. A massive four-story hotel was constructed, along with a bank and store and a club with a bowling alley. A going concern by 1890, Cascade awaited the arrival of the Burlington & Missouri River Railroad on its way into Hot Springs. Alas, the syndicate, banking on its confidence the railroad had no other way to go, demanded too high a price. The Burlington selected another route. By 1900 the town's population had withered to twenty-five.[12]

The railroad was slow to penetrate the Black Hills but, once there, extended its reach swiftly. The first locomotive was hauled in by bull train from Bismarck in 1879, a tiny Baldwin weighing five tons with a wheel gauge of twenty-two inches. With two wax candles mounted in its headlight for emergency illumination, it hauled ore for twenty years on tramways linking various Homestake installations. The diminutive *Haggin* calls to mind the locomotive Faulkner pictures entering the great woods with its "shrill peanut-parcher whistle" in *The Bear*. "It had been harmless then," Faulkner observes, leaving the reader to contemplate what has taken place in the interim. Since 1932 the *Haggin* has been a shiny relic on display in the Adams Museum in Deadwood.

The great transcontinental railroads bypassed South Dakota to both north and south. The first true railroad in the Black Hills was the Black Hills and Fort Pierre, a narrow gauge line launched in December 1881 to transport wood to Lead from nearby Woodville. Its engine, the *George Hearst*, was hauled in by mule team. Eventually the line was extended to Piedmont, where it connected with the Chicago and Northwestern working up from Nebraska along the eastern edge of the Hills. The Deadwood Central was launched in 1888 to connect Deadwood with Lead. A branch of the Chicago, Burlington and Quincy entered the Hills at Edgemont, snaking its way up through Custer into the Central Hills—Hill City, Keystone, Rochford.[13]

On the testimony of de Mandat-Grancey, who returned from France in 1887, the Fremont, Elkhorn and Missouri River line played a cruel trick on the citizens of Buffalo Gap. The town, he remarked, had experienced its ups and down: "*boome* and *deboome*, to employ a local expression." Twelve hundred inhabitants waiting for the railroad to reach them discovered, to their chagrin, that the company had run the line three miles away. Undeterred, they transported their houses to the vicinity of the station.[14]

On December 29, 1890, on the same morning as the slaughter at Wounded Knee, the first train arrived in Deadwood. The band struck up *The Star-Spangled Banner* even as the Hotchkiss guns were cutting down men, women, and children on the plains to the east. Thundering up the grade, recalled Estelline Bennett, the daughter of Judge Granville Bennett, the train pulled up alongside the platform "panting and heaving just as the six white stage horses had done the day before. . . . It closed the era that had made Deadwood famous. . . . It was a dream come true," she said, "a whole shaft-full of hopes realized, but it had plunged us—people of the mountains and gulches and stagecoaches—into a new order of things we didn't quite understand."

"Well," Judge Bennett told his family that evening, "we'll have to lock our doors now." The old stagecoach aristocracy, once forced to eat humble pie in the company of the rough pioneers who'd come in on foot or horseback, could now lord it over the tenderfeet arriving spic and span via the effeminate luxuriousness of the railroad. But with the coming of the railroad, observes Watson Parker, something passed out of the life of Deadwood, leaving it a step closer to being merely the center of an industrial area whose product happened to be gold.

For Estelline Bennett, the message was more personal: "You're not a little girl any more. You are grown up. You can't walk stilts or play hop-scotch in the street. You mustn't dance on the sidewalk to the music of the Gem Theater band, and you should give your dolls to your little sister."[15]

The demand for beef in the mining camps fostered the growth of ranching in and around the Hills. It also encouraged cattle rustling. By 1891 the losses to rustlers in western South Dakota had become so great that notwithstanding their stout individualism some of the leading ranchers decided to band together. Their local associations lacked the reach to be effective; common sense economy dictated that they concentrate their efforts. A call went out for a meeting in February to form a general organization of Black Hills stockmen, and the Western South Dakota Stock Growers Association was born.

The forty charter members voted to assess themselves two cents on cattle and one cent on horses—"very liberal" in the count, too, quipped Ed Lemmon, "a lot more so than when the tax assessor came around." The rustling was so pervasive that eventually they had to boost the assessment to three cents. The association hired Sam Moses as detective at a salary of $125 a month and expenses, with a $750 bonus for each conviction secured. Within two years Moses obtained thirteen convictions. Rustling declined significantly.[16]

As the 1890s opened in the Black Hills, Luther Standing Bear's indictment of the white man was clearly justified. The ravages of mining threatened to transform the Northern Hills into a barren waste. A field inventory for the Department of Agriculture reported in 1892 that in large tracts only "stumps, fallen logs, and the underbrush" remained. It would be "no wonder," the report editorialized, "if in a short time the dark pine forest is gone and the name 'Black Hills' has become meaningless." In 1899 an official investigation by Henry S. Graves, first dean of the Yale School of Forestry and later chief of the U. S. Forest Service, reported that the laws were so loose, the provisions for enforcing them so weak, that there had been "no check to the reckless waste of timber which has been going on for years. . . . [T]he exhaustion of the timber supply is merely a matter of time."[17]

Where were the conservationists, as the Progressive Era was getting under way? Mostly scarce, and out of public view. In 1874 Franklin B. Hough, a pioneer environmentalist, had petitioned the government to take action against wanton destruction of timberlands, especially in the West. The following year Hough organized the American Forestry Association and established a one-man forestry research office, the forerunner of the U. S. Forest Service, within the Department of Agriculture. By 1889 Carl Schurz, Secretary of the Interior, warned that the destruction of the forests would kill future prosperity in the United States. Schurz saw a public opinion looking with indifference on "this wanton, barbarous, disgraceful vandalism; a spendthrift people recklessly wasting its heritage; a Government careless of the future and unmindful of a pressing duty." On such matters he found himself all but alone: "Deaf was Congress, and deaf the people seemed to be."[18]

Then in 1891 an amendment quietly slipped through Congress without debate—the most important legislation in the history of forestry in America, in the view of Gifford Pinchot, the father of forestry in America. The Forest Reserve Act, an amendment to an act repealing the Timber and Stone Act, authorized creation of the reserves that formed the basis for the entire system of National Forests. Ten days before he left office in 1897, President Grover Cleveland created thirteen Forest Reserves. First on the list: the Black Hills Reserve, with 967,680 acres.[19]

The most flagrant violators, of course, had been the mining companies, especially the Homestake. In 1894 Homestake was charged with illegally cutting 6,828,160 trees from public land. Instead of the $688,804 in damages sought by the government, a Deadwood judge fined the company $75,000 on lumber valued at two or three million dollars. Three years later Gifford Pinchot discovered a vigorous and beautiful forest near Spearfish filled with fraudulent mining claims, all ascribed to men working for Homestake. The company skirted the law because the profits from doing so exceeded the cost of litigation and punishment.

The Forest Reserve Act had made no provision for *regulated* use of the Reserves. Fierce protests rose across the West. In response, Congress passed the Forest Management Act of 1897. Pinchot favored a European management system that would allow regulated timber cutting. Working for the Secretary of the Interior, he proposed to Homestake officials a system of permits for legally cutting timber. Homestake, previously undeterred by litigation and penalties, now came around to support conservation in principle for the simple reason that it assured continual use of public forests at minimal cost. Thus arose Timber Case No. 1, the first regulated timber cut on a public forest reserve—the beginning of modern forestry practices in the United States.[20]

From the earliest days a resource fought over was water, a critical element in gold mining. The struggle to control the supply led to "The Great Water Fight" between Homestake and its most serious rival, the Father DeSmet Mine. Homestake seems to have fired the first volley by secretly buying a water company coveted by the DeSmet. In a bitter war of litigation both companies went to the extreme of purchasing newspapers to sway public opinion. The Deadwood civic authorities were caught in the middle. A referendum was scheduled—a "glorious" election, as Joseph Cash calls it. "[W]ater was the issue, but alcohol was the means. Both sides furnished copious amounts of whiskey, wine, brandy, cordials, and beer in an attempt to woo the voters. Some teetotalers, immune to the charms of John Barleycorn, had to be bribed. Some men with no ethical standards at all," Cash notes, "sold votes to both sides."

The Homestake came out ahead, and the case ultimately had to be settled by Judge Gideon C. Moody, who ruled in favor of Homestake. A Republican, Moody later resigned to become chief legal counsel for the Homestake. After statehood he joined his employer, George Hearst, a Democrat, in the United States Senate. In the end the Homestake bought out the DeSmet and used all the water.[21]

The first cutting on Case No. 1 began southwest of Nemo on Christmas day 1899. Pinchot sent Edward M. Griffith, "a partly trained forester like myself," to the Black Hills the following May with a "fine collection of spirited young colts" to develop the first working plan for a Forest Reserve. The plan prescribed no duties for rangers, though there must have been rangers because one was fired for turning his marking hatchet over to the lumbermen busily cutting the timber. Nor did the working plan provide for sustained yield. Said Pinchot, "We had first to save the forests from immediate destruction" by fire and bark beetles. Case No. 1 was completed in 1908. Essentially a clear cut, it neverthe-less marked a beginning, a triumph for the Progressive Era: resource conservation to enhance the local economy, an alliance between a cor-poration and men trained in forestry, an alliance that began in the Black Hills.[22]

When the Virginian, that mythic figure from Owen Wister's novel, stepped down from the train in Wyoming, he found the field swept clean:

no untidy remnants, precious few "savages" lurking about, no corpses to stumble over but those of his own making. Wyoming was open space, where a man could do what a man had to do.

The self-reliant cowpoke takes over from the vanishing American. We know the script. The Indians put on their ghost shirts to dance back the buffalo and rid the world of whites. Then the guns of the Seventh Cavalry speak, and the old life is gone. The trail ends, the Indian slumps over his horse. Curtain.

We dab at our eyes. It's unbearably sad. And convenient.

Convenient? The death of a people?

Yes, because the stage is cleared for the next production. Still, the actual drama is far less tidy, for despite hunger and Hotchkiss guns and the death of any hope of resuming their old free life, most of the Lakotas survived and endured. Many histories end with Wounded Knee. What about those *unvanishing* Americans?

Their prospects were desperately bleak. After Wounded Knee the acting agent who took over at Pine Ridge reported that the people "seem to be fenced in with no future and nothing to do but draw and eat their rations and then die." Crazy Horse was long dead. Spotted Tail had been murdered by a Lakota rival, Sitting Bull by the Indian police. Of the great chiefs who had led them, only Red Cloud remained. Wrinkled and stooped, nearly blind, Red Cloud was honored as a symbol of an earlier day, but his glory was gone. "You see this barren waste," he told an anthropologist. "Think of it! . . . I, who used to own rich soil in a well-watered country so extensive I could not ride through it in a week on my fastest pony, am put down here! Now I," Red Cloud lamented, "who used to control 5000 warriors, must tell Washington when I am hungry. I must beg for that which I own. If I beg hard, they put me in the guardhouse." Lakota girls were "getting bad." Every winter the "coughing sickness" was carrying away their best people. "My heart is heavy, I am old, I cannot do much more. . . ."[23]

In 1894 Red Cloud was arrested in Wyoming for killing game out of season on lands where he had once held sway. Jailed in Casper, he had to pay his fine with two of his horses. In 1903, in his last appearance in tribal council, he was reduced to begging a congressman for money from the Black Hills treaty "because we need it now." After he and his wife had driven a hundred and ten miles to Rosebud in an old lumber wagon, a friendly officer described them as "dirty and desperate," and Red Cloud as virtually blind. It was "a pathetic sight to see him led about by his 4 year old grandson."[24]

Red Cloud's death in 1903, at eighty-eight, drew widespread national attention, but the man who had fought so many rearguard actions defending his people's territory, had lost influence with the government. In the aftermath of Wounded Knee a delegation of Lakota chiefs was sent to Washington to visit the Great Father—"some of the best and wisest counselors," General Miles called them. Red Cloud was left behind. He wrote the Commissioner of Indian Affairs to ask for an audience at some later time. The Commissioner's response is recorded on the letter: "File." Red Cloud's active career, observes James C. Olson, ended not in violence like those of his fellow chiefs, but in a government file.[25]

The government's paramount objective with the Lakotas was to "civilize" them, which is to say remold them into whites of a darker hue. A number of strategies were brought to bear, notably education and the encouragement of agriculture. Some of the most gifted young were sent off to distant government schools designed to acculturate them to a new mode of living. In 1879 the first school, Carlisle, opened in Pennsylvania.

Efforts to convert Lakotas into farmers ran into all but insurmountable obstacles from the outset. In the same year Carlisle opened, a new agent was installed at Pine Ridge, Valentine T. McGillycuddy, the surgeon who had attended the dying Crazy Horse. McGillycuddy called the principal chiefs together to enlist them in a plan. He displayed a map of the reservation and urged them to move to the outlying valleys and grow crops. But "Father," Red Cloud told him in a classic utterance, "the Great Spirit did not make us to work. He made us to hunt and fish. He gave us the great prairies and hills and covered them with buffalo, deer, and antelope. He filled the rivers and streams with fish. . . . The white man owes us a living for the lands he has taken from us."[26]

More promising than farming was introduction of the "spotted buffalo," cattle. At first put off by the stench of the corrals, so unlike the open prairies, the Lakotas thought beef inedible, but they came to like it. On ration day a head of household found great sport in going after a steer on horseback and bringing it down with a rifle. The women would butcher it, as they always had with the buffalo, and load it into wagons. The men fared worse with reservation life than the women. Except for the ration day "hunt," Lakota men were cut off from all their traditional activities. "So they sat around in idleness," wrote Clark Wissler in the 1930s. "On the other hand, the Indian woman had no time to loaf. As of old, she was the housekeeper, gathered the wood, reared the children, cared for the sick and made most of the clothing." The women's morale was "far less shattered and it was they who saved tribal life from complete collapse."[27]

The true role of Lakota women has been difficult for non-Indians to see in its own light. As the Lakota anthropologist Ella Deloria has written, "Outsiders seeing women keep to themselves have frequently expressed a snap judgment that they were regarded as inferior to the noble male. The simple fact," she says, "is that woman had her own place and man his; they were not the same and neither inferior nor superior. . . . Both had to work hard, for their life made severe demands. But neither expected the other to come and help outside the customary division of duties; each sex thought the other had enough to do."[28]

A corrosive cycle of dependency became imbedded in reservation life. If the white man owed the Lakotas a living, as Red Cloud said, work was uncalled for. Not only were there few jobs at Pine Ridge, there was no need for them; the Bureau of Indian Affairs would take care of everybody. "Moreover," Marla Powers points out, "any enterprising Oglala man or woman who wanted to become an entrepreneur was criticized by fellow tribesmen for 'selling out to the white man,' for the only way anyone can make a living on the reservation is at the expense of the Indian."[29]

A noteworthy exception was stock raising. Those Indians who had accepted reservation life found opportunity in raising cattle. By 1885 there were ten thousand head on the reservation. In 1900 a new agent came to Pine Ridge, John R. Brennan, a Rapid City businessman and one of its founders, the same man who ten years earlier had referred to a Lakota corpse as a good Indian. During his seventeen year tenure Brennan gave fresh impetus to cattle ranching. By 1912 the Lakota herds had grown to forty thousand.[30]

Through these years the cattle roamed over open range. Great roundups were held each spring and fall. The Pine Ridge Reservation, says Gordon Macgregor, "became steeped in the life of the cowboy, his existence in the open, his dress, his skill with horses—all of which would be extremely attractive to people who had been great horsemen and lived the life of the Plains Indians." By 1914 rations became so unnecessary that they were in effect only token payments.

These bonanza years brought on a catastrophe. With the onset of World War I, cattle prices soared. Drawn by the high prices, white cattlemen pressured the Lakotas to lease their lands. In 1914 only one lease had been made to a white man; by 1917 virtually the entire reservation had been leased to large cattle operators.

The loss of their own herds swept away the foundation of Lakota society along with its economy. Sudden wealth lured many into an orgy of spending on all the gadgets of civilization, especially cars. When white cattlemen defaulted on their leases in the postwar depression, the Lakotas were encouraged to sell their allotments, sometimes fraudulently, to speculators preying upon ignorance and inexperience. Completing the disaster, the government then promoted an economy of dry farming on the eve of the great dust bowl of the 1930s.

The personal story of Luther Standing Bear reflects the profound changes taking place during these years. Born in the 1860s, he was the first son of *Mato Najin*, or Standing Bear, a mixed-blood Sicangu, and Pretty Face, his beautiful young wife. The boy was given the name Plenty Kill by his father, who had killed many enemies. He passed the early years of childhood living the old free life of the Lakotas.[31]

One day Pretty Face went to visit her mother and never returned to his father's tipi. Two other women came. They were kind to him, but when an uncle took the boy to see his mother it was "a wonderful feeling . . . again to be with my own mother." She petted him and combed his hair and gave him moccasins, but she never said she was coming back.

His father introduced the other women, who were sisters, as his new wives. "[T]hey were both very good to me. But when their own children came, there was a difference." Yet because there was no trouble between his parents the boy was able to go back and forth between them as he pleased, and he had four grandparents.[32]

His father taught him to use a bow with arrows tipped with knobs instead of points. He was given his own pony, and one proud day he killed his first bird, which made his father so happy he gave away one of his horses. Watching some of the older boys dress up and show off in front of the girls, young Plenty Kill wished he too could "ride a perfumed horse, all fixed up, and go see a pretty girl." But first he would have to learn to kill game and handle a horse, and be able to go on the war-path.

Standing Bear mentions a sun dance his mother told him of, held when he was an infant, alongside a rain-swollen stream at their summer camp in the Black Hills. The tribe entered the Hills through Buffalo Gap, as wild animals did in winter for protection from the cold blasts. There were springs with clear water and plenty of wood. "Nature seemed to hold us in her arms," he remembered. "And there we were contented to live in our humble tipis all through the rough weather." As the season warmed, with new tipi poles cut from the pines, the tribe moved to its summer camp on the Niobrara, in northern Nebraska where buffalo were plentiful. The hunting was very dangerous. In a cloud of blinding dust the hunters rode into a stampeding herd, watchful to avoid being "surrounded and trampled beneath the hoofs of the ponderous beasts."

One day a small man of slight build was invited into his father's tipi, a man with very dark skin and fine light hair. He carried nothing and was poorly dressed. What little he had to say, he said in a quiet tone. It was Crazy Horse. The next day they learned Crazy Horse had been killed by the soldiers.

Plenty Kill first experienced cattle at the agency. What a terrible odor! It was awful! Were the Indians going to be forced to eat those animals? The white people ate them, his father said. All the white people the boy saw were bald. Could it be from eating those vile-smelling creatures? Buzzards were bald-headed too, and lived on carrion. Plenty Kill felt sorry for the white people who "had to live on such stuff."

When he killed his first and only buffalo, it took him five arrows. That shamed him, but he felt his father was proud of him because he told the truth. Another chance to please his father came on a raid to count coup on the Poncas. Plenty Kill was the only boy on the expedition. His father urged him, when the opportunity came, to ride into the Ponca camp and touch a man with his stick. If he fell in the enemy's midst, he should keep his courage.

"That is the way I want you to die. I will be with you, my son."

The words brought tears to the boy's eyes and made his heart thump, "but I was willing to do my father's bidding, as I wanted so much to please him." When the raid was called off, he was chagrined that he had to go home "without having taken a chance of getting killed."

Before long he had a fateful chance to please his father. A group of white people came out from the East to find some Lakota boys and girls to take back with them. The only reason he knew for white people to want Indian children was to kill them. When his father asked him if he wanted to go, Plenty Kill said yes. He thought he was going East to be killed. His father had always counseled him to be brave and die, and he dreaded being called *can'l wanka,* a coward. He decided to honor his father by being a brave son.

When his group arrived at the Iron Road, they encountered a long row of little houses, all in a line, standing on long pieces of iron. Climbing into one of the houses, Plenty Kill found himself in a beautiful little room with soft seats. Then suddenly the whole house began to move away and he hung on for his life. Coming into the "smoky city," Chicago, he was astonished to see so many people. The big boys said the *Wasicun,* or Long Knives, were "like ants; they are all over—everywhere." The big boys sang brave songs and told the little fellows they were all being taken to the place where the sun rises, where they would be dumped over the edge of the earth.

At Carlisle, placing a pointer on one of the names on the blackboard, Plenty Kill selected Luther and became Luther Standing Bear. Shorn of his hair, he felt funny and bald-headed—no longer an Indian, but an imitation of a white man. His new clothes, like his boots, were too big, though he was proud to have clothes with pockets and he liked the way his boots squeaked when he walked.

The school's operating principle was total immersion. "I am a Baptist," said the army officer who founded it, Richard Henry Pratt, "because I believe in immersing the Indians in our civilization and when we get them under holding them there until they are thoroughly soaked." Soaked he was, young Luther. Like the others, he was forbidden to speak his own language. When the elder Standing Bear, who spoke no English, came to visit him after a year, Luther had to ask permission to speak Lakota to his own father.

Captain Pratt was very kind to his father and took him to visit Boston, New York, Baltimore, Philadelphia, and Washington, an experience that affected his father much the way Spotted Tail had been influenced years earlier, witnessing the number and power of the whites. His father saw nothing but the Long Knives wherever he went. They kept coming like flies. The Indians, he told his son, would have to learn their ways. "Some day I want to hear you speak like these Long Knife people, and work like them."

Luther determined to learn all he could, and in time he achieved remarkable success in the white world. With Buffalo Bill's Wild West Show, he danced before King Edward. Utimately he went to California to become one of the first Indian actors in Hollywood. He wrote four books. And he remembered his father's advice: "He did not say that he thought the white man's ways better than our own; neither did he say that I could be like a white man. He said, 'Son, try to be like a white man.' So, in two more years I had been 'made over.'"

Looking back half a century later, he felt that the pressure brought to bear to "enforce conformity of custom and habit has caused a reaction more destructive than war, and that the injury has not only affected the Indian, but has extended to the white population as well."[33]

The Black Hills figure in the stories of Luther Standing Bear as a sometime place of shelter and comfort in the embrace of Mother Earth. In those of Black Elk they are identified as the domain of *Wakan Tanka,* the Great Spirit, Grandfather. With Black Elk we are in the presence of a holy man, a seer. At the center of his vision: *Ophata I,* the Mountain at the Center Where One Comes to Speak—Harney Peak.[34]

A contemporary of Luther Standing Bear, Black Elk was born in 1863 on the Little Powder River, the son and grandson of medicine men and second cousin to Crazy Horse. As a boy he too lived the old free life, but he felt set apart from other children, burdened by secret knowledge of the Other World. When forced onto the reservation, he adapted to the pressures of the white world in his own singular way. He never went to Carlisle, and he learned only a little English, yet he left a most powerful legacy.[35]

What set him apart was the vision he experienced at the age of nine. It seemed to the boy that everyone should know about his great vision, but he was "afraid to tell, because I knew nobody would believe me, little as I was." For years he kept it entirely to himself. Then on rare occasions his strange powers began to emerge. One afternoon while he was hunting deer with his father a remark escaped him that made him feel weird. Wait here, said his father, who had seen some deer ahead, while I go to round them up. "No, father," the boy said, "you stay here, they are bringing them toward us and we'll get them here." When he realized what he had said, Black Elk felt strange. His father looked at him oddly but said nothing. The deer came closer, though they proved to be antelope.[36]

Black Elk remembered camping up in the hills along Spring Creek, cutting tipi poles in the forests on Rapid Creek, making camp near Buffalo Gap and on Horsehead Creek, south of the Black Hills. When the sale of the "Hunting Ground" arose as an issue, young Black Elk told his fellows, "When we grow up, boys, we'll have to help hold the Black Hills." He was present at the Battle of the Little Bighorn. Too young and small to be in the thick of the fight, he participated in the aftermath, and though the smell of gunpowder and blood soon sickened him he was not sorry for the soldiers who had so foolishly attacked the people and been wiped out: "I was a very happy boy."[37]

After Crazy Horse was killed, Black Elk's family fled with Crazy Horse's band to join Sitting Bull in Canada. One winter day, hunting buffalo over the line in Montana, his party was attacked by Crows. His cousin Hard to Hit was killed. Black Elk cried all day. "It was hard work crying all day," he said later, "but this was the custom. This is the way I had to cry: 'Hownh, hownh—My cousin, he thought lots of me and I thought lots of him.' I did not feel like crying, but I had to do it all day."

Game was scarce and the people were very hungry. For a year Black Elk forgot all about his vision. Then one night he heard a coyote howling and a voice telling him there were buffalo nearby. Next day, out of a snow haze, a buffalo appeared, followed by seven more. The party managed to kill four and celebrated with a feast.

His powers seemed to be growing. Tired of the hardships in Canada, he left with a small group of men and women in the spring of 1880. While they were camped at All Gone Tree Creek in Montana, Black Elk heard a voice say, "Be careful and watch. You shall see." Scouting from a hilltop, he spotted two Blackfeet warriors observing their camp. "Grandfathers," he prayed to the spirits, "something may happen to me. They will come. But I will depend on the power you have bestowed upon me. Hear me!" He went to warn the others. Leaving their tipis behind, they escaped just in time, which told Black Elk he truly had powers, because for the first time his prayer was answered.[38]

At sixteen he developed an obsessive fear of the Thunder-beings, who were directing him to *do* something, he didn't know what. Concerned about their son's behavior in the presence of lightning and thunder, his parents invited a wise old medicine man, Black Road, to talk to him. Black Elk confessed his vision to Black Road, who told him to dance the horse dance, demonstrating the first portion of his vision. Thus began his career as a medicine man.

In 1887 he went to England with Buffalo Bill's Wild West Show for the Golden Jubilee of Queen Victoria's reign. Becoming separated from the party when it sailed for America, he found himself stranded. He joined another wild west show and traveled through Germany, France, and Italy. "All the time I was away from home across the big water," he recalled, "my power was gone, and I was like a dead man moving around most of the time." When he was able to remember his vision, it seemed only a "dim dream."[39]

In the fall of 1889, returning to Pine Ridge, Black Elk addressed a letter to the Lakota people about his time across the water. He told of having wanted to see the place "where they killed Jesus . . . to go over there to tell about it myself." But it was far, and there was no railroad. It would have taken a lot of money. He quoted the opening verses of I Corinthians 13: *Though I speak with the tongues of men and of angels, and have not charity, I am become as sounding brass, or a tinkling cymbal.* . . . "So Lakota people," he urged, "trust in God!"[40]

At Pine Ridge he found the hunger severe, worse than when he had left. The people were in despair, but there were stories about news coming out of the West, the promise of a Messiah who would save the Indians and bring back the buffalo. At first Black Elk was skeptical. Maybe only the despair led people to believe such a thing. But they were saying it was the son of the Great Spirit out there, who had been killed by the *Wasichus* and was coming now to help the Indians. So Black Elk went to watch them dance near Manderson.

The people were dancing in a circle around a sacred pole, and he recognized the sacred hoop, the tree that never bloomed. Everything was from his great vision. A great happiness overcame him: "I was to be intercessor for my people and yet I was not doing my duty." Next morning, dressed in his sacred clothes, he joined the dance, thinking of his father who had died, the sister and brothers he had lost, the people in despair and poverty, who had gone on the wrong road but would be brought back into the hoop. He asked the Great Spirit to help him make the tree bloom again. He could not stop crying.[41]

The slaughter at Wounded Knee brought the curtain down on the ghost dancing. Black Elk came upon the scene right after the massacre. Forty years later, in a passage that has so often been cited, he described to John Neihardt what he had witnessed: "When I look back now from this high hill of my old age, I can still see the butchered women and children lying heaped and scattered all along the crooked gulch as plain as when I saw them with my eyes still young. . . . A people's dream died there," Black Elk said. "It was a beautiful dream. And I, to whom so great a vision was given in my youth,—you see me now a pitiful old man who has done nothing, for the nation's hoop is broken and scattered. There is no center any longer, and the sacred tree is dead."[42]

In 1889 the Great Sioux Reservation had been reduced—again, this time by more than half, and broken up into five smaller, isolated reservations. The intervening lands were then opened to white settlement. Black Elk turned from the white man's ways following the massacre and settled down nearby, conducting traditional healing ceremonies. In 1892 he married Katie War Bonnet, who bore him three sons, all baptized Catholic. The youngest, Ben, was born in 1899.

After Red Cloud's repeated requests for the "Blackrobes," Holy Rosary Mission was established near the agency in 1888 by Jesuit missionaries. As first in rank among his people, Red Cloud was baptized Peter. According to Lucy Looks Twice, the devoutly Catholic daughter of Black Elk by his second wife, whom he married after Katie died, her father had a pivotal experience in 1904, three years before she was born.

A few miles north of the mission Black Elk was doctoring a very sick little boy in a tent. He was singing and beating his drum, shaking his rattle, when along came one of the Blackrobes, Joseph Lindebner, known as Short Father.

Father Lindebner had already baptized the boy and had come to administer the last rites. Seeing what Black Elk was doing, he threw the drum and rattle out of the tent and—according to Lucy Looks Twice—seized Black Elk by the neck and said, "Satan, get out!" Black Elk withdrew and sat down, feeling "downhearted and lonely, as though he lost all his powers."[43]

The priest took him back to Holy Rosary, where he was fed and housed. After two weeks of preparation, on December 6, the feast day of Saint Nicholas, he was baptized Nicholas Black Elk. Though *Black Elk Speaks* mentions it not at all, he served as a catechist for the church for the rest of his days, which makes his sessions with John Neihardt all the more remarkable. Black Elk's conversion was likened by his daughter to Saul's on the road to Damascus. One of his greatest rewards, she attests, was the "little ones," who listened to him and loved him. His principal teaching, taken from Matthew 18:3: "Unless we become as children, become like these little children"—and he would point to some—"we cannot enter the Kingdom."[44]

During these desperately troubled years after Wounded Knee, the Black Hills claim endured as a tenuous but vital link to Lakota tribal identity—one of the few bridges, Edward Lazarus notes, to the cherished past. As early as 1891 a group of some three hundred non-progressive old chiefs and headmen came together to organize the Oglala Council. They began meeting about once a month to discuss the old treaties, to calculate what the government owed them for the Black Hills and, in the view of agent John Brennan, to "make life as unpleasant as possible for the agent and other employees."[45]

In 1903, at the same meeting of the tribal council in which Red Cloud made his final appearance, the tribe presented its claim for the first time not merely as recollection, but as a specific indictment. "We do not mean that we will take back the Black Hills and drive the white people away," Edgar Fire Thunder told Congressman F. W. Martin. "But we would like to have something for the Black Hills treaty." American Horse, one of the first progressive chiefs, pointed to the many houses he believed the whites had filled with gold. He asked Martin to "find a way to get some food for our children."[46]

Congressman Martin took no action. When the tribal council selected an attorney in Washington to represent them, the Indian Bureau,
seeing no merit in the claim, used a regulation designed to *protect* Indians
from legal predators to deny them the right to counsel. But in 1911 the
tribe found a white advocate, its first, in a surprising place—South
Dakota's official state historian. "The Sioux Indians," wrote Doane
Robinson in the *Deadwood Pioneer Times*, "have a highly interesting
and equitable claim to the Black Hills which they assert they have never
relinquished . . . [They] have no thought that they can regain possession
of the Hills but they think they have an equitable claim against Uncle
Sam for the value of the property, and they propose to push for it until
they obtain justice."

Seven months later, a group of elders from the Rosebud Reservation met with a young lawyer named Ralph Case who felt an affinity
with the Lakotas. When they asked him to help, he promised to do so.
Another who contacted Case was Henry Standing Bear, the younger
brother of Luther, a progressive who championed the Black Hills cause.
On Columbus Day, a day chosen by design, a small group of progressives that included Standing Bear founded the first nationwide pan-Indian
political organization, the Society of American Indians.

Approaching the incoming Wilson administration with tact, the
progressives struck a responsive chord. After Henry Standing Bear led a
delegation to Washington in 1914, they found that a degree of official
sanction encouraged mainstream progressives to come flocking to the
cause. In part because of the debt owed relatives of the ten thousand
Indians who had died fighting in World War I, their lobbying produced
results: a Sioux Jurisdictional Act was passed by Congress in June 1920.

On May 7, 1923, Ralph Case filed the Black Hills claim, hand-
delivering it to the Court of Claims. Hailed as the "Moses of the Sioux,"
Case was inducted into the tribe, given the name Young Spotted Tail. He
promised to help them to the end of his days. Case cautioned them they
could never regain the Black Hills because the government had the right
to take anyone's property. What made its actions illegal was the failure
to pay compensation. But "the promise of victory," says Edward Lazarus,
"delivered with such kindness, confidence, and seeming expertise in the
unfathomed world of law, must have kindled extravagant hopes" in his
naive clients, who prepared to follow their Moses.

The years in the wilderness began.[47]

Even as the Sioux began the attempt to regain the Black Hills, new enterprises were under way by others, with other aims. In 1905 came the first trip from the Missouri to the Hills by automobile. A well-driller in his mid-thirties set out from Pierre with two friends in a single-cylinder Cadillac, a "one lunger" generating only nine horsepower. They chugged their way on unmarked stagecoach trails across a hundred and fifty miles of gumbo prairie. When they found no bridges or ferries across rivers and streams they crossed on railroad trestles, taking their chances, or had to be hauled out of the mud with lariats by cowboys on horseback. The trip took three days.[48]

It proved to be a fateful expedition because the well-driller was Peter Norbeck. What left a lasting imprint on Norbeck was the heart of the uplift, the beautiful Southern Hills, with their rugged granite mountains and timbered uplands, their wildlife. He came away with a passion to create a game sanctuary there. And as the world would come to learn, what Norbeck wanted, sooner or later, Norbeck usually got.

The first son of Scandinavian immigrants, Peter Norbeck was born in 1870 in the cellar beneath the unfinished house on the family homestead near Vermillion. The oldest of six children of George Norbeck, an unordained Lutheran minister who spent much of his time off missionarying, Peter learned hard work and responsibility early. His sporadic schooling consisted mostly of the "three R's," though he received valuable attention at home. His mother read to her children from *Pilgrim's Progress* and *Uncle Tom's Cabin.* His father required young Peter to memorize long passages from both the Old and New Testaments. He was almost sixteen when George Norbeck received a "call" from a congregation one hundred and thirty miles to the west. Over the next six years Peter managed to enroll for three terms at the struggling University of Dakota at Vermillion, returning to the farm during the long intervals. At that point his formal education ended, though in time he built up a library and read widely in history, philosophy, and science. Most of all, he enjoyed the Norse sagas.

George Norbeck was more interested in the search for "a well of water springing up into everlasting life" than in tapping the rich artesian water basin underlying the farm, but he turned over to his son a crude well-drilling machine he'd purchased without any intention of using it. Eventually, after hitting dry hole after dry hole, Peter struck water and established a successful well-drilling business in Redfield.[49]

The Southern Hills had been spared the worst of the excesses taking such a toll on the north. What saved them—and the source of their wealth, ironically, after the excitement stirred up by the Custer expedition—was their paucity of gold. The riches of the Southern Hills lay in the weathered foundation rocks of the central core, the dark robe of pines overlaying the slopes, the lush grasses of the valleys and foothills, and the abundant wildlife. In the part of the Hills that evoked Norbeck's passion, the early promise of gold simply never panned out. The only gold mine of consequence operated for three years but recovered little gold. Mica and feldspar mines were more numerous but like cattle raising disturbed the natural order less. Lumbering had greater impact.[50]

The survey conducted on the eve of the new century by Henry S. Graves found a landscape in the Southern Hills markedly different from the one Custer and Dodge had encountered earlier. Graves found a forest "irregular and broken, and composed in many places of defective and scrubby trees," primarily the effect of destructive fires that had swept the Hills for centuries. Many if not most could be ascribed to the Indians, who in certain times of the year had set lines of fire to drive out game. On Lame Johnny Creek virtually the entire district had been cut to supply Buffalo Gap, with all the best lumber removed. On lower Bismarck Creek, south of Sylvan Lake, the forest had been heavily thinned. Along Upper French Creek the once fine forest of old timber had been largely cut over. Sawmills were already pushing into the good timber on the upper reaches of small tributary streams. On Lower French Creek there had been less cutting. Many slopes and ridges showed severe injury by fire, but most of the mature timber in the bottoms had escaped. The old trees along Grace Coolidge Creek were scarred by a fire dating back a hundred and sixty years. Graves estimated that in the timbered area of the Black Hills there were some four hundred and fifty ranches, stitched together in long strips out of contiguous placer claims along streams and valleys. The rich grass sustained about five thousand head of cattle, but no sheep. The most extensive grazing lands lay in the open parks and prairies of the Southern Hills.[51]

One ranch in the southeastern portion had been operating for fifteen years—the Fleur de Lis, already the subject of an acclaimed book published in France. In the summer of 1885, drawn by the opportunities for stock raising unveiled to him by de Mandat-Grancey's *Cow-Boys and Colonels,* Raymond Auzias de Turenne journeyed to the Black Hills to establish the Percheron and Arab Importing and Breeding Company. He brought along four full-blooded stallions—two Percherons, an Arab, and a fast Anglo-Arab named El Mahdi.

Astride El Mahdi, de Turenne arrived in Custer at sunset wearing a Parisian riding suit. His display seems to have pleased the ladies but drawn flak from the men. A bronco buster named Spurlock challenged "Frenchie" to come down off his "high-fallutin critter" and prove his mettle on Pinto, an undersized mongrel of Spurlock's. The Frenchman took up the challenge and was promptly "thrown eight feet to the side," said a witness, "and crashed down like a corpse," whereupon Pinto bounded off into the woods biting the saddle.[52]

De Turenne was game enough to stand the company a few rounds at a Custer saloon and was eventually adopted as a regular cowboy. Two weeks after his arrival he was accidentally shot in the face by his partner. Operated upon without anesthesia on a billiard table by the only doctor in Custer, who chanced to be sober at the time, de Turenne survived. In the good mountain air of Custer, reported the *Chronicle*, the wound quickly healed.

Locating a site near Lame Johnny Creek, de Turenne and his partner built a two-story frame house and established the Fleur de Lis Horse Ranch. Putting their stallions to work, they charged fees only when foaling occurred. Their growing herds roamed all the way from Custer to Buffalo Gap. The Fleur de Lis attracted French visitors by the dozen—barons, counts, marquises. "[T]oo many aristocrats," said an old-timer, "though clean bedfellows, if you ask me."

The "great success of the season," de Mandat-Grancey observed drily, was the housewarming ball laid on by de Turenne. Three Frenchmen in formal evening clothes and white gloves stood on the porch to receive the guests, which must have impressed the four Walsh daughters, who had come twenty-five miles on horseback and arrived drenched in perspiration. A waitress from "the inn of Buffalo Gap," the beautiful Laura, attended as well, along with five or six farmer's wives and a cowgirl or two from neighboring ranches. The cowboys consigned their revolvers to the cloakroom, and twenty or twenty-five of them joined in as a three-cowboy "orchestra" enlivened the festivities with music. The Mlles. Walsh danced all night, then saddled up at seven a.m. for the return trip.[53]

The great actress Sarah Bernhardt missed a visit to the Fleur de Lis only because the cowboys who had planned to kidnap her at Sidney en route to San Francisco flagged down the wrong train. Later told of the plan, she deplored having missed the thrill of it.

In 1890 the house burned to the ground. Another building was constructed in its place, but now covered wagons by the hundred were appearing on the prairie. One cowboy remarked that the barbed wire fence was beginning to "infest the open country." The ranch was sold to Herbert "Shorty" Mann, who homesteaded it in 1908. A mound of stones alongside the road still marks the grave of a Mann baby. Gus Miller, one of the cowboys, purchased the Fleur de Lis brand and became known for the fine horses he raised. De Turenne himself left the Black Hills and became a bank president in Seattle.[54]

What Peter Norbeck saw when his Cadillac went chugging into the Hills on a primitive road was not wildlife in profusion but *habitat*, an ideal sanctuary for native game that had been all but eliminated. The area's scenic values have been extolled in terms extravagant enough to raise doubt in those who have never seen it. A good corrective appears in a study in the 1920s. Cleophas C. O'Harra, a geologist, and Joseph P. Connolly, a mineralogist, place the region in the context of such works of nature as the Grand Canyon, Yosemite, the Rocky Mountains, and Niagara Falls: "Its mountains are not as high as the highest, its valleys are less deep than the deepest. It has not the icy waters of glacial streams, nor the heated steam of boiling springs. No waterfall of surpassing magnitude decorates its craggy precipices, it is far from the tang of the ocean, and, until recent years, the world knew little of its existence" Still, observe O'Harra and Connolly, "Here one may close at hand study to his heart's content the makeup of mountain, park, and valley, the peculiarities of topography, the course of the swift flowing streams, the coloring of the many kinds of rocks, the great variety of interesting minerals and the unending array of plant and animal life native to the region."[55]

Lovers of the Black Hills know it comes to a question of scale. The mountains Norbeck discovered for himself were accessible—accessible and finite. Climbing Harney Peak, he would have left Sylvan Lake behind and wound his way among lichen-encrusted knobs and spires of granite through a forest of spruce with almost no underbrush except along a rivulet flowing from a spring. At the summit he would find himself on a rough mass of granite, the highest point in the Lower Forty-Eight east of the Rockies, with an unobstructed sweep offering a glimpse of three states: a scene both intimate and grand, the forest rolling away over the heart of the uplift in descending undulations broken by immense gray whaleback bodies, one of which nearby had acquired the name Rushmore.

Habitat and great beauty: that was the vision Norbeck took away with him. The native wildlife had been reduced or utterly exterminated. The profusion of deer, elk, and pronghorns that Custer and Dodge had encountered in and around the Black Hills had been swept away in little more than a decade. The grizzlies were gone. In 1881 four mountain lions had been killed in the area, but soon even that wary creature was all but eliminated. The last buffalo native to the Hills was killed in 1884, the last free-roaming native elk four years later. The once plentiful beavers were almost gone, along with the bighorn sheep. Deer in scant numbers remained, as did a few gray wolves and coyotes despite a hunter's war against them.[56]

A hopeful precedent for Norbeck's dream of a wildlife sanctuary had recently been established just to the south, Wind Cave. "Discovered" in a prairie ravine in 1881, it had long been known to the Plains Indians: a hole in the rocks eight inches by ten, the wind blowing out or in according to variations in atmospheric pressure. The Lakotas knew it as *Washun Niya,* the breathing hole, the link between the underground and upper world through which their legends said the buffalo and other game animals emerged. The sounds made by the wind were the whisperings and singing of the under-the-ground people.[57]

Its proximity to Hot Springs had made the cave a growing tourist attraction, threatening its natural wonders. One scheme proposed to mine its formations of lattice box work for sale as curios. Then in 1903 Wind Cave National Park came into being with the signature of President Theodore Roosevelt, part of the conservation legacy of the Progressive Era, followed in 1906 by establishment of Devil's Tower, the first national monument.[58]

Two formidable obstacles stood in the way to Norbeck's dream of a game sanctuary. First, except for a few dozen homesteads and one section from each township given the state for common schools, the land belonged to the federal government. Second, Norbeck himself hadn't risen to a position from which to exert leverage. As a progressive Republican, however, he had a significant advantage in South Dakota. Supporting the party gubernatorial candidate in 1906, he gained admission to the inner circle. With the help of Republican friends he was elected state senator in 1908, beginning a public career that made him lieutenant governor in 1914, governor in 1916, and United States Senator in 1920. Now he could go to work.[59]

Custer State Park was produced through a complex series of land swaps. In 1912 the state surrendered title to its widely separated sections within the Black Hills National Forest in exchange for the "in lieu lands," 61,440 acres in Custer County. When the State Game and Fish Commission had been created in 1909, federal authorities had urged the state to establish a game preserve in the Harney National Forest. In February 1913, at Norbeck's suggestion, State Senator John F. Parks of Custer County introduced a bill creating a state game preserve out of the "in lieu lands" and appropriating $15,000 from the game fund to fence and stock it with big game. The bill failed in the house. When a temperance bill favored by its opponents came up short of votes, wrote Doane

Robinson, "Mr. Norbeck suggested that it might be possible to make an exchange of votes that would carry both through." So it came to pass: "wet" votes for temperance, temperance votes for the Game Park Act: done!

Homesteaders raised objections. Some did not welcome the prospect of buffalo and elk roaming freely through their farms and ranches. In a letter to the editor of the *Custer Chronicle*, William F. Sayars, whose homestead is now bisected by the Wildlife Loop Road, attacked his "bonehead senator" for having sponsored "the greatest menace and imposition ever forced upon the people." With these "pestiferous and vicious animals" turned loose, Sayars warned of serious and fatal accidents. He was not about to shinny up a tree; he knew "a safer, surer, quicker and easier method of dealing with these pestiferous interloping quadrupeds." A Custer resident observing the goings-on remarked that along with buffalo and elk the state had "attorneys and other wild beasts" with which to "make life miserable for the unfortunate farmers it has corraled."[60]

One thing Peter Norbeck had learned in his years in public life was patience. He knew how to wait. He was the driving force behind a push to persuade more than fifty settlers to sell their farms and ranches to the state. In 1919, when the Custer State Park Board was established at his urging, Governor Norbeck became its chairman, in position to influence developments. He personally supervised the construction of a forty-mile fence within the Park. Ranchers frequently cut the fence to let their cattle into the preserve. In 1913 twenty-five elk were brought in from Wyoming. In the following year buffalo were introduced, transported in a special wagon from rail cars at Hermosa in a process that took twelve days. Pronghorns arrived in 1916.[61]

The buffalo that would become the central attraction of Custer State Park are widely believed to owe their existence to James C. ("Scotty") Philip, the legendary rancher who had died three years earlier, though the idea of "saving" them originated with Fred Dupree, who, with little fanfare, developed a small herd from calves roped along the Grand River.[62] Scotty Philip, an immigrant from Scotland, had acquired a big ranch near Fort Pierre by the mid-nineties. Perhaps urged by an Indian wife, determined to save them from extinction, he bought the Dupree herd and built it up to almost a thousand. Thirty-six were purchased for the Park.

Philip admired the buffalo for its hardiness, for the way the bulls would form a protective triangle in a blizzard to shelter the cows and calves, the "boss bull" at the apex "doggedly holding his head against a

Dakota blizzard," as Philip told a Kansas City reporter. Challenged by visiting Mexican officials unimpressed by the seemingly indolent bulls, Philip transported two of them to Juárez in 1907 for a showdown. In the bullring there, the buffalo bull Philip called Pierre, using its massive head as a battering ram, scarcely stirring from its position, took the heart out of four Mexican fighting bulls in succession.

When Philip died in 1911 at fifty-three, his funeral was attended by cattlemen, Indians, and dignitaries from all over, but the most significant onlookers, in the view of Wayne C. Lee, were the shaggy dark four-leggeds he had saved from extinction. "Hundreds of them," says Lee, "attracted perhaps by the huge crowd gathered at the cemetery just outside their high fence, came slowly and quietly down from the hills to the north and west and bunched up on the hillside directly above the cemetery." The buffalo stood motionless during the services. When the coffin was slowly lowered into the grave, they "turned almost as one and moved slowly and again without any sound back over the hill and out of sight."[63]

Until 1920 the most beautiful part of the Black Hills—Sylvan Lake, the Needles, and Harney Peak—remained outside the park boundary. In that year Norbeck, with the support of Congressman Harry Gandy of Rapid City, secured legislation to enclose them in the park, some thirty thousand acres, under joint federal and state management. Norbeck himself was gaining wide attention. Yet when legislators wanted to name the park for Norbeck, he declined such personal advertisement: "it stands in the way of getting further work done."

By 1921 there were eighty thousand tourists in the Black Hills. The inadequacy of roads and accommodations was becoming a major problem. With Scovel Johnson, state engineer, and Cecil Gideon, construction foreman on the preserve, Norbeck tramped on foot, with his two hundred and forty pound frame, over trails that horses could not traverse, to lay out the Needles Road, which was completed in 1922. A few years later he walked and rode over Iron Mountain some twenty times to find an artistic route to Mount Rushmore. The Iron Mountain Road, says Gilbert Fite, has few equals for design and architecture. Its most spectacular feature is "the framing or telescoping of Mount Rushmore through three different tunnels several miles away. Superbly designed, the highway [winds] over pigtail bridges and through virgin forests, presenting one naturally-framed picture after another." The Iron Mountain Road, said Gutzon Borglum, the monument's sculptor, "promised to become an integral part of the memorial."[64]

The resort at Sylvan Lake, a Victorian-style hotel built in 1895, was acquired by the state in 1920. It was destroyed by fire in 1936. A new hotel was constructed out of native rock. The State Game Lodge, built by prison inmates, was completed in 1921. Two months later, it burned down. Rebuilt, it opened again the following summer. Bluebell Lodge, constructed by a Bell Telephone executive in the early twenties, was acquired by the Park in the thirties, as was Legion Lake Resort.

In 1921 the legislature authorized the Park Board to offer leases for cabin sites in areas near the resorts "to encourage the erection of summer cottages." Implemented in 1924, this policy was continued for more than a decade. Congressman William Williamson was one beneficiary. Another was Peter Norbeck. People were induced to build on the assurance of ninety-nine year leases. Over the next decade several dozen summer cabins were constructed. The name Norbeck gave his summer home echoed the feeling many people had about their cabins: Valhalla.[65]

Officials saw the cabins as a good way to foster development of the Park. In time the long-term leases would become a problem; in the twenties the focus was short-term. And Custer State Park was preparing to welcome a new summer resident—Calvin Coolidge, the President of the United States.

Chapter Seven: Monumental Dissonance

In the heart of the uplift, to the east of Harney Peak, the faces of four presidents carved in granite stand out from the mantle of green, reflecting the morning sun: Washington in the lead, followed by Jefferson and Lincoln, with Teddy Roosevelt wedged in between. Sixty feet from crown to chin, they preside over an apron of boulders blasted from the mountain. Ten miles to the west, beyond Harney Peak, or the Center of Everything That Is, the colossal figure of Crazy Horse emerges slowly from the granite after half a century of work. Together they mark the Black Hills as contested territory, settled and occupied by whites, claimed by natives of the continent. A more resounding clash of symbols would be difficult to find. From around the world millions come to see them. Both represent tremendous expenditures of energy and will. What drives mortal men to such exertions?

Crazy Horse, we know, was launched as a direct response to Rushmore, but why Rushmore to begin with? Why carve the faces of presidents on a mountain? Why deface the natural order of things? One explanation that has been offered: "The Euro-American culture used the construction of Mount Rushmore to stamp the Hills with a symbol of U.S. ownership and control and to create the aura that the Black Hills were sacred in the white culture."[1] A neat explanation, certainly; maybe a little too neat. Can motives be so elegant? Monuments are created by human beings, not by collective abstractions. And most Americans who come to gaze at the images of their presidents would be astonished by the twists and entanglements in the story behind the carving of Mount Rushmore.

It begins in the South. In early 1915 a Georgia newspaperman suggested carving a monument on Stone Mountain, a huge crescent-shaped granite mountain near Atlanta. His editorial stirred the elderly leader of the United Daughters of the Confederacy to imagine a "great tablet . . . carrying some record of the war between the states." Could the head of Robert E. Lee be carved on the side of Stone Mountain? wondered Mrs. C. Helen Plane. She invited Gutzon Borglum, the noted sculptor, to Georgia and posed the question to him.[2]

Borglum may have been the wrong man for the task. This son of Danish immigrants had an exuberant imagination. To carve the head of Lee on a working face eight hundred by fifteen hundred feet, in his view, would be to paste a postage stamp on the side of a house. Borglum saw an opportunity to carve the largest monument in history on Stone Mountain. Why not create something grand? Why not the legions of Lee on the march, a panorama of Southern military might: marching men and horses and rolling guns, trailing across the mountain for more than a quarter of a mile?

"I am celebrating an idea," he was to say of Stone Mountain, "the idea of strength, courage, self-sacrifice and love. These men who fought for a lost cause went forth fearlessly to do their best as they saw it." That was what he wanted to perpetuate on the rock, "the going forward to meet the unknown at the call of right and truth as one sees it."

After three days in Atlanta, Borglum returned to his home in Connecticut, his plan approved, as official sculptor of Stone Mountain. Now the Daughters of the Confederacy confronted the challenge of raising millions to implement the plan. By chance, a source of help was stirring to life. On a cold and pitch-black Thanksgiving night that same year, fifteen men gathered on top of Stone Mountain, dressed in bedsheet robes and hooded caps. They formed a semicircle in front of a stone altar where an open Bible lay alongside an unsheathed sword. Following a prayer, "Colonel" William Simmons lighted a huge cross and, by the light of its flames, took an oath administered by Nate Forrest, grandson of the famous Confederate cavalry general Nathan Bedford Forrest, founder and Grand Wizard of the Ku Klux Klan. Simmons was made Grand Dragon of the reborn Klan.

Mrs. Plane then wrote Borglum that the Stone Mountain project would receive a percentage of the ticket receipts for *Birth of a Nation,* D. W. Griffith's epic film of Reconstruction. Featuring black villains and Klan heroes, the film was playing to record crowds across the South. She asked Borglum to incorporate a tribute to the KKK into Stone Mountain, "a small group of them in their nightly uniform" approaching in the distance to "[save] us from Negro domination and carpetbag rule."

The sculptor must have been perplexed. The Klan hadn't existed when he went to Georgia. Reluctant to offend Mrs. Plane, he included a KKK altar in his plan for the memorial and moved his family to Georgia to begin preparations for construction. A dedication ceremony was held the following spring. Then in less than a year the U. S. entered the "War to End All Wars." When his superintendent at Stone Mountain enlisted, Borglum closed the operation down for the duration.[3]

The scene shifts to South Dakota, where in the early 1920s the State Historian, Doane Robinson, was wrestling with a challenge: how to draw more tourists into the Black Hills. You needed something more than beautiful scenery, he felt, "something of special interest connected with it." Alerted to the work being done at Stone Mountain, which was under way again following the war, Robinson conceived the idea of a great monument carved in the Hills. It came to him in 1924—in a flash, he claimed—during a talk he was giving to a tourist promotion meeting in Huron. He straightaway proposed it to his audience and subsequently asked Borglum to undertake its creation.

In fact, he had proposed such a monument weeks earlier to Lorado Taft, considered by many the leading American sculptor. Robinson had in mind the figure of "some notable Sioux" such as Red Cloud carved in the Needles, on the flank of Harney Peak. When Taft hesitated, Robinson sought to keep the possibility alive by enlarging his dream. He could see "all the heroes of the old west peering out" from the Needles, he wrote Taft, column after column: the figures of Lewis and Clark, Fremont, Jed Smith, Bridger, Sakakawea, and Red Cloud, even an equestrian statue of Buffalo Bill and the overland mail.[4]

Wanting influential support for his idea before going public, Robinson sent a copy of his first letter to Taft to a man whose opinion would carry weight, Peter Norbeck. Norbeck usually reacted cautiously to new proposals. It was a new suggestion, the senator replied. He had never thought of it, but he saw a "wonderful opportunity to work out among the Black Hills Needles the very thing you suggest." With Norbeck's support, Robinson went ahead and presented his plan to the meeting in Huron.[5]

Lovers of the Needles today would gasp at what Robinson envisioned. Indeed, when the press reported that he proposed to convert a portion of the Needles into "massive and spectacular figures of sculpure," the response was predominantly negative. Presumptuous, observed one

editor, "painting a lily." The "bunk," said another. Commercial rape of
the Black Hills, desecration of a "noble work of nature with a puny work
of man," as ridiculous as "keeping a cow in the Capitol rotunda." In the
Hills the bitterest opposition came from Cora B. Johnson, who rebuked
Robinson in the *Hot Springs Star:* "Man makes statues but God made the
Needles. Let them alone."

Robinson countered that he had no intention of desecrating the
Hills. He proposed only to commemorate the heroes of the Old West
while bringing in a flood of tourist dollars. If his critics thought they
could wring a nickel's worth of gold out of each ton of granite, he scoffed,
they would happily grind up the Needles and wipe them off the face of
the earth." His plan would not only leave them in place but bring in an
"annual harvest of gold" for a thousand years.

In Sioux Falls, on the main tourist route to the Black Hills, the
press welcomed his proposal. The *Daily Argus-Leader* found it excellent. Throughout the state most commercial clubs thought it grand. The
secretary of the Rapid City club cautioned Robinson that the Needles
were not soft and easily worked, "but we needn't advertise it." The
impracticality of the proposition mattered little; what mattered was the
enormous free publicity with which it would be attended.

By early spring Robinson's dream had evolved further: "Custer
and his gold-discovering cavalcade winding its way through the Needles,
with Red Cloud and a band of Sioux scouts, resentful and suspicious,
spying on it through rifts in the pinnacles of the opposite wall, while
above, a great mountain buck, wary but unafraid, inspects the pageant
with curiosity."[6]

While controversy was building in South Dakota, events at Stone
Mountain were reaching a crisis. Borglum, at work on the head of General
Lee, was beset by a swarm of troubles, many of his own making. He had
always found it difficult to work with anyone else. To Peter Norbeck his
unwillingness to cooperate with others was simply astonishing. But
Borglum's fatal mistake, little known, may have been taking up with the
Ku Klux Klan. The Klan had made spectacular gains following the war,
and not only in the South. It had become a force to be reckoned with. In
1922 the largest Klan gathering ever was held in Kokomo, Indiana, a
gathering impressive enough to arouse jealousy in the Southern hierarchy.
Two hundred thousand robed Klansmen assembled in Kokomo to honor
the Grand Dragon of the Northern Realm, D. C. Stephenson, who was to
become a close friend of Borglum.

What ever drew Gutzon Borglum, artist and sculptor, a man who admired Michelangelo and had worked with Rodin in Paris, into the Ku Klux Klan? The promise of financial support for Stone Mountain, of course; funds were always a problem. But beyond that, the Klan's willingness to help finance such an ambitious monument led Borglum to believe it could be molded into a power base, an organization powerful enough to win the White House, and malleable enough to enable Borglum, working behind the scenes, to shape national policy. Borglum had no wish to wear a hood and robe himself, or to join in a campaign of fear and flogging. But in 1923—out of public view, for he could not risk being openly connected—he was named to the Klan's executive board, its cabinet.

Gutzon Borglum was a complex man, an impassioned political animal with marked agrarian leanings, and an activist. He had supported agrarian causes in North Dakota with some success. To Borglum the farmer was the heart of the nation. He reasoned that the KKK, with its primarily rural base, would be beyond the control of international bankers, most of whom he believed to be Jews. In the intellectual climate of the 1920s Borglum felt free to express anti-Semitic feelings. The Jews, Borglum believed, were greedy and anti-social except with their own kind. They had no rightful place in the family of man. In a paper titled "The Jewish Question" he laid out his views with unblinking candor: "Jews refuse to enter the mainstream of civilization, to become producing members of the world community. They do not share or create, but choose instead to clannishly hold onto their old ways and with mere money buy and sell the efforts of others."

Ironically, notwithstanding such sentiments, Borglum had close Jewish friends who somehow overlooked his outbursts, even defended him—such men as Felix Frankfurter, Paul Warburg, and Bernard Baruch. And to do him justice, when Hitler began uttering much the same sentiments in the 1930s, and *acting* on them, Borglum denounced him as barbaric. His vehement attacks provoked Hitler, after the Nazis had invaded Poland, to destroy Borglum's statue of Woodrow Wilson in Poznan. An eyesore, said the Fuehrer, all out of proportion.[7]

In 1923 the Stone Mountain Memorial Association was taken over by a leading supporter of the Klan. The state of Georgia officially recognized the memorial. The legislature authorized $100,000 for the project, to be matched by the county. Confident he could convince wealthy patrons to finance the project, Borglum went on with the work. As rivalries within the Klan began to tear the organization apart, he tried without success to intercede. Then bitter internal rivalries turned to open war.

When Borglum himself began receiving publicity, he vociferously denied he was a Klan leader.[8]

On January 19, 1924, the hundred and seventeenth anniversary of General Lee's birth, a crowd gathered at the base of Stone Mountain beneath two huge flags. Borglum personally carried Mrs. Plane, now ninety-four, to the rostrum. The crowd fell silent as she gave the signal. Slowly the flags parted to reveal the portrait of Robert E. Lee.

"My God," an elderly veteran exclaimed over the awed hush. "It's the General!"

So at last the Stone Mountain Memorial was under way. Work began on the head of Andrew Jackson, to be followed by that of Jefferson Davis. But Borglum himself was in deep financial difficulties, being sued by his Jewish friend Eugene Meyer. Twelve years earlier Meyer had lent him the money to buy his Connecticut estate but had yet to receive any payment. Even Borglum's friend Stephenson, about to be sentenced to thirty years in the Indiana State Penitentiary for crimes unrelated to his Klan involvement, was filing suit against him.

In 1924 the Republican candidate for president was Calvin Coolidge. Borglum found little in Coolidge to respect. When he tried to close his mind around the man, he wrote a friend, he found "nothing within." A staunch Republican, Borglum could never back the Democrat, Bill McAdoo. The Klan openly supported McAdoo, which doomed him to drown in chants of "Ku Ku McAdoo." The delegates nominated John Davis instead, and the Klan was finished as a significant political force.[9]

Borglum's final break with the Stone Mountain Association came over a Confederate Memorial half-dollar he was designing. Five million coins were to be minted and sold for a dollar each, which would yield the Association at least two million dollars as a working fund. To achieve a model acceptable to him, Borglum made nine different bas-reliefs, but then in February 1925, feeling betrayed by the Association, he blocked release of the coins. The executive board fired him.

Enraged, Borglum ordered his model of the memorial's Central Group smashed with a hammer. He rushed to Stone Mountain and pushed his working models of Lee's shoulder and Jackson's head onto the rocks below. The executive board swore out a warrant for his arrest. Pursued by the sheriff, Borglum fled by automobile and escaped into North Carolina, a fugitive from Georgia justice.[10]

Fugitive or not, Borglum had another card up his sleeve, his invitation from Doane Robinson to carve a monument in the Black Hills. He'd paid a visit to South Dakota the previous September. When

Robinson's letter of August 20, 1924 arrived at Stone Mountain, Borglum was in Connecticut. Jesse Tucker, his assistant, received it and forwarded it to him with a message scribbled across it: "Here it is, Borglum! Let's go!"

On condition there would be no publicity about his visit until he had seen the mountain, Borglum traveled to Rapid City in late September. He told Robinson he opposed carving Western figures in the Black Hills. That would be too local. The monument must be national, commemorating America's founders and builders. On a pocket pad he sketched the lonely figure of George Washington standing heroically above the surrounding mountains. When he was taken to the summit of Harney Peak, Borglum sighted a great line of granite domes and pinnacles along the mountain's south flank. He gasped.

"Here is the place! American history shall march along that skyline!"

He'd found "a veritable garden of the gods," he told a banquet in Rapid City. He knew of "no grouping of rock formations that equals those found in the Black Hills . . . nor any that is so suitable to sculpture." Money would be no problem, he assured his audience. He had come at the request of men of substance, men with an interest in the country's history and founders. The monument would bring the Black Hills community a golden harvest from tourism.[11]

The Mount Harney Memorial Bill was introduced in the legislature in January 1925. It would grant permission to carve a monument in Custer State Park and establish a Mount Harney Memorial Commission to be headed by the governor. It would also, and this was the hitch, appropriate $10,000 for surveys and planning—an unfortunate bit of timing, especially west of the Missouri River. After a severe drought in 1910-1911, West River had come to see itself as "next year country." This year might be hard, but next year would be better. In the aftermath of the war, crop prices had plummeted. Loans were going bad. In 1924 more than a hundred South Dakota banks had failed. Farmers in danger of going under were in no mood to finance some hazy project to bring in tourist dollars. Even Peter Norbeck thought Borglum's grandiose plans "too dreamy." The bill died in committee. With the appropriation reduced to $5,000 it was reintroduced into the senate. A fuss stirred up by attacks on Borglum emanating from Georgia contributed to its defeat on February 24.[12]

Ironically, salvation arrived with those very assaults. The executive council of the Stone Mountain Association sent a copy of their resolution to virtually every official and community leader in South Dakota, condemning Borglum for a wide range of sins and failings. The members proudly listed their pedigrees: all Southern-born, most of distinguished ancestry, bankers, lawyers, capitalists, men of unassailable integrity and judgment—to Southerners.

South Dakota is not Georgia. Most Dakotans of the 1920s were laconic folks who considered overstatement a vice. This windy barrage of purple prose from a committee "fairly dripping with aristocracy," as Rex Alan Smith put it, struck many Dakotans as one of those childish temper tantrums embarrassing in private, unforgivable on display in public. These farmers and ranchers and shopkeepers, many of them descended from peasants who had come to America to *escape* aristocratic domination, found it small wonder Borglum had run afoul of the Georgians.

In the week following defeat of the Harney Bill, headlines in the *Rapid City Journal* roused controversy: Borglum fired for wrecking plans for Stone Mountain; four states looking for him; the sculptor vowing to "rot in jail" before he would surrender the plans. On March 1 the rumpus mounted to an out-and-out false report:

BORGLUM FOUND
AND ARRESTED
Georgia Will Try Him For
Malicious Mischief

Four days later, the Harney Bill passed and was signed into law.[13]

Borglum traveled to the Black Hills in August with Lincoln, his son, to find a suitable cliff to carve. The summer of 1925 had been a good one for South Dakota agriculture, a favorable omen for the project. Here in the Black Hills, Borglum told a welcoming luncheon, he would build the true American memorial. The Needles would not be touched. He would venture back into the Hills to find "some now unknown massive stone" on which to carve the figures of Washington, Jefferson, Lincoln, and Theodore Roosevelt. South Dakotans wouldn't be asked to spend a dollar on the project, only to understand it.

Malarkey has often accompanied accounts of his search: the sculptor picking his way through "a pathless . . . almost impenetrable wilderness" for two weeks before finding, and instantly recognizing, his mountain. On the third day, in fact, Borglum was led to a place publicly identified months earlier by the State Forester as a good place for him to work. The great cliffs of Rushmore exhilarated Borglum, with their main wall big enough for his dream, all framed in green timber and wildflowers—and facing *east*, the best direction for the play of light and shadow! When he returned to climb the peak and plant the American flag on its crest, the scale of what he beheld simply awed him:

> We looked out over a horizon level and beaten like the rim of a great cartwheel 2,000 feet below. We had reached upward toward the heavenly bodies . . . and it came over me in an almost terrifying manner that I had never sensed what I was planning. Plans must change. The vastness I saw here demanded it.

Plans must change: a key to what Borglum came to envision, so very different from the idea propounded by Doane Robinson. Borglum's initial theme had been a memorial to the founding and preservation of the Union: thus, Washington and Lincoln. For setting forth American ideals in the Declaration of Independence and securing the Louisiana Purchase, Jefferson was brought into the scheme the following year. Theodore Roosevelt, who had died only six years earlier, was included despite repeated challenges because Borglum and Norbeck were ardent fans. "TR" was something of a "native son" as well, a "local" choice for the memorial, and in building the Panama Canal, Borglum maintained, he had joined the waters of East and West and thus belonged in the final Rushmore theme—commemoration of "the founding, preservation, and continental expansion of the United States."[14]

The *Rapid City Journal* hailed the carving of the monument as a thing of the ages, "the most stupendous undertaking of its kind in all history." The idea alone "has turned our minds from the small things of today and given us a vision of the great things of the past and of the future." The *Lead Daily Call* sounded a cautionary note: the memorial was not an advertising scheme. It should be "more than a commercial proposition to the Hills, it should be their ideal too."[15]

So, stamping the imprint of ownership on the Black Hills no doubt constitutes a motive for the creation of Mount Rushmore, but other elements went into the mix: commerce, the ideals and aspirations of the dominant culture, pride in the establishment and preservation of the Union as well as its expansion, and commanding personal ego. Yet despite Borglum's showmanship and assurances, a shortage of funds stalled the work and almost proved fatal. At the colorful dedication pageant on October 1, 1925 Borglum vowed the statue of Washington would be completed "within a twelvemonth," but the struggle was scarcely under way. The following year passed with no significant work on the memorial. Then in 1927 the President of the United States came to the Black Hills for the summer.

On August 10 Calvin Coolidge, son of Vermont, in full Western attire, including boots and a ten-gallon hat, mounted a horse in Keystone and rode three miles to the base of the mountain. "We have come here," he announced to some seventeen hundred people in attendance, "to dedicate a cornerstone that was laid by the hand of the Almighty."

For the first time the eyes of the nation turned to a place called Mount Rushmore. Three years passed before the figure of Washington began to emerge from the rock. Its unveiling on July 4, 1930 was designed to be a memorable occasion. Across the valley from a huge American flag draped high over the mountain, a crowd of twenty-five hundred waited, along with representatives of four motion picture companies and the *New York Times*. Presiding was a Texas oil millionare, Joseph S. Cullinan, a friend of Borglum's, who chaired the Memorial Commission. Given the great need for funds, men of wealth were increasingly being sought out for the commission. Before introducing the sculptor, Cullinan spoke of the memorial as "American's Shrine for Political Democracy," a phrase that would evolve into the now familiar "Shrine of Democracy."

The aim was not mere "bulk form," Borglum told the gathering, "but rather to give form and intimate personal character, while yet being colossal and heroic in dimension." He was attempting to carve "a head in sculpture as vital as one can hold, produced at arm's length." Washington's brow had now emerged. "When the great sockets below [it] were cut to their proper depth, the eyes seemed unnecessary; the great face seemed to belong to the mountain; it took on the elemental courage of the mountains surrounding it."

When Borglum concluded his remarks, the enormous flag was drawn slowly upward, inch by inch. As the spectators looked on in amazement, the features of Washington stood forth rough-cut, sixty feet high, still in the keeping of the mountain. Rifle salutes were fired; airplanes roared overhead; cameras whirred. An account of the ceremony made the front page of the *Times*.[16]

Among those looking on as the monument progressed was Henry Standing Bear, Luther's younger brother, leader of the Great Council of American Indians. In November 1931 Henry Standing Bear wrote Borglum a letter in which he shared a dream—an *Indian* dream:

> I have started . . . a memorial association among my people to further the project of having an Indian head carved on the rock in the Black Hills. . . . The propriety of this idea coming from the Indians is what I am careful

about in this matter. . . . I would ask all white men to be kept out of this idea and the details of the same . . . .

As the Depression deepened, Borglum was moved by conditions he saw on the nearby reservations. People were starving. Borglum wired President Hoover about the Lakotas "marooned . . . on a vast barren area, timberless and practically gameless . . . ." Even their streams had dried up. Borglum sought to shame Hoover into action by confessing that he himself, even knowing "our historic record" of destroying the Indians and stealing from them, had come to think "something like contentment had been developed in those we had not killed off . . . . "

The situation was too critical to await government action. Borglum organized a local relief effort. He donated his own cattle and asked Norbeck to send six buffalo from the Custer State Park herd, securing blankets and medical supplies from Fort Meade. His efforts saved many lives. To express their gratitude the Lakotas made him a blood brother and honorary chief. At a ceremonial dance and buffalo roast on the Rosebud Reservation, he was installed as Chief *Inyan Wanblee*—Chief Stone Eagle.

Though Borglum must have received Standing Bear's request with sympathy, the timing could not have been worse. What had been tough times in next year country had subsided into the Great Depression and the Dust Bowl. Rushmore itself was struggling for funds. Given Borglum's difficulty in working with anyone else, it is all but inconceivable he would accede to what Standing Bear outlined in his next sentence: "I have great things planned for this project I want to explain to you . . . ."[17]

Nothing came of Standing Bear's request, but at least the Black Hills claim was in the courts, thanks to their champion, Ralph Case, their Moses in this new legal wilderness. In reality, however, no matter how many long-haired old men sat around waiting for yesterday, expecting the white man's courts to make them rich, that claim was stalled, if not foundering. Its prospects were further hindered by infighting between mixed blood progressives and fullblood traditionals, especially on the Pine Ridge Reservation. In 1931 the traditionalist Oglala Council declared itself the official council, and dissolved the progressive Council of 21. The progressives countered by denouncing the Oglala Council as vainglorious: "All the old fellows like to do is feast and sleep."[18]

In 1934 an "Indian New Deal" was launched following the revelations of Indian poverty in the Meriam Report in 1928 and the election of Franklin Delano Roosevelt. Its cornerstone was the Indian Reorganization Act designed by the new Commissioner of Indian Affairs, John Collier. The act halted the allotment program and sought to implement a measure of tribal independence by introducing a form of representative democracy. The policies of assimilation enacted in the General Allotment Act of 1887 had been well intended in part, though more sinister motives were clearly at work. "If this were done in the name of greed," one congressman protested at the time, "it would be bad enough; but to do it in the name of humanity, and under the cloak of an ardent desire to promote the Indian's welfare by making him more like ourselves, whether he will or will not, is infinitely worse." Theodore Roosevelt later called the act a "mighty pulverizing engine to break up the tribal mass." The Indian Reorganization Act of 1934 was considered by some a mere façade, perceived on the reservation as a way of further eviscerating traditional tribal government by instituting elections, white man's style, and employing English and the written word.[19]

Yet it was the written word that would capture a fading Lakota vision before it was lost to the world. In a luminous moment in that dark time, the white poet John Neihardt made contact with old Black Elk, now almost seventy, his eyes failing. From that conjunction came the extraordinary book we know as *Black Elk Speaks*.[20]

Neihardt was then at work on *The Song of the Messiah,* a long narrative poem concerning the Ghost Dance movement. He wanted to meet someone who had been involved in it, who could interpret its deeper spiritual significance. Neihardt had the facts; he needed "something to be experienced through intimate contact, rather than to be received through telling." He learned of an old Lakota named Black Elk, "kind of a preacher," who had been involved in the movement, a second cousin of Crazy Horse who had known him well.

As Neihardt drove up the dusty road to a log cabin near Manderson, he saw the old man sitting in a pine shelter nearby, watching his approach. Black Elk seemed to know Neihardt was coming. With other visitors he had declined to speak of important things, but in Neihardt he sensed something rare. "As I sit here," he told the interpreter in Lakota, "I can feel in this man beside me a strong desire to know the things of the Other World. He has been sent to learn what I know, and I will teach him." And hours later, as the sun was about to set, Black Elk asked Neihardt to come back in the spring. "What I know was given to me for men and it is true and it is beautiful. Soon I shall be under the grass and it will be lost."[21]

The old man Neihardt returned to interview in May 1931 was not the Black Elk we know from the book, but *Nicholas* Black Elk, a baptized Catholic, well known on the Pine Ridge Reservation as a catechist for

Holy Rosary Mission. A man of medium height, very dark from working in the sun, his short hair graying at sixty-eight, he wore a rumpled white man's suit and tie. Effective leadership among the Lakotas during the early reservation period had shifted from the political sphere to the religious, and Black Elk was fully engaged in the process as a catechist. "[L]et us not talk of our ways of the past," he wrote in a letter to the *Catholic Herald* in 1911, "but think about the new ways our Savior has given to us."[22]

For sixty years his great boyhood vision had lain dormant. Then in 1931 it came vibrantly to life. At his first meeting with Neihardt, each time he had mentioned the vision an air of deep sorrow seemed to envelop him: *he had failed his vision.* Now as Neihardt returned, with his son and two daughters, Black Elk would send it out to all the world. It was for all mankind.

His son Ben, later such a familiar figure at Mount Rushmore, where he posed for tourist photos for a price, served as interpreter. Standing Bear, a Minnecoujou Lakota, his oldest and closest friend, was constantly in attendance to assure Neihardt that Black Elk spoke the truth. At first, other old Lakota men participated. As Ben Black Elk translated each of his father's statements into idiomatic "Indian English," Neihardt would repeat it, and rephrase it for clarity into standard English. His daughter Enid would then record it in shorthand.

The painstaking process continued, with interruptions, for three weeks. In a naming ceremony Black Elk took Neihardt as his son, Flaming Rainbow—one who would make his vision go out to the people, like the flame from a rainbow. During an intensive period of three days, in a dramatic unveiling, they completed Black Elk's great vision. "All the listeners were excited and amazed by the great vision," writes Raymond DeMallie. "Black Elk had not revealed it before, so even Standing Bear and Ben Black Elk were hearing it for the first time. Ben could hardly find the English words to translate his father's account, for this was all new to him."[23]

Black Elk's vision eludes any attempt to suggest more than a few outlines here, but recently Neihardt's daughter Hilda, who witnessed the scene, recalled Black Elk's effort to convey the Lakota worldview. She offers only an approximation, filtered through time, of what Black Elk presented one day to the Neihardts and Standing Bear, who were seated on blankets next to a small fire. The old man raised his arms and held them out to represent a great circle as Ben earnestly, sometimes haltingly, sought to translate:

"Imagine a hoop so large that everything is in it—all two-leggeds like us, the four-leggeds, the fish of the streams, the wings of the air, and all green things that grow. Everything is together in this great hoop. Across this hoop, running from the east where the days of men begin to the west where the days of men end, is the hard black road of worldly difficulties. We must all pass along this road, for it represents the world of everyday life. . . . It is not easy to live in this world. . . . [B]ut there is another road," continues Hilda Neihardt's representation of the vision. "It is the good red road of spiritual understanding, and it begins in the south where lives the power to grow and proceeds to the north, the region of white hairs and death. Where this good red road crosses the hard black road, *that place is holy,* and there springs the sacred tree that shall fill with leaves and blooms and singing birds. . . . And that is the sacred hoop."[24]

In the bottomland of Wounded Knee Creek one day, Black Elk spoke of Neihardt's coming in relation to the sacred tree. After Neihardt told Black Elk of a dream he himself had experienced at the age of eleven, a dream that to him constituted a mandate for his literary life work, Black Elk responded, "You are here and have the vision just the way I wanted, and then the tree will bloom again and the people will know the true facts. We want the tree to bloom again in the world of true that doesn't judge."

Next day the small party moved to some property Black Elk owned in the Badlands. Speaking of the Black Hills, he identified Harney Peak as the peak where he was taken in his great vision—the center of the world. As they sat gazing at the Black Hills silhouetted blue against the western sky, Black Elk felt sad thinking of old times. "[B]ut I hope that we can make the tree bloom for your children and for mine," he told them. "We know each other now, and from now on we will be like relatives; and we have been that so far, but we will think of that deeply and set that remembrance down deep in our hearts—not just thinly, but deeply in our hearts it should be marked." He named the place where they were sitting Remembrance Butte.[25]

On May 28 Black Elk completed his story. With the other family members all gone to a council at Holy Rosary, the Neihardts found themselves alone with Black Elk and Ben. Neihardt asked Black Elk why, with the beliefs he had revealed, beliefs of such spiritual beauty and meaning, he had put his old religion aside. Black Elk thought for a moment, then replied in simple words Hilda Neihardt would never forget: "Because my children have to live in this world."[26]

One mission remained, before they parted: Black Elk wanted to return to the center of the earth, where the grandfathers had taken him in his great vision. So on their final day the party made a pilgrimage to Harney Peak. Pausing at times to rest, Black Elk made it to the top. Modestly he went behind a rock to put on a suit of red flannel underwear representing the color his body was painted in his vision. Then, raising his right hand while the left held his pipe, he addressed *Wakan Tanka*, the Great Mysterious, praying that the sacred tree might be nourished to bloom again.

> *Hear me, not for myself, but for my people; I am old.*
> *Hear me that they may once more go back into the sacred*
> *hoop and find the good red road, the shielding tree! . . .*
> *In sorrow I am sending a feeble voice. O Six Powers of*
> *the World. Hear me in my sorrow, for I may never call*
> *again. O make my people live!*[27]

Published the following year, *Black Elk Speaks* was in effect an elegy, the faithful elegy of a pitiful old holy man who has failed in his life work and of a people whose lifeway has passed—moving images of the Vanishing American. The story ends with Black Elk's well known reflections on the death of a dream at Wounded Knee: "[T]he nation's hoop is broken and scattered. There is no center any longer, and the sacred tree is dead."

The book was favorably reviewed but a financial failure, soon remaindered. The strongest response came from the Jesuits at Holy Rosary, whom it shocked and offended. In those pre-ecumenical days it had to be either/or: either the Catholic faith to which Black Elk had dedicated thirty years of his life, or reversion to primitivism. In the first of a series of actions that may never escape controversy, Black Elk made a "final speech." In a letter from Holy Rosary Mission dated January 26, 1934, he reaffirmed his belief in "the true faith of God the Father, the Son, and the Holy Spirit" and the seven sacraments of the Catholic Church. "While I live I will never fall from faith in Christ."

The letter was signed by Nick Black Elk, Lucy Looks Twice, his daughter, Joseph A. Zimmerman, S.J., and *Wanblee Wankatuya*, or High Eagle. Nevertheless, when Ben Black Elk's wife gave birth to a boy the following year, the boy was named John Neihardt Black Elk. Black Elk never denied the sincerity of his appeal to the grandfathers.[28]

What to make of such seeming contradictions? In the 1990s two Jesuit anthropologists examined the paradox posed by Black Elk's religion. Paul B. Steinmetz suggests that Black Elk fluctuated between the two positions, repressing his Lakota religion when talking to the priests, but consciously integrating it privately with his Catholic faith. Michael F. Steltenkamp maintains that Black Elk's passage "from medicine man to catechist, from horseback to motorcycle and cars, from forager to successful rancher, from buffalo subsistence to sauerkraut, and from buckskin to three-piece suits" provides a more accurate picture of Lakota culture than does the image of a warrior society. His "completed biography," says Steltenkamp, reveals the old Lakota culture to be *adaptive*, and Black Elk as typifying its essence: "flexible and responsive to the demands of changing conditions."[29]

The work of art Neihardt shaped out of Black Elk's story is clearly what N. Scott Momaday terms "an extraordinarily human document— and beyond that the record of a profoundly spiritual journey, the pilgrimage of a people towards their historical fulfillment and culmination, towards the accomplishment of a worthy destiny." An observation of Raymond DeMallie's deserves underlining here: that notwithstanding Neihardt's deep sounding of the tragic theme in *Black Elk Speaks*, Lakota culture "does not emphasize the irreversible, but rather the opposite: *what once was is likely to be again*."[30]

One supporter of Mount Rushmore who proved vital was Franklin Delano Roosevelt, whom Borglum and Norbeck convinced of its inspirational value for years to come. At a critical juncture the President threw his support behind a bill funding $200,000 to complete the monument. Even FDR knew about the stresses arising from Borglum's refusal to submit to control by the commission. The Jefferson face, begun to the right of Washington, had become a problem. It had to be removed and carved on his left, but by 1936 the Jefferson figure was ready. The President was invited to the dedication, which Borglum had scheduled for noon on August 30.

Fuming that Roosevelt had decided to come later, after shadows fell over the face of Jefferson, the sculptor nevertheless held off until the President arrived, on his own schedule, promptly at 2:30. Among the dignitaries present, with only a few months to live, a scarf around his neck to conceal the ravages of throat cancer, was Peter Norbeck, a man without whom there would have been no monument. Five charges of dynamite were detonated. A huge flag swung aside to reveal Jefferson's face. Borglum asked the President to dedicate the memorial as a "shrine to democracy."

Roosevelt had not planned to speak, but he could not ignore such an invitation:

I had seen the photographs, I had seen the drawings, and I had talked with those who are responsible for
this great work, and yet I had no conception, until about
ten minutes ago, not only of its magnitude, but also of its
permanent beauty and importance. . . . I think that we
can perhaps meditate on those Americans of ten thousand
years from now . . . . Let us hope . . . that [our descendants]
will believe we have honestly striven every day and
generation to preserve a decent land to live in and a decent
form of government to operate under.[31]

The previous September another visitor of note had come to see
the monument—Frank Lloyd Wright. The great architect thought it fitting that among the abundant rock masses sculptured in nature's own
style "some hand of man should brush aside the realistic veil of a stained
weathered rock and let the mind of man himself envision his own greatness
and his fate alongside the titanic handiwork of nature." The "noble
countenance" of Washington emerged from Rushmore, he wrote, "as
though the spirit of the mountain had heard a human prayer and itself
became a human countenance."

Wright rhapsodized about the Black Hills. In the Badlands he
found "an indescribable sense of mysterious otherwhere . . . an endless
supernatural world more spiritual than earth but created out of it." The
Black Hills themselves had "a more flesh and blood kind of beauty. . . .
All has the charm of human scale which many great Western scenes lack.
. . . an ideal home; these Black Hills." They stirred the heart. In Spearfish
Canyon he found himself in the land of the Sung and Ming masters, "the
great Chinese painters, the greatest painters who ever lived . . . a stately
exposition of what decorated walls on an enormous scale can do and be."

When he asked his host why he'd heard so little in the East of
this miracle, the spiritual quality of the Badlands, Wright was told slyly,
"Oh, we are not on the through line to the coast." Wright remarked that
he would be "burned for a heretic" in saying so, but in the "softly modeled
brown surfaces of South Dakota binding these three wonders together
[was] a terrain greater in charm" than any to be found in California and
Arizona. To "that jaded public who have 'seen everything' and stick to
the 'through lines,'" he advised: "Go to South Dakota, but drive there."[32]

At the New York World's Fair in 1939 a young sculptor of Polish extraction won first prize, by popular vote, for his portrait in marble
of Paderewski, the great Polish pianist and patriot. That summer Gutzon
Borglum met the thirty-year-old Korczak Ziolkowski on a speaking trip

to the East. Needing a highly skilled assistant, Borglum invited him to come work at Mount Rushmore. They quickly became friends—two like-minded, opinionated men of the most independent temperament. But within a few weeks Ziolkowski tangled with Gutzon's son, Lincoln, to the point of physical violence. Lincoln was his father's project manager. Borglum had no choice but to fire Ziolkowski, who went back to Connecticut and resumed his sculpture.

Meanwhile Henry Standing Bear, who had never given up his dream of an Indian memorial, learned of Ziolkowski's prize at the World's Fair. Hearing that Ziolkowski had worked briefly at Mount Rushmore, Standing Bear wrote him a letter that fall, repeating the request he'd made of Borglum seven years earlier: he and some of his "fellow chiefs" would like to have the head of an Indian chief carved in the Black Hills. "This is to be entirely an Indian project," Standing Bear made clear, "under my direction." Hardly a man to be directed by anyone, Ziolkowski failed to take the request seriously, but Standing Bear wrote him again: "My fellow chiefs and I would like the white man to know the red man has great heroes, too."

"That was the line that got me," Ziolkowski recalled.[33]

The following year, still undecided, he visited Standing Bear on the Pine Ridge Reservation before undertaking an ambitious project in Connecticut. In 1941 he put a thirty-three ton block of Tennessee marble in place near the city hall in West Hartford and began work on a statue of Noah Webster, the largest statue hewn from a single block of marble since Michelangelo's *David* in 1504. Thirteen and a half feet tall, with an inscription implying that Webster's fellow townspeople had neglected and misunderstood him, the statue drew both praise and criticism. Some of the criticism was insidious and personal. Ziolkowski was accused of arrogance. More than likely, some of the town's long-established Yankees considered it impertinent of a transplant, especially a young man of Polish origin whose name they could not pronounce, to lecture them on their greatest native son.[34]

As the shadows of war in Europe moved closer to America in 1941, work on Rushmore was drawing to a close. Cancer had carried off Peter Norbeck. The Lincoln figure had been dedicated in 1937 and that of Theodore Roosevelt in 1939. The final appropriation for the monument's completion, $86,000, was authorized in August 1940. Weary from all his battles but still full of fight, Borglum warned against appeasing Hitler. When work for the 1940 season ended, he held a party for the entire crew at the Alex Johnson Hotel in Rapid City. He shook hands with each man, inscribing for each a copy of the *Saturday Evening Post* featuring the Rushmore profile of Washington on the cover.

On a speaking tour of the East in February 1941 he was hospitalized for surgery in Chicago. There he learned that President Roosevelt was cutting non-defense spending deeply in order to fortify the "Arsenal of Democracy." There would be no more money for Rushmore. A week later, Borglum died. Though Congress authorized burial for him at Mount Rushmore, the family decided to honor a wish he had expressed in a letter: burial in California. There his soul had awakened, in earlier days; there his spirit had been born: "I have loved her ever since . . . . A little prayer whispers to me now and then 'may I be buried there?'"

He was laid to rest at Forest Lawn in Glendale. The true memorial service for Gutzon Borglum may have been the one held earlier in Keystone, attended by his workers and other members of the Mount Rushmore family. "I ask only one favor," Borglum had once told a friend who was writing about him. "[F]or God's sake don't cover me with the twaddle and gush usually written about artists." His workers had found him demanding and tough, but big-hearted and generous. He cared about them. In all the years of hazardous work at Rushmore there had been only one serious injury. As the old-timers used to say, observed Rex Alan Smith, "he was somebody you could ride the river with."[35]

Lincoln Borglum, respected and competent in his own right, took over the task of winding down. On October 31, 1941, the monument was left as it remains. The Hall of Records was never completed. The entabulature was abandoned—a fortunate outcome, in the view of the monument's first biographer: "The worst blunder of all would have been to carve any history on Mount Rushmore where it might have stood for half a million years."[36]

In 1943 Ziolkowski, at thirty-four, enlisted in the army. He landed on Omaha Beach on D-Day as sergeant of an anti-aircraft gun crew. He was wounded twice. Finally, after the war, he decided to take up Standing Bear's invitation to carve an Indian monument. Ziolkowski would have preferred to locate it elsewhere, perhaps in the Tetons, rather than in proximity to Rushmore, but the Indians insisted it should be in the Black Hills, their *Paha Sapa*. So he went to South Dakota, where he and Standing Bear found a mountain six hundred feet high, north of Custer. Ziolkowski staked a mining claim on it and named it Thunderhead Mountain.[37]

In May 1947 he arrived in the Black Hills to begin work. The monument would be big, that was certain. If Borglum had been out to achieve large scale, Ziolkowski came to be obsessed by it. Initially planned as a less ambitious undertaking, it grew into the most colossal mountain carving ever attempted, carved in the round. At the insistence of the Indians it was to feature Crazy Horse astride his horse. His arm would be outstretched and pointing east, in accord with Crazy Horse's response to a white trader's mocking query as to where his lands were, now that most of the Indians had gone on the reservation: "My lands are where my dead lie buried."

Word of Ziolkowski's plan preceded his arrival in South Dakota and elicited a negative response. The *Rapid City Journal* editorialized, in effect: we already have Mount Rushmore; we don't want the Black Hills turned into a sculptors' gallery. When Bob Lee, then a young reporter for the *Journal*, went out to interview Ziolkowski, he found him stripped to the waist, wielding an ax, cutting timber to build a cabin. Ziolkowski was a powerful man, visibly hot-tempered. Lee feared he might take after him with the ax.

"You blankety-blank newspapermen!" Ziolkowski growled. "You smear me and what I'm doing without even talking to me! You never got *my* side of it!"

"I'm a reporter," Lee told him. "I'm here to get your side of it."

Ziolkowski fumed and Lee listened. Eventually Ziolkowski calmed down. "Wait here," he said. He went into his tent and emerged with a pitcher of manhattans: "Come on in." After a drink or two Lee had his story, and Ziolkowski and Lee became Korczak and Bob, friends for life.[38]

Among those from West Hartford who helped Ziolkowski in his move west was Ruth Ross, one of the student volunteers who aided him on the Noah Webster statue. She stayed on as a fellow pioneer, peeling the logs he felled for the cabin, collaborating in the development of a master plan for the memorial. In 1950, twenty-four to his forty-two, Ruth Ross became Mrs. Korczak Ziolkowski, with full understanding and agreement that Korczak had to keep his promise to the Indians. The mountain would always come fiirst.

The master plan embraced three goals: the mountain carving itself, a North American Indian museum, and a university and medical training center. Ziolkowski's design envisioned a treasure house of Indian culture where Indians could meet whites on an even plane, honorably and with pride. On that basis the federal government granted the Crazy Horse Memorial Foundation nonprofit status in 1949.

From the beginning Ziolkowski insisted the memorial would be constructed, or not, with private funds: no federal dollars. The story has it that he twice refused offers of ten million dollars in "potential" federal funds. One such offer seems to have been based on a casual statement by a friendly senator or congressman to whom he remarked that if he had ten million dollars he could finish Crazy Horse: "I'll put in a bill for ten million."

The official dedication took place on June 3, 1948. As four hundred Indians stood by, including five survivors of the Battle of the Little Bighorn, Henry Standing Bear touched off a charge blasting ten tons of rock from Thunderhead Mountain. The next year Ziolkowski blasted twenty thousand tons more. *Time* and *Life* carried pictures of the occasion. The *Minneapolis Sunday Tribune* ran a full page in color.

The project encountered resistance as well as support. Ziolkowski saw racism. His "biggest surprise out here," he said, "was how they hated Indians with a purple passion." He was no "Indian lover," just a storyteller in stone, but a lot of people hated him for wanting to tell the story. He thought Borglum had been treated even worse. Without what Borglum had accomplished, Ziolkowski knew, he would never have been able to move one rock for an Indian memorial.[39]

No doubt Ziolkowski, like Borglum, brought some of it on himself. Reducing the opposition to racism surely made few friends, even among those sympathetic to the cause. Like Borglum he often seems to have placed blame elsewhere, though some of it was home grown. Rumor held that the rock on Thunderhead Mountain would never support the design. Grumbling was heard that the sculptor had set himself up with a good thing for life. Once when he labored for two years out of public view, tunneling through a hundred and ten feet of rock, some said he had quit working on the mountain.

No one who knew him in the slightest would label Ziolkowski a slacker. His labors were simply prodigious. After a couple of land exchanges in the early 1950s, the foundation acquired more than a square mile of land. Ziolkowski cleared roads and built a staircase seven hundred feet long to the top of the mountain, always with Ruth working along with him. Over the years they had ten children, one of whom was delivered by Ziolkowski himself. Most would ultimately stay on to help complete the project.

One irony Ziolkowski could never escape: the carving of a mountain to honor a people whose traditional lifeways do not countenance major carving on Mother Earth. A final irony lies in the boasts of comparative scale, the number of Rushmore heads that would fit in the face of Crazy Horse, and so on—an American obsession with size reflected in one son of immigrants who honored another, with a distinctly American competitive edge that was thoroughly naturalized.

Chapter Eight: Threats and Promises

On a cold February night in 1972 four local roughnecks in a car spotted a lone Indian walking along the main street of a small town in the Nebraska sandhills. Visiting from Colorado, where they were living at the time, they had been hunting coyotes. Gathered in a bar earlier that evening, they had come up with the idea of "busting an Indian." Here was a target of opportunity! One of them got out and yelled at the Indian and gave him a shove. The man simply walked on, but not long afterward they found him slumped in the cab of a pickup. They roughed him up, took off his pants, and threw him in the trunk of their car. After further deliberation while driving around town with their captive bouncing around in the trunk, they decided to add to the fun. Why not toss him into the American Legion Club, nude from the waist down?

Around midnight they shoved him into the club through a side door and took off. Two men standing inside tried to help him as he covered his face with one hand, pulling his shirt down with the other. Seconds later he escaped by the same door. As he walked back toward the center of town his attackers spotted him again. This time they forced him into their car and drove him to a laundromat, where they put his clothes back on and let him go. At a truck stop afterward, they talked freely about their bit of fun. Next morning they all went back to Colorado. A week later the object of their amusement was found dead in the cab of a pickup. He was fifty-one years old. His name was Raymond Yellow Thunder.[1]

So much for the rudimentary facts of the episode, as clearly as they can be made out. But an event, Marshall Sahlins has said, is a "happening interpreted." What to some might seem only a date for lunch, to others may be a radical *event.* What happened that night in a little prairie town soon became an Event—the first in a chain leading to rekindled anger and violence over the Black Hills. As interpretation was compounded by interpretation, then acted upon as *fact,* what might have been put down as a sadistic happening soon became a *cause célèbre.*[2]

Response to the crime reflected the early 1970s, with embers glowing in the winds of change. Some of the developments in Indian affairs preceding Raymond Yellow Thunder's death have been outlined by Vine Deloria, Jr. In 1963, Deloria says, only a few Indians had attended the March on Washington where Martin Luther King gave his most famous speech. The following year a "fish-in" was staged by tribes in the Pacific Northwest, with a celebrity boost from Dick Gregory and Marlon Brando. After King's assassination in 1968, perhaps a hundred Indians joined the Poor People's March on the nation's capital. Then in 1969 some three hundred Indians seized Alcatraz, the recently abandoned federal prison in San Francisco Bay, and demanded title to it.

This illegal invasion of government property brought public expressions of abhorrence from tribal elders who had long sought restoration of tribal lands, though privately they were delighted by such a bold thumbing-of-the-nose at federal authority. The occupation of Alcatraz lasted eighteen months. Its notoriety brought an influx of Indians from the cities to the reservations in search of identity. As the militants sought to eject their more accommodating relatives from the premises, the progressive middle ground eroded. The strategy turned to confrontation.[3]

The wild card among national Indian organizations was AIM— the American Indian Movement. The name was perfect, its chroniclers point out: it suggested "action, purpose, and forward motion." For a few weeks the movement called itself Concerned Indians of America, until the acronym—CIA—showed the leaders their blunder. Formed in Minneapolis in 1968, AIM was composed mainly of Chippewas, most notably Dennis Banks, but urban Lakotas soon joined. "In this family," observe Paul Chaat Smith and Robert Allen Warrior, "AIM was the second cousin you knew growing up . . . charming, rowdy, a bit wild, who later did three years at the state prison for stealing cars."

One Oglala who enlisted had been born on the Pine Ridge Reservation but grown up in California, a swaggering and charismatic figure with a gift for capturing attention. Living in Cleveland, he'd offered his resignation from AIM shortly before Yellow Thunder's death for a remark he made about the Chippewas, or Ojibwas, ancient enemies of the Sioux, who had driven them out of Minnesota. The Chippewas had done nothing in earlier days, he said, but "hang around the fort." His resignation was rejected. His experience and talents were needed, and the circumstances surrounding Yellow Thunder's death could not have been better tailored for a man like Russell Means.[4]

The drama erupted in Gordon, a community of about twenty-five hundred inhabitants, most of them white, best known as a backdrop for the works of Mari Sandoz, daughter of "Old Jules," who had homesteaded in the sandhills south of town. Few communities have been so thoroughly maligned, or so poorly defended. Gordon became a free-fire zone for anyone with a charge to make, or a score to settle, with no risk of counterfire. The brutal assault on Raymond Yellow Thunder could not have left the town more vulnerable. Given the version of events accepted as gospel by supporters of AIM and the consequences it provoked, we need a clear look at the version that propelled them into action.[5]

The setting was defined as a "whiskey town" where nothing was cheaper than Indian lives but the fortified wine that was "the center of a border town's character and identity." Indians visiting Gordon or neighboring Rushville, it was said, were waited on by "rednecks who hated Indians and who probably hated themselves because they made their living from the very Indians they despised." Killing Indians was "a favorite sport" in those parts, where "liquored-up cowboys display[ed] their manhood by hunting down and stomping homeless Indians to death." In this instance the victim had been forced to dance naked from the waist down before two hundred people.

Gordon officials had done nothing, this story said, until AIM invaded the town with nearly a thousand Indians. Peter Matthiessen's best-selling *In the Spirit of Crazy Horse*, the most influential of many accounts, maintains that Yellow Thunder had been "severely beaten for the fun of it by two white brothers named Hare, then stripped from the waist down and paraded before a patriotic gathering at an American Legion dance in Gordon, Nebraska; the merry crowd," Matthiessen adds, "was invited to join the Hares in kicking the Indian, after which the brothers stuffed him into a car trunk, where he perished."[6]

A graphic sequence, and the past sins of towns like Gordon were enough to give it plausibility. As an image of the town it may have had as much validity as most generalities applied with an angry brush. It was a happening interpreted, an *event,* with violent repercussions. And it was *believed*, and acted upon.

A careful sifting of the evidence reveals a different set of facts. Corrections are in order. After being released at the laundromat on that Saturday night, February 12, Raymond Yellow Thunder found his way to the county jail. He asked to sleep there, as he had done many times before. The deputy sheriff on duty had already heard about the Legion incident. He saw bruises and scratches around Yellow Thunder's right cheek. Next morning at 7:00 Yellow Thunder left the jail with a staggering gait. George Ghost Dog saw him later that day in a pickup cab, with a swollen lip and blood on his face. Yellow Thunder said he'd been beat up by some white guys but was all right. A few days later Ghost Dog saw him lying down in the truck but left him undisturbed, thinking he was asleep.

When his body was found on February 20, a pathologist from Scottsbluff, Nebraska determined by autopsy that Yellow Thunder had died of a subdural hematoma, a slow internal bleeding caused by a wound on the forehead, a wound inconspicuous on the surface but spreading slowly inside, caused by an instrument other than a fist. County Attorney Mike Smith had already been investigating the incident in the Legion parking lot. An eyewitness had stepped forward. On February 22 Smith filed a manslaughter and false imprisonment complaint against five persons living in Colorado. Three days later they were brought in for a preliminary hearing on both charges and released on a bond of $6,250 each.

Two weeks after manslaughter charges were brought against the five men, AIM entered the picture. Rumors were circulating that Yellow Thunder had been mutilated, burned with lighted cigarettes, maybe castrated. Desperate and weeping, his three sisters went to Severt Young Bear, their nephew, at Porcupine, on the Pine Ridge Reservation. Severt had friends in AIM. Couldn't he ask them for help to get justice for their brother? So Young Bear drove to Omaha, where AIM leaders were meeting, and told them about Yellow Thunder.

What Raymond Yellow Thunder had suffered was a story, say Paul Chaat Smith and Robert Allen Warrior, that "reached out to every Indian person who could see in him not just another Indian drunk, but a brother, a father, an uncle, or a cousin." AIM chartered two buses to Pine Ridge, where Young Bear had arranged a rally at Billy Mills Hall. More than five hundred people attended. County Attorney Smith and an investigator for the Nebraska State Patrol went up to face the angry charges and accusations.[7]

On March 6 a caravan of about three hundred American Indians, flying the Stars and Stripes upside down as a distress signal, came over the hill into Gordon, accompanied by network television crews. A big story was in the offing. After securing food and camping privileges from town authorities, AIM took over the Gordon Community Hall. Alarmed by highly colored television and radio bulletins, Gordon residents half expected a siege. Some wanted to oust AIM physically from the Community Hall. One World War II veteran had to be forcibly restrained from attacking Russell Means, who had draped himself in the American flag. County Attorney Smith insisted on negotiations.

After three days of demands and negotiations widely publicized by the mass media, having secured a seven-point agreement, AIM left town declaring victory, convinced they had turned a routine bit of racist thuggery into an object lesson for a community of rednecks who would otherwise have shrugged it all off as nothing of consequence. Gordon residents say the invaders had urinated on buildings, stuffed all the toilets, and left behind an enormous mess. On the way back to Pine Ridge the caravan stopped off at the Wounded Knee Trading Post, where some of the caravanners stole merchandise. The white owner was warned they would like to do to him what white men had done to Yellow Thunder.

Many of the visiting reporters were impressed by the moderation and skill with which Gordon's leadership had handled the situation. Residents felt stunned—defamed and violated by the inflammatory national coverage. The weekly *Gordon Journal*, which on February 23 had cited "evidence of foul play" in reporting the manslaughter charges, deplored what it saw as distortion "beyond all belief." A second autopsy conducted in front of many witnesses, including a lawyer from the Native American Rights Fund, found no evidence of mutilation. A jury convicted the Hare brothers of second degree manslaughter and they were sentenced to one to five years in prison.

Intoxicated by success, AIM leaders informed the press that from ten to thirty thousand Indians from across the country would soon be arriving to raise consciousness in towns along both sides of the Nebraska-South Dakota border. They invited presidential candidates, the BIA Commissioner, and the Secretary of the Interior to attend. None came, nor did the Indians, but AIM had made its name.[8]

If any of the movement's leaders questioned their own version of happenings in Gordon, no evidence has surfaced. To them, rednecks and whiskey towns were just that. The citizens of Gordon had views and feelings of their own, of course, seldom vocalized beyond the immediate surroundings. *The New York Times* briefly noted the results of the autopsy and the storming of the Wounded Knee Trading Post but, as usual, the national media showed no further interest in matters of local concern.

As events moved on toward the Black Hills, divergent stories flourished in a sort of compound interest of interpretation. Positions hardened, generating a counterreaction that would soon come into play. A few weeks later the AIMsters, as they came to call themselves, followed their Gordon triumph with a fiasco in Minnesota, a standoff with a tribal council in which guns were drawn and roads blocked. No gunfight ensued, but the pattern of violent confrontation and a willingness to use arms became part of AIM's modus operandi.[9]

The movement slumbered uneasily through the summer. In August the leaders gathered at Crow Dog's Paradise, the home of spiritual leader Leonard Crow Dog on the Rosebud Reservation. AIM seemed to have exhausted its store of ideas, but a former tribal chairman at Rosebud, Robert Burnette, came up with a fresh proposal: a march on Washington. The Trail of Broken Treaties would be a peaceful caravan for Indian pride and dignity—their "finest hour," if they could maintain a discipline of no drugs and no liquor. Three separate caravans would move across the country, gathering adherents along the way, to converge on the nation's capital.

They did precisely that. The caravan arrived in Washington on November 1, 1972, the eve of the election, with a list of twenty points to take up with federal officials. Led by AIM, ready to die if necessary, they seized the Bureau of Indian Affairs building, calling themselves the Native American Embassy. For a week they occupied the building, a week in what degenerated into "a sort of indoor Indian Woodstock," according to Burnette, "with just enough threat of violence to keep everyone's nerves tingling." Some of the occupiers loaded furniture and artwork into trucks, along with cartons of official documents. An orgy of "revolutionary hooliganism" and destruction secured mixed publicity, a few promises from officials, and a major haul of BIA files, but the diverse groups representing Indians found themselves divided against each other, the "gang of thugs" that AIM had become set against "pawns" and "hang around the fort Indians." A year that opened with "visions of unprecedented unity," note Smith and Warrior, "ended with bitter recrimination."[10]

The next opportunity for AIM was not long in coming. Soon its triumph in Gordon was amplified by a timely incident in Buffalo Gap that yielded dividends in the heart of the Black Hills, with explosive potential far exceeding Gordon's. On the edge of the Hills south of Rapid City, Buffalo Gap was no longer the enterprising place satirized by de Mandat-Grancey in 1889 but a declining town of fewer than two hundred residents, with "rickety fences, dusty dirt streets, post office, bank, liquor store, and bar," a tiny prairie burg known thereabouts for its bar.[11]

On January 21, 1973, an Oglala named Wesley Bad Heart Bull died from a wound inflicted in Buffalo Gap by Darld Schmitz of Custer. Bad Heart Bull had grown up in nearby Hot Springs, where he was known for a nasty temperament when drinking. He had a record of nineteen arrests and was being sought at the time for a brutal beating in Hot Springs. On the night in question he got into a fight with Jim Geary, a former high school wrestler nicknamed "Mad Dog." They were both thrown out of the bar. Bad Heart Bull somehow got hold of a truck chain. He knocked Geary unconscious with it and went on beating him.

Schmitz was leaving with his date, a woman who knew Bad Heart Bull. She tried to stop him but was pulled back. Schmitz, who had put away half a dozen drinks, evidently thought Bad Heart Bull was threatening her. He stepped in, ducking the chain, and took out his pocket knife. Grabbing Bad Heart Bull by the shirt, he stabbed him in the chest. Schmitz saw blood on his knife but left the scene. "I've been stabbed," Bad Heart Bull said. He collapsed.

The knife had penetrated his aorta. The car in which he was rushed toward Hot Springs broke down near the Maverik truck stop. Bad Heart Bull, picked up by the same car carrying Geary to the hospital, died on the way in from loss of blood. Both men were dead on arrival.[12]

At first glance the death of Bad Heart Bull looked to be just one more instance of an Indian killed by a white man in a drunken brawl. The absence of any thorough coverage of the incident left the field open to improvisation. A reporter for the Associated Press actually went to Buffalo Gap to investigate, but his story, filed early in February, was carried in full only by the *Aberdeen American News*. Grossly distorted accounts have been propagated by AIM ever since. In 1974 Clyde Bellecourt told college audiences in South Dakota and California that Bad Heart Bull had been "set upon by four whites [and] stabbed a total of twenty-seven times in broad daylight, [then] tied to a bumper of a car and drug down the main street, fifty to sixty people witnessing it." As recently as 1995 Russell Means, citing an eyewitness, reported that "Mad Dog," whom he confused with Schmitz, stabbed Bad Heart Bull seven times while his mother was forced to watch.[13]

Clearly designed to inflame, such accounts find no support in the ascertainable facts. On the morning after Bad Heart Bull's death, State's Attorney for Custer County Hobart Gates received an early call from the sheriff of Fall River County. A man had died from a scuffle in Buffalo Gap, just over the line in Custer County. Gates promptly drove to Hot

Springs to interview witnesses, both Indian and white. As prosecutor in the case, he decided the only charge he could bring against Schmitz was second degree manslaughter. Absent premeditation or malice afore-thought, a murder charge was out of the question. Manslaughter would be difficult enough to prove. A coroner's journey might return a verdict of justifiable homicide and that would be the end of it.[14]

Schmitz was arrested. He admitted killing Bad Heart Bull and surrendered the knife he had used. A preliminary hearing was set for February 26, with bond set at $5,000, presumably enough to assure he would not run off and leave his business and family. When Banks and Means learned of the light charge, they issued a furious protest and called for a day of reckoning. Banks called the Custer County Sheriff to demand a meeting with Gates, which was set for 9:00 a.m. on February 6 at the Custer County Courthouse. In the view of Smith and Warrior, the issue was not Bad Heart Bull but South Dakota "and all it stood for." And *Custer,* of all places—the very name despised by Indians![15]

Authorities in Custer, like the town's residents, knew of AIM's recent moves and methods. Law enforcement people familiar with AIM's tactics elsewhere called for a show of force. The governor and the U.S. Justice Department urged everyone to "play it cool." On February 5 a meeting of about sixty civic leaders was held to discuss preparations. Jessie Sundstrom, the formidable editor and publisher of the *Custer Chronicle,* who had often clashed with some of them, was not invited, but attended anyway. A John Birch Society film, *Anarchy-USA,* was shown by a man alleged to be a society member. Gates said that the movie had nothing to do with the present situation and that half the audience soon became bored with it and left.

February 6 brought a snowstorm. Nine o'clock passed, with no AIM caravan. A camera crew from Salt Lake City set up across the street from the courthouse, headed by a woman friend of Dennis Banks who sometimes acted as his chauffeur. The crew told reporters they were planning "footage for a movie of the 'Billy Jack' type." Late in the morning a caravan of about two hundred Indians rolled into Custer. They had paused in Hill City to burn a chuck wagon, a symbol of the pioneer tradition. The first thing Mary Crow Dog saw as they came into town was a big sign: "WELCOME TO CUSTER—THE TOWN WITH THE GUNSMOKE FLAVOR." They hadn't come to riot, she said, but to see justice done. They were fed up with what they saw as a judicial double standard. Too often a white would be charged with only a misdemeanor for killing an Indian, where an Indian would be condemned death for killing a white.[16]

A "young Indian hobo girl" at seventeen, in her own words, and seven months pregnant, Crow Dog had joined the caravan after a wild night in Rapid City in which eighty years of resentment had boiled over in "a kind of insane rage," a rage fueled by the case of Raymond Yellow Thunder. At first, as the Indians gathered in front of the Custer County Courthouse, says Crow Dog, everything was dignified, even jolly. Four or five spokesmen—and she notes they all *were* men—went into the courthouse. Soon an official came out on the front steps to assure the crowd Schmitz would be vigorously prosecuted—*for second-degree manslaughter!*

The last words brought a "deep growl" from the Indians, "like a knife stuck into our bellies." Another Indian-killer would go free! In the melee that followed, the outlines of what happened are blurred. Gates reported that a television man came into his small office with Banks and Means and two others, where a television camera was set up, and that all of them were "extremely belligerent." Banks demanded the charge be changed to murder. Absolutely impossible, Gates said, unless new evidence was presented. "At no time," he said, "did any of them endeavor to find out any facts in the case."

Finally Means went out into the hall and signaled others to come on into the courthouse. Scuffles broke out with fists and clubs. The camera turned from Gates to the fighting in the hallway. Rocks came crashing through the windows. A molotov cocktail was tossed in. Gasoline from a nearby station was poured and set afire. Gates escaped the flames by jumping out the window of an adjoining office. Mary Crow Dog says that Banks followed Leonard Crow Dog out another window with a big grin: "I'm following my spiritual leader."

Troopers outside went after the protesters with batons, deploying tear gas as they fought for control of the street. Across the street the small log structure housing the Chamber of Commerce blazed up. An Indian woman ran from behind the building, clothing on fire, but was rescued before she was seriously injured. The courthouse fire was quickly suppressed, but the Chamber of Commerce building burned to the ground. Two police cars were set afire. In the conflicting accounts of what happened, some say Sarah Bad Heart Bull, Wesley's mother, was choked with a nightstick and shoved down the stairs. Gates believed she was too drunk to stand up. Mary Crow Dog saw a young Indian girl, her clothes torn off, dragged almost naked through the snow. Russell Means claimed the troopers made women their first targets: "The troopers tore off the women's clothes to fondle their breasts, then clubbed them."[17]

No one can say with assurance precisely what happened. An officer of the Highway Patrol pointed to the difficulty of fighting "that kind of battle when they've got women and children out there in the street with you." In the end, no one was killed, though eleven troopers were injured, along with many of the protesters, twenty-seven of whom were arrested. The riot marked the first time in a century, writes Peter Matthiessen as if describing a grade-B Western, when "the white people could holler, 'Injuns comin'!'" A historic event rich in symbolism, he asserts—an Event, we might say—the Custer courthouse riot was "the first outbreak of violence between white men and Lakotas since the Wounded Knee massacre in 1890."[18]

For Mary Crow Dog it had been "quite a day." She left Custer in at a car whose bumper sticker read "CUSTER HAD IT COMING!" Back in Rapid City, the protesters watched themselves on television. Residents of Custer were alarmed and outraged. The *Custer Chronicle* and the South Dakota dailies reported fully on the details, but the enormous national coverage framed the encounter, in effect, as a confrontation between brutal racist oppressors and native warriors fighting for justice. The most objective editorial in South Dakota, ironically, appeared in Custer. The *Chronicle* editorialized that after so many frustrations it was only natural some of the Indians had become militant. History would decide whether it was justified, but "right or wrong the tactics used by AIM do succeed in focusing national attention on the Indian and his problem." Facing community criticism for such comment, Jessie Sundstrom stood firm: "As long as the news is being made it will be reported in the *Chronicle* and every attempt will be made to be completely objective in reporting and fair in editorializing."[19] Custer residents went about repairing the damages, nursing raw feelings. Some armed themselves, predicting bloodshed if AIM came back as rumored. In Rapid City, meetings of the Racial Reconciliation Commission were convened. Backed by cheers from a hundred and fifty AIM people and the beating of a drum, Dennis Banks voiced charges of racial discrimination. Indian people seldom complained, he said, because in the past their complaints had always fallen on deaf ears: "We've carried signs to protest illegitimate acts against our people, but they have never listened to us, but they did listen to us February 6 in Custer."

Despite a moratorium AIM declared on all violent activities in the Black Hills, some of the rank and file launched an offensive of their own in Rapid City, "three minutes in, three minutes out," ransacking taverns, breaking windows. An all-woman commando team smashed up one bar with clubs and made it out in time to pick up others fleeing as the sirens wailed. It felt good, said the leaders: "To say, hey we can do this and we can do it again. I think they learned a heck of a lot from that."[20]

To the north, Sturgis prepared for violence as Banks led more than two hundred supporters into town to protest the bond for an Indian charged in the death of an elderly woman. When the Circuit Court judge informed AIM representatives that the bond for a white man charged with raping an Indian woman was three times that for the Indian in question, the caravan left town peacefully, honking horns. "Custer obviously was not prepared," commented the *Sturgis Tribune*. "Sturgis was." A similar welcome greeted an AIM caravan of twenty-four cars that rolled into Hot Springs and found themselves in an armed fortress. In the charged atmosphere Banks conferred with officials, to little effect. The trial of Darld Schmitz, held in Rapid City, was prosecuted by Hobart Gates and a veteran trial lawyer from the Attorney General's office. Schmitz was acquitted of manslaughter in the death of Wesley Bad Heart Bull on the ground of self-defense.[21]

The confrontations at Gordon and Custer had repercussions, intended and unintended, in questions relating to the Black Hills. They provided vital impetus for the most violent encounter yet between American Indians and the federal government—the occupation of Wounded Knee. The siege at Wounded Knee has been recounted from every angle, in scores of books. Symbolically powerful though it was, the takeover lies beyond the scope of the story here. A summary will have to do.

Three days after the raids on Rapid City taverns, with increasing threats of a confrontation between AIM and tribal officials on the reservation, the federal government sent sixty-five U.S. marshals into the town of Pine Ridge and set up a command post. The FBI and BIA reinforced their personnel. A group of traditionalists joined by newly formed chapters of AIM launched impeachment proceedings against tribal chairman Dick Wilson, who had strong support on the reservation and considered AIM part of a communist conspiracy. On February 22 their impeachment attempt failed.

Four days later, hundreds of people turned out for the funeral of Ben Black Elk, now a revered elder. The AIM activists and the traditionalist group then went to nearby Calico, where a series of meetings produced a decision. The town of Pine Ridge was too well fortified; they would go to Wounded Knee. In that decision, Oglala women were a powerful voice. Gladys Bissonette spoke for twenty minutes in Lakota, then turned to address the uncomprehending AIMsters in English. The Oglalas had lost their way, she told them. They had forgotten how to fight. Ellen Moves Camp lamented that most of those demonstrating against Wilson were women and old people. "Where are our men?" she demanded. "Where are our defenders?"[22]

The question touched a chord in most of AIM's young men. Few spoke their tribal languages. What the traditionals had, they lacked: ceremony, wisdom, ancient knowledge. "To them their lack burned like the theft of something priceless, irreplaceable," say Smith and Warrior, "and with it came a smoldering resentment they felt nearly every waking moment. This, more than any specific grievance, fueled their bold activism." A dissonant note from offstage was sounded by a ninety-year-old cousin of Black Elk, a forceful woman who believed Black Elk's message was that only Almighty God could change the way things were: "Younger ones now don't tell the truth. They never believed. People heard him but did not listen."[23]

What the AIMs, as the old people called them, brought to the struggle was secret knowledge of their own, garnered in the cities. They knew the power of publicity, especially Russell Means, with his flair for the dramatic. *Wounded Knee!* What better place to stage a protest under the eyes of the world? The caravan of fifty-four vehicles rolled right through the fortified town of Pine Ridge and on to the place where so many had died back in 1890. Reporters and television journalists soon flocked to the scene from around the world and were treated as royalty— eyes through which the world would see.

"Armed Indians Seize Wounded Knee, Hold Hostages," the *New York Times* proclaimed on the front page. CBS Evening News led with Russell Means issuing demands by telephone. *Time* found the events surreal, as if "history had been hi-jacked by a band of revisionists armed with a time machine." There was little or no mention of the Black Hills. Before long the journalists began to realize, uneasily, that they had become central players in the story, that without the cameras there might have been no story at all. Terry Schultz, a young free-lance reporter returning to Pine Ridge after an absence of eighteen months, found only a game of charades. Instead of the "noble warriors and tragic heroes with tongues of gold" in which she had once believed, she found a "pseudo-event in which the world press responded with all the cautiousness of sharks scenting blood."[24]

For AIM the cause had expanded beyond Gordon and Custer, beyond the Black Hills. They proclaimed an Independent Oglala Nation, "a stand for all Indian people, everywhere," somewhat ironically, since most of the Oglalas left despite Russell Means' pleas for them to stay. Replacements streamed in from other parts of the country, scores of them non-Indian. A delegation of Iroquois arrived in support. The Grand Council of the Iroquois issued a plea addressed to whites that strangely parallels a view Thomas Jefferson had once expressed on the evils of slavery: "For your children learn from watching their elders, and if you want your children to do what is right, then it is up to you to set the example." The occupation elicited widespread sympathy but lost focus as it wore on, drawing radicals of every stripe—national liberationists, countercultural folks who had always "liked Indians," Vietnam Veterans Against the War, even a few Chicanos, Asians, and Blacks.[25]

For seventy-one days it dragged on. For those inside the perimeter it was frequently marked by hunger, often by "stupefying boredom." A poll found ninety-three percent of Americans following events, with fifty-one percent supporting the occupation, but news coverage was declining. A bloody firefight was now given a mere ten seconds, maybe twenty, on the evening news. When the occupation finally ended after seventy-one days, the television cameras filmed scenes of mindless destruction that made the scene look like an abandoned war zone.

One federal marshal had been fatally wounded. A member of the tribal council was found burned to death in his car. The occupiers had suffered two dead, one of them a Cherokee scarcely known to the others. The second was Buddy Lamont, a local boy everyone knew, a Vietnam veteran and the only son of Agnes Lamont. Dressed in his uniform, in moccasins and beadwork, a pipe in his hands, he was buried next to the mass grave of the victims of 1890. His coffin was covered by the American flag and the flag of Wounded Knee—red, yellow, black, and white, for the four races and the four directions. His fellow warriors honored him with a hundred-gun salute.

Another casualty may have been the American Indian Movement, always more a movement than an organization. With the occupation of Wounded Knee AIM had reached its zenith and seemed to have nowhere to go but down. Many Indians as well as whites would witness its decline without sorrow. A loss that would endure is memorialized in the inscription on Buddy Lamont's grave:

"Two thousand came to Wounded Knee in 1973. One stayed."

Three years before the seizure of Wounded Knee, soon after the occupation of Alcatraz and unbeknown to the warriors of AIM, a talk by an Interior Department official in Omaha cast a menacing shadow over the Black Hills. The Assistant Secretary for Water and Power Development, addressing the major suppliers of power in the North Central United States, outlined a proposal to meet the growing demand for electric power. His remarks launched what became known as the North Central Power Study. The times called for "broad, imaginative and sophisticated" approaches, James R. Smith declared. The nation would not countenance a "static or repressive society" in which American citizens were forced to curtail their use of electric energy. The industry would be "hard put to find excuses" if it failed to utilize every tool at its command to prevent recurrent power shortages.

Not far to the north and west—in Montana, Wyoming, and the Dakotas—lay massive resources of coal and lignite. The challenge in tapping them was imposing because, for the first time in our history, irreparable harm to the natural environment had "captured the attention of our citizens." Smith proposed that the power industry, in concert with the Department of the Interior, "forgetting political considerations" in the interest of maximum economic benefit to their customers, should apply "innovative and imaginative thinking" to the development of those resources. In so doing they must of course "protect and enhance the environment in which we live."[26]

The *North Central Power Study* was published by the Department of the Interior in October 1971. It proposed construction of forty-two stations at the mouths of strip mines to generate electricity from coal and transmit it by high voltage lines to Midwest cities. The Black Hills would become the nucleus of a vast energy complex. The study made no reference to nuclear power, only to coal, lignite, and hydropower. The power generated would be immense. The Environmental Defense Fund calculated that it would be exceeded only by the total electric energy production of the United States or the Soviet Union and would emit far greater quantities of nitrogen oxides, sulfur dioxide, and particulate matter than were released into New York City and the Los Angeles Air Basin combined. Twenty-one sites were to be located in Montana and fifteen in Wyoming, directly upwind of the Black Hills and the Pine Ridge Reservation.

When a full-page ad in the *Billings Gazette* declared the plants would meet all federal and state requirements for air and water quality, the *Gazette* editorialized: "What might be highly desirable standards for Chicago, Gary, Indiana, or Birmingham would be an atrocious deterioration of the air quality in Montana." Ship the coal, if need be, and burn it elsewhere. "Let those who need it pay the air degradation price." A common sentiment was "Don't make Montana another Appalachia," a reference to the once-green valleys of Kentucky and West Virginia laid waste by strip mining. The Black Hills would be black, all right—with soot![27]

Engineers and power executives could be expected to take a narrowly utilitarian view of such an area, especially those with no connection to it. They saw a sparsely populated wasteland good only for grazing cattle, a remote, undeveloped region ripe for exploitation. But this "wasteland" had its defenders. Remote from whom? These were the sacred lands of the Crows. Ranchers cherished the "psychic income" of life in Montana and were ready to fight for it. Terms such as "overburden" and "spoilbanks" were alien to free and open spaces. With resources sufficient for thirty-five years, as the study concluded—or for *only* thirty-five years, as its critics saw it—the scheme promised to turn the whole area into the Ruhr Valley of America, a kind of hit-and-run proposition designed to fill a gap until unlimited nuclear energy could come on line.

The study itself cited difficulties. Adequate water supplies had been located, but minimizing water use was desirable, since "NCPS water supply is expensive." The participants "fully recognize the very real concern for the environment . . . and will incorporate whatever methods and facilities are necessary to minimize this impact." Many air pollution problems had yet to be solved. Aesthetic concerns dictated that high voltage transmission lines go around mountains rather than through them. In outlining a massive grid of power lines, not surprisingly, the study neglected to point out that several would cross Indian reservations. What with the escalating cost of uranium for nuclear power, federal officials saw development of the area's coal resources as urgent, simply inevitable. No thought was given to lower consumption of power, or to the recommendation by a presidential commission that consideration be given to "limiting growth where [growth] does not add demonstrably to quality of life."

The demand for water alone in such a semiarid region might have torpedoed the project, had it gone ahead as planned, but fourteen of the utilities declined to participate in the second, more detailed phase of the study. The first phase had stirred withering criticism, including a statement by Montana's Senator Lee Metcalf that he had "never seen another resource report that so casually disregarded the water needs of farmers, ranchers and local governments of the entire region." The strip mining rampage was halted in 1977 when the state of Montana, unwilling to risk letting the Yellowstone River run dry in time of drought, issued a moratorium on water permits. In the end the study was shelved because the utilities hoped to find a cheaper source of power. Reluctant to invest immense sums in transmission lines, they preferred to ship the coal out of state.[28]

Still, the alarm had been sounded. Ranchers, environmentalists, and Indians had been alerted to the threat behind an alliance of multinational corporations with public power districts and the federal government. Meanwhile, as the price of uranium rose higher and higher, leases on Black Hills land were being quietly issued to big energy consortiums. Colossal Kerr-McGee turned its attention to the Dakotas, as did the Tennessee Valley Authority, a government-owned corporation— a "fitting symbol," says Peter Matthiessen, of the corporate state, considered by AIM "the monolithic enemy of the Indian nations."[29]

One fear of Dennis Banks was becoming real. As AIM leaders contended with almost two hundred federal indictments arising from the occupation of Wounded Knee, they had to focus attention on their own defense. "I was real apprehensive by what I saw in the beginning," Banks recalled, "not at the attorneys but at the situation . . . . I was not afraid of a poor defense, but I was afraid that the political struggle would be lost because of now being tied to the courts." Banks took some of the blame for a leadership vacuum and assigned some to Russell Means. With AIM unable to provide continuous leadership to the Wounded Knee Legal Defense/Offense Committee, dissension among the defendants shattered the illusions of those who saw Indians as spiritually superior.[30]

Post mortems on AIM pointed to weaknesses that hampered its effectiveness. Jerry Wilkinson, the executive director of the National Indian Youth Council, a Cherokee, praised the organization for making Indians visible but cited criticisms often heard of its leaders: they "gave big speeches about the earth and the sacred Indian way by day and then got drunk or took dope in the disco by night." The civil rights movement benefited from clear goals and achievements, Wilkinson observed, but for Indians "it was generally more important to throw these [demands] in somebody's face than to get them to act on it." The movement had manifestoes aplenty but failed to "create a tradition of people relentlessly, ceaselessly, and uncompromisingly pursuing a long-range goal," and it became "terribly anti-intellectual." Wilkinson counseled a group of students that the modern world called for "a new kind of warrior," a warrrior who could acquire skills and work hard in support of his community, who could benefit from "intangibles the last movement sorely lacked, things like tolerance, kindness, good humor."[31]

Most South Dakota citizens would have welcomed those intangibles. A backlash had sprung from AIM's use of violence and threats of violence, and the profligate charges of racism flung about as if they were revealed truth. Speaking of the commando raids that had ransacked local taverns, a Rapid City woman voiced a common sentiment: "It set [the Indians] back a hundred years." Many citizens of Custer armed themselves against another assault on their town. Mrs. Hobart Gates, wife of the prosecutor who confronted AIM in the Custer riot, expressed frustration: "They came here because of our name. How can we possibly negotiate a symbol?"[32]

The political struggle continued at the leadership trial in Saint Paul in January 1974. As the law and order administration of Richard Nixon was unraveling in the Watergate scandals, Means and Banks aimed to try the case through the media. They sought to base their defense on the Treaty of 1868, reviewing the injustices of the previous century. "Let the public determine who is guilty at Wounded Knee," Banks told a rally on the eve of the trial. Eight months later Judge Fred Nichol, a lifelong resident of South Dakota, dismissed the case with an angry blast at government misconduct. Nichol accused the prosecutor of deceiving the Court. He found it hard to believe that the FBI he had revered for many years had fallen to such a low estate. "I guess this has been a bad year for justice," he said, "a bad year for justice."[33]

A major reverse for the Indian cause came soon thereafter in Federal District Court in Lincoln, Nebraska. A number of lesser cases had been consolidated in a hearing to determine if the treaty barred federal jurisdiction for crimes alleged at Wounded Knee. If so, some cases would be dismissed. In a case brought by the Cherokees in 1831, Chief Justice John Marshall had ruled that Indians comprised "a dependent domestic nation . . . in a state of pupilage." In January 1975, after an extended hearing in which dozens of witnesses testified, Judge Warren Urbom ruled for the government: "The conclusion that Indian tribes do not have complete sovereignty is irresistible," he wrote. White Americans might "retch at the recollection" of a history "pocked by duplicity" on the part of the United States government, Urbom acknowledged, but "recognizing what was wrong did not necessarily determine what was right." The courts could not apply remedies reserved to the executive and legislative branches. The defendants were addressing the wrong forum.

The truly devastating blow came in 1980 when the Supreme Court affirmed a Court of Claims decision that the 1877 act had violated the Fifth Amendment in taking the Black Hills, but awarded not land but money—roughly $105 million.[34]

Uranium finally brought the cowboys together with the Indians. After World War II uranium was discovered in the southwestern region of the Black Hills, near Edgemont. The Atomic Energy Commission established a station there in 1953 and began searching in other parts of the Hills. The birth of a domestic uranium market stirred a feverish interest in the Black Hills. With federal encouragement, prospecting intensified.

Soon more than a million acres were claimed or leased by twenty-five corporations. Widespread exploratory drilling showed great promise. Governmental agencies were quietly making preliminary surveys on Indian reservations.

The keen interest in uranium caught the attention of Dennis Banks, who issued a statement that was highlighted in a 1974 FBI document: AIM now intended to shift its emphasis to halting exploitation of resources on Indian land. The Federal Energy Commission reported that Indian lands had produced $349 million in uranium alone. The Northern Cheyenne Tribal Council unanimously voted to cancel existing coal leases. The Crow nation followed suit. Nevertheless, the Interior Department endorsed the grand design of the North Central Power Study in its final environmental impact statement in 1977. It would inflict enormous damage, most likely irreparable, on the Great Plains, the NCPS statement acknowledged. In the shift to "mineral extractive use," Indian people would lose their "special relationship to the land," but they would also lose their "isolation" and be brought more into the "mainstream" of American life—the kind of talk that AIM leaders denounced as cultural genocide. Meanwhile, the power industry, undaunted by scarce water resources and stout popular resistance, kept to its plan to establish thirteen coal-fired plants.[35]

Potentially far more lethal was the proposal for a nuclear energy "park" with as many as twenty-five reactors. Atomic scientists at the time were debating whether the pile of tailings from a typical uranium mine would kill three hundred and ninety-four people in a gigawatt-year or a mere two hundred, asking themselves if we had the right to impose the lethal consequences on thousands of future generations for a few decades of electric power. The Tennessee Valley Authority and Union Carbide went on drilling exploratory holes in the Black Hills, leaving most of them unplugged. They proposed to "dewater" the Madison Aquifer, the great underlying reservoir fed by the Black Hills. *Water, the very source of life!* The holes they were punching threatened to contaminate the aquifers and release radiation into the atmosphere. When Union Carbide, without a permit, sank a two thousand foot hole alongside ancient petroglyphs in Craven Canyon, near Edgemont, the opposition mobilized.[36]

In March 1979 a mixed group alarmed by the threat met to organize resistance. Two days before the meeting, a major nuclear accident took place in Pennsylvania. The Black Hills Alliance was born in the wake of Three Mile Island. For the first time Indians united with environmentalists and a few ranchers to employ all legal means to slow or halt the destruction, though the Western South Dakota Stockgrowers Association opposed the move. In defining their mission the Alliance coined a term, National Sacrifice Area—an area singled out for devastation for the greater good of the nation. The heart of it would be the Black Hills.

The Black Hills Alliance drew support from a wide range of environmentalists and antinuclear and anti-powerline activists. They opened an office in downtown Rapid City and set out to educate South Dakotans on the dangers they saw in nuclear mining and milling, water depletion and contamination, and other environmental threats. One position that complicated their efforts was their decision to support the Black Hills claim of the Sioux. AIM was specifically excluded from the Alliance, as poison to white South Dakotans, but its sister organization joined—WARN, or Women of All Red Nations. One of WARN's leaders was a cousin of Russell Means, who had resigned from AIM once again after his leadership had been questioned. When Means was released from prison, he enlisted on his own. He found the Alliance doing well, supported by white ranchers, "an entire generation of feisty, independent-minded people who didn't want to see multinationals come in and pillage the Black Hills. . . . I loved shaking the callused hands of those old ranchers."[37]

The Alliance's most heralded project was the International Survival Gathering in July 1980. Widely publicized in advance, it drew participants from all over the world to the Kammerer ranch northeast of Rapid City, adjoining Ellsworth Air Force Base. Part of the ranch had been taken by eminent domain to expand the runways. Third generation on his land, Marvin Kammerer is a rancher who inherited a sense of responsibility from his German forebears. He has played a leading role in causes such as Ranchers for Peace as well as the Black Hills Alliance, and served on the board of South Dakota Peace and Justice.[38]

The International Survival Gathering opened in mid-July, shortly after the U. S. Supreme Court affirmed the Court of Claims award of seventeen and a half million dollars to the Sioux for loss of the Black Hills. With the accrued interest, the sum now totaled one hundred and six million dollars. The Oglala Tribal Council filed a claim in federal court for eleven *billion*. The Survival Gathering followed upon festivities in Deadwood, where a parade had just been held on behalf of a famous brothel, recently shut down. There was nothing of Woodstock about the Gathering, Molly Ivins observed in the *New York Times*. Entering the ranch beneath a sign reading "No alcohol, no drugs, no firearms," she said, participants mingled with a "wonderfully eclectic gathering, featuring old left, new left, Indians, earnest academics, the straightest of straight farmers and ranchers (slightly bemused to find themselves fallen in with long-hairs) and one busload of fine, old-fashioned furry freaks from California."[39]

Security was provided by ex-Green Berets with walkie-talkies. As the proceedings got under way, B-52s often roared over the tents and tipis—good visual aids, a reporter noted. There were teachers from Sweden and Germany, film crews from Amsterdam and Japan. One of the displays was a traveling exhibit sponsored by the Department of Energy and TVA. Workshops and presentations focused on alternative energy sources, the effects of radiation, the corporate grab for land and water, defense of the family farm, low-key discussions that impressed visitors by their seriousness and concentration. A California professor drew contrasts between community accountability for the future and short-term corporate exploitation. A representative from the American Friends Service Committee spoke on the hazards of transporting nuclear waste. Indian activists lamented the destruction of families by social service agencies. The local media apparently ignored a speech by Russell Means in which he vociferously damned Marxism along with capitalism: just another expression of genocidal European mind-set, he said, both of them singing the "same old song." Evenings featured concerts by pop celebrities like Jackson Browne and Bonnie Raitt.

At one time or another, ten or twelve thousand people attended over the ten days. Business picked up in Rapid City, though the call was more often for salads and juices than for meat and potatoes. The apprehensions of neighboring ranchers, by their own testimony, proved needless. A spokesman for Ellsworth Air Force Base said, "We haven't had problem one with them." The only damage left behind was wear and tear on the roads and on some grass on the host ranch. Yes, said Marvin Kammerer, as the tents were folded up on the last day, his pastureland had suffered from the tramping of thousands of feet. But what was important, "whether I've got grass now or whether I've got a place to live on, and my kids have got a place to live on, years from now?"[40]

During the year to come, the Black Hills Alliance showed signs of fraying around the edges. For their part, the AIMsters were attempting to clean up their image on the reservation. They established an Indian-run health center and a radio station at Porcupine and worked to ban alcohol, the source of so much trouble. During a discussion of the Black Hills question, a white lawyer working with the Alliance informed Russell Means there was no law against camping in the Hills. "Suddenly," Means says, "I knew what to do—just set up a camp and reclaim the Black Hills. Possession is nine-tenths of the white man's law." They would go in unarmed, with the sacred pipe, to make clear they had peaceful intentions. Most Lakotas greeted the idea with skepticism, unwilling to "risk their lives for the Black Hills, which seemed far from their homes," but the Means brothers were determined. Since Russell was on parole and could not involve himself in anything that might result in law-breaking, brother Bill took over management of the venture.[41]

On April 4, 1981, the anniversary of Martin Luther King's assassination, a caravan of cars with some fifty people, about half of them Indians, drove into the Black Hills and set up a camp at Victoria Lake, twelve miles southwest of Rapid City. In lightly falling snow they pitched a couple of tents and christened the place Camp Yellow Thunder, after Raymond Yellow Thunder, who had died at Gordon. The lake was more nearly a pond, its dam having been breached after the Rapid City flood of 1972. It was situated on federal land in a beautiful small canyon encircled on three sides by cliffs. The camp was seen as the first step in regaining the Black Hills. Matthew King, a Lakota elder, filed a claim for eight hundred acres of surrounding federal land, based on the Fort Laramie Treaty of 1868 and the Freedom of Religion Act. AIM proposed to establish a church and school to instruct their children in traditional Lakota ways.

Camp Yellow Thunder soon became known around the world. Initially, local authorities reacted with watchful waiting. The governor was unruffled: "just a bunch of kids camping out." A friendly ranger came by to suggest they get a permit for open fires. The supervisor of the Black Hills National Forest announced they could stay as long as they wished, provided they broke no laws. Response from Indian sources was more complicated. Vine Deloria termed the idea "one of the most progressive proposals to be received by the federal government in the last century of Indian relationships," but Women of All Red Nations withdrew from both the Alliance and Camp Yellow Thunder. Tribal officials reacted strongly, accusing AIM of creating division, jeopardizing the Sioux attempt to reclaim the Black Hills. The days of confrontation and demands were over, said one. "We must deal with the courts and the politicians on a professional level." More critical yet was Mario Gonzalez, tribal attorney for the Oglala Sioux, who had been working quietly within the legal structure. Now "AIM comes along and jeopardizes the lawsuit . . . and they're splashed all over the front page."[42]

A "more mellow and cagier" movement now, in a reporter's phrase, AIM took pains to comply with Forest Service regulations and the letter of the law. Bill Means told a group at the camp that the courts had done nothing but legitimize theft of the Hills. Now the tables were turned; they were going to use some of the laws the white man had used against the Indians. Ironically, being anything but woodsmen, they had to call upon a bearded white mountain man to show them how to put up the tipis they'd purchased from hippies in Washington state.

Still, said Russell Means, it proved to be the finest and most important time in his life. He felt a sudden love for the land, for their "leafy U-shaped valley." Watching the play of fireflies, he began to grasp "the beauty and grace of being in the present, of living in harmony with everything in the natural world." Then in June his son Hank, drunk out of his mind, was arrested for a robbery during which a priest had died of a heart attack. Means found it hard to forgive himself for all the years he had not been around for Hank, "all the times when my drinking provided him with the wrong example to follow."[43]

The camp's occupants stayed on for the summer and through the following winter. The Forest Service, refusing to grant them a special-use permit for a permanent settlement of eight hundred acres, took them to court in November 1982 to secure an eviction. In lengthy proceedings a district judge in Sioux Falls ruled in 1987 that the Service must allow establishment of a religious settlement, a ruling overturned on appeal. In 1989 the U. S. Supreme Court refused to hear any further appeal, and the occupation ended.

Along the way the camp's population had dwindled from forty to twenty-five. Interest gradually fell away. The district ranger's routine winter visits to assess environmental damage, always with advance notice, would find only two or three tipis. Several sun dances were approved during the summers, with fire permits and arrangements for sanitation and parking. When the camp was finally closed, all that was left in the valley was a guard shack and a tipi or two. The cleanup required was insignificant by one account, an ecological disaster by another.[44]

A casualty along the way was the Black Hills Alliance. For Russell Means its purpose had always been about "Indian people returning to our holy land." Soon after his son's sentencing he addressed the Alliance's board of directors. They had achieved a moratorium on strip mining, Means told them, and driven out the big corporations. The ranchers had what they wanted. The focal point and priority for all funding now should be Camp Yellow Thunder. Some of the white directors raised objections, whereupon the Means brothers staged a coup, removing all the non-Indians except Marvin Kammerer. When the always sympathetic Peter Matthiessen told Russell Means it was a pity the Alliance had lost its biracial balance, Means snapped at him harshly: suggestions unwelcome! For a year Kammerer stayed on the board to see it through, but when it became clear their only interest was Camp Yellow Thunder he left to devote his energy to other causes.

Thus did the Indians rid the Alliance of its last cowboy.[45]

Whatever symbolic resonance Yellow Thunder Camp may have had elsewhere, it was all but ignored in the Black Hills. To the Forest Service the camp was a very minor episode in Black Hills history, as evanescent as the flash of fireflies along Victoria Creek. From the outset the Black Hills National Forest had been unusual among the national forests, established not in a remote area but in one where development was well under way, a more complicated challenge. Managing timber, mining, water resources, and grazing rights, while providing fire protection, took all its energies, especially with growing pressures for recreation and development. A dramatic challenge soon appeared in the offing, threat or promise, according to your point of view—a bill introduced in the United States Senate.

In the nineteen-seventies Bill Bradley, a professional athlete before he became a U. S. senator from New Jersey, began giving basketball clinics for young Lakotas at Pine Ridge. Troubled by what he saw there, and by federal policies that he felt had turned descendants of the original Americans into relics, Bradley wanted to do something to remedy the injustice of it. "Confronting the dark pages of our history," he wrote, "is essential to getting beyond them." In 1983 he was visited in his Senate office by a delegation of Sioux headed by Gerald Clifford, the well educated mixed-blood Lakota coordinating the Black Hills Steering Committee. With one representative from each Sioux tribe, the committee was charged with drafting and securing passage of legislation to return most of the Black Hills to the Sioux. Their suggestion, in Bradley's words: "a big-picture reform that remedied injustice."[46]

On July 17, 1985, with the most generous intentions, Bradley introduced the bill drafted by the Black Hills Steering Committee, Senate Bill 1453. The Sioux Nation Black Hills Act would return more than a million acres of federal land in western South Dakota, including most of the Black Hills, to the Sioux. This "re-established area" would become the Sioux Black Hills Forest and the Sioux Park. Mount Rushmore would be exempt, as would all private land and all existing timber, mining, and grazing rights. No mention was made of Custer State Park. The Sioux would also receive almost two hundred million dollars, the money allotted them by the Court of Claims.

The response in South Dakota was furious, if not contemptuous. Generous indeed, with other people's land! An outsider like Bradley had no business meddling in matters he knew nothing about. The state's congressional delegation came out in fervent opposition to the bill. The governor challenged its constitutionality. A Wyoming senator threatened to introduce a bill returning a million acres of New Jersey, along with the Statue of Liberty, to the Leni-Lenape Indians. Bradley had accepted as fact a claim rejected by historians: that the Lakotas had been in the Black Hills long before the Chippewas pushed the Sioux out of Minnesota. He may have been swayed by Clifford's belief the Sioux had been there for at least ten thousand years. Presented in 1997 with the views of historians on tribal origins, Gerald Clifford told me simply, "We have a different view."

Prospects for passage of the bill were very slight, "like crossing a vast attitude desert," said Bradley, "an inch at a time." Then a millionaire businessman from California made his appearance, Phillip J. Stevens, who claimed to be part Sioux, announcing he had come to save his people. The Bradley bill was a sellout, Stevens declared. The tribes should put him in charge and demand three billion dollars, along with the Black Hills. His agents managed to persuade two of the eight Sioux tribes to withdraw their support, which doomed the bill.[47]

The Bradley bill was expressly designed to "preserve the sacred Black Hills from desecration." Its first congressional finding declared the Black Hills the "sacred center of aboriginal territory of the Sioux Nation." Today the word "sacred" is often linked with Black Hills as if three words had been fused: *sacredblackhills*. But such a coinage seems to be recent. The Fort Laramie treaties of 1851 and 1868 make no reference to the Black Hills as sacred, nor apparently did the negotiations with the Allison and Manypenny commissions. The argument then centered around provisions and price—in dollars. Red Cloud told the Allison Commission that in exchange for the Hills he wanted seven coming generations to be fed. Spotted Tail wanted the money left in trust with the President; the Lakotas would live on the interest. Little Bear wanted forthrightly to "get rich" on the Black Hills, their "house of gold."[48]

The chiefs weren't holy men, of course, but tribal leaders endeavoring to get the best deal they could under impossible circumstances. But historians find little or no hard evidence that nineteenth century Lakotas regarded the Hills as sacred. One historian suggests the theme surfaced in the 1970s, when their descendants devised a new strategy. Having failed to get the land back by legal argument, Donald Worster concludes, they attempted a "second maneuver," one designed to "touch the sensibilities of a nation of churchgoers where legalisms had failed." In their Senate testimony and during interviews with journalists, he notes, Lakotas often "fell back on this religious argument like a speaker slipping into his native dialect, weary of speaking a foreign tongue." The Black Hills were more than property, they declared, they were "sacred space . . . the heart of everything that is." One elder said they were "the heart of our home and the home of our heart," an exalted, holy place—their Jerusalem, their Mecca, "beyond any form of compensation."[49]

A useful observation in 1996 by Dave Ruppert, an ethnographer for the National Park Service, finds an artificial distinction at work here. Referring specifically to a district court ruling on the use of Devils Tower, Ruppert suggests such places are better seen as critical *cultural* sites: "The judge and the climbers see it as 'religious,' but Native Americans don't make a distinction between secular and sacred. They call it 'sacred' because they figure it will make more sense to us—it fits our lexicon."[50]

Clearly this religious argument is also a sincere cry of frustration and longing, with faint echoes of the yearning for a Messiah that led to the Ghost Dance. If any Lakota in more recent times embodied it, surely it was Black Elk, the revered holy man born into the old free days. Nowhere in *Black Elk Speaks* or *The Sixth Grandfather* does Black Elk explicitly designate the Black Hills as sacred land, though he once told Neihardt in passing that he thought the Black Hills were the place the Thunder-being told an early chief would be their promised land.[51] As a boy, when Red Cloud heard the *Wasichus* wanted to take the Hills away from them, it only made him sad: "It was such a good place to play and the people were always happy in that country." As an old man he spoke of Harney Peak as "the center of the world," where the spirits took him in his great vision, the place from which he beheld "the whole hoop of the world" below. He went there in person with John Neihardt to address the Grandfathers. To hear Black Elk's plea, in his old age and sorrow, to "make my people live" is to experience great depth and power.

Such feelings cannot be disregarded or brushed aside. Nor can the assertion by historians that the Lakotas never regarded the Black Hills *in their entirety* as sacred deny the possibility that *particular* sites served them for what we think of as religious purposes. New evidence continues to surface. In 1986, after extensive research into Lakota oral tradition, Charlotte Black Elk, a great-granddaughter of Nicholas Black Elk and the wife of Gerald Clifford, testified before the Select Committee on Indian Affairs of the United States Senate. In her prepared statement, along with six designations for the Black Hills as a whole, she lists forty distinct

Lakota names for specific places in the Black Hills: five names for Devils Tower, four for Harney Peak and Bear Butte, three for Inyan Kara and Reynolds Prairie, and two for Wind Cave. More recently, Linea Sundstrom, a professional archeologist then on contract with the Forest Service, identified sixteen locations as traditional Lakota sacred places. In 2004 Sundstrom reinforced the case with persuasive evidence in her book *Storied Stone.*[52]

Forest Service policy today calls for rangers, when they come upon places where Indian people go for "medicine," to inquire of local native people where the boundaries are, in order to respect those sites. The locations are not made public. The *Cultural Resources Overview* of the Black Hills National Forest lists dozens of prehistoric sites. In a joint effort to identify and protect sacred places, the Historical Preservation Officer meets regularly with Lakota traditionals and tribal officials. To date no "hard" sites have been established—public sites that can be protected and interpreted.[52]

Whatever the merits of their wider claim, one conclusion is inescapable, on firm historical grounds, beyond argument: Lakota people cherish distinct, particular places in the Black Hills that can be called *sacred,* often places valued by whites as well.

Mitakuye oyasin: "all my relatives" or "we are all related," as it comes across in the cumbrous ways we have of interpreting one language and its people to another. I cannot speak the words as a native, but I want to conclude this final chapter of a long story with a personal anecdote that suggests how we can indeed all be related to one another and entangled, people to people. Some years ago I set out to track Ben Mills, Red Cloud's choice for his agent. Mills may have been my grandfather's Uncle Ben back in Pennsylvania, who "went out west and lived with the Indians." Both men had blue eyes and red hair. The descendants of Red Cloud's Ben knew little of their white progenitor but were intensely curious to learn. They offered me all the leads they could, particularly the elders, who still spoke Lakota and remembered their parents, if not their grandfather.

One granddaughter was especially helpful, Lucy Mills Hall, one of the dearest old women I've ever known. She was so kind and generous to me that sometimes I was reluctant to visit her, because she always loaded me down with gifts. Lucy had some personal quality I've never found words for. She lived in a small town in Nebraska, south of the Black Hills. Well into her eighties she still drove to Pine Ridge alone in her battered little blue Datsun. Her mother had toured with Buffalo Bill's

Wild West show. The day I first called on Lucy she entrusted me, a man she had never met, with her only photo of her mother all decked out for the show. In my annual pilgrimages to the Hills I always dropped in to see her.

Then one year Lucy wasn't there. I felt her loss as if she were a member of my own family. In a very real sense she was, because in the process of tracking down Ben Mills I found all his descendants I met to be welcoming and helpful. I've never been able to establish definitively that he was, or was not, my own blood relative, but over the years I've come to feel they are *family*, these Lakota Millses. It's painful to see the old ones dying, even as the young move on with their lives.

Crossing the reservation one day on my way to Gordon, I saw an elderly Lakota woman standing alongside the road with a small overnight bag. I stopped for her. She was going to Gordon, she said, to clean houses for some white ladies. As we rode along I told her I had been born in Gordon, though I'd never lived there. I mentioned the name Raymond Yellow Thunder—how terrible it was, what they'd done to him."He was my cousin," she said, or maybe it was brother-in-law. "He was a nice old man. He never hurt anybody."

I dropped her off at the house of one of those white ladies and went out to the cemetery to visit the graves of my parents and grand-parents and five uncles and aunts who had died in infancy. Then I headed west to Chadron to call on Lucy in her little house on the wrong side of the tracks and take her out for pizza, a favorite of hers. After more talk in her tiny living room, I loaded up the gifts she had for me and set out for the Hills as dusk settled in.

That elderly woman who rode with me into Gordon comes to mind whenever I see the name Yellow Thunder, but I miss Lucy, and now, if you'll pardon me, or even if you won't, I'm going back on the road west to see the dear old woman whose mother toured with Buffalo Bill. Onward!

PROSPECTS

There they stand, looming over the plains in all their grandeur and mystery, their mantle of woods and meadows prey as always to fire and storm. Now even their granite foundations are subject to depredation. In their timeless wisdom we can imagine these mountains contemplating the vanity of human claims like an exasperated parent, an indulgent mother with a band of squabbling adolescents. Children, she pleads, what are you *thinking*? If you love this place, if you cherish my woods and streams, my four-leggeds and wingeds and my other human children—yes, if you *love* me, you have a home here.

If you don't, keep out!

Is anyone listening? The contention never ends. Ironies abound. The Black Hills were assigned to the conquerors who drove out the Kiowas and the Crows in a treaty violated by random Lakota bands even before they were unlawfully seized by the United States. They were then promised to settlers and prospectors, who built homes and businesses and undertook mining, ranching, and timbering. On those promises, towns were built, national forests and parks established, granite monuments, state parks, summer cabins. Tourists were beckoned. After a century of settlement the Supreme Court, while deploring the way the Black Hills were seized, affirmed a cash award to the Sioux for their loss, an award refused by the tribe to date.

A Lakota tribal judge and law professor, Frank Pommersheim, has called the Sioux claim on the Black Hills a "sleeping giant." While it slumbers, this giant, real or imagined, the pressures on the Hills increase relentlessly, year after year. Tourism gathers force, "ranchettes" proliferate.

In time the Black Hills as we know them will be overwhelmed by what we choose to call progress. The pressures to make them a wasteland for the greater good of the nation seem to have been eluded for the time being, but to what purpose, if they are to be converted into a Regional Sacrifice Area from within? Ghosts emanate from the very images employed to promote business—the staged powwows, the fake Indian gewgaws, even the artful tributes in sculpture and oils depicting bygone days. The Lakotas are an enduring people with a long time horizon. No one who knows them believes they will leave things unruffled forever. There will be no truly *quiet* title to the Black Hills.[1]

What's to be done, at this point? One proposal, advanced by historian Donald Worster: return them to the Lakotas. And why not? he asks. Has the stewardship of the white settlers been exemplary? Can anyone say justice has been done to the dispossessed? Would such a move heal a deeply felt wound among the Indians without hurting the whites? Surely yes, Worster replies. "The Black Hills, or some significant portion of them, should be returned to the Lakota people."[2]

A neat solution: simple, even beguiling to those removed from the scene, with no stake in the outcome. What could be better for the Hills than the Lakota principle of respect for the earth? Recall the wisdom of the old Lakota articulated by Luther Standing Bear: "He knew that man's heart, away from nature, becomes hard; he knew that lack of respect for growing, living things soon led to lack of respect for humans too." The story of the Black Hills can only reinforce the view that "the white man," that mythical creature, has given himself a lofty place in nature, arrogating the right to "conquer" her. Yet no living person had a hand in the seizure of the Hills. After more than a century the resident population has rights of its own.[3]

A few years ago, to satisfy my curiosity, I paid a visit to the abandoned site of Yellow Thunder Camp. No sign of its activity remained. As I clambered over the small dam of huge boulders and walked along Victoria Creek in a beautiful canyon surrounded on three sides by cliffs, I came under the spell of what Russell Means called "our leafy U-shaped valley." It was impossible not to empathize with the aspirations and hopes inspired there. Dreams die hard.

Who *owns* the Black Hills? Many have cherished them, whites as well as Indians. In 1861, on his way to Washington to assume the presidency as the South was proclaiming the Union dissolved, Lincoln asked rhetorically if the United States belongs to *all* the people. "Where is the mysterious, original right, from principle," Lincoln asked, "for a certain district of the country, with inhabitants, by merely being called a

State, to play tyrant over all its own citizens and deny the authority of everything greater than itself?" Substitute "tribe" for "State," and the issue is joined. Can a tribe deny the final authority of the United States?[4]

Legally, the courts have put the issue to rest. The moral question comes down, finally, to contending myths. On the basis of revered oral tradition handed down through the generations, one party claims possession since "time immemorial," its people having emerged from the Earth on this very spot, the Center of Everything That Is. The other, founding privilege upon a doctrine of discovery propounded centuries ago by European powers, holds that manifest destiny, Biblically sanctified, confers the right to possess "unused lands" and turn them to the purposes of the Almighty.

Once digested by a people, notes Ronald Wright, most history becomes myth, "an arrangement of the past, whether real or imagined, in patterns that resonate with a culture's deepest values and aspirations. . . . [Myths] are the maps by which cultures navigate through time." The myth of the invader is triumphalist; the myth of the dispossessed has to explain catastrophe and find ways to overcome it. A generous view would take both myths into account, recognizing, as Wright points out, that if "the vanquished culture is to survive at all, its myths must provide it with a rugged terrain in which to resist the invader and do battle with *his* myths."[5]

Until recent years the histories have been written by the victors. Given the impasse, where to begin? Perhaps with the third party in this fray—the silent one, the Hills themselves, with what we might call practical love. Why not listen to the mountains? Who *cares* for them, in either sense? How can their finite resources and limited expanse best be preserved for another day and generation? What wealth of generosity and imagination exists to be drawn upon?

A glance at the map offers a leading clue. Most of the Black Hills is colored green: National Forest. Though it shares responsibility with parks and monuments, as well as with private land, the chief steward for the past century has been the United States Forest Service. How well has it managed that challenge? Before establishment of the Black Hills Reserve in 1897, exploitation was ruinous and shameful, as it was in the country at large, where the Secretary of the Interior saw "wanton, barbarous, disgraceful vandalism; a spendthrift people recklessly wasting its heritage." How much have actions and attitudes changed since that time?

The Black Hills National Forest is distinct in that its stewardship began in a region already under development, which makes its mission uniquely challenging. Resistance to managerial schemes from people living in the Hills has taken many forms. Perennial feuds pit landowners against the Forest Service on matters of access, grazing, lumbering, and land use. In 1970 a Colorado corporation proposed a recreational and cultural development featuring a visitor's center on top of Harney Peak. Sylvan Lake was to feature a Plains Indian cultural center, state historical museum, and amphitheater. The Forest Service appeared to favor the plan. No thanks! said a citizens campaign that produced a Sierra Club chapter, and the proposal died in the planning stage.[6]

Fire control illustrates the complexities. The Jasper fire, set by an arsonist in 2000, burned 84,000 acres west of Custer, the worst fire in recorded Black Hills history. In a sparsely settled area, luckily, it took only one summer cabin and damaged two houses. But the favored policy of letting fire take its natural restorative course can hardly be applied in wooded areas where people have built homes. Nor does fire respect jurisdictions. The Cicero Peak fire in 1990 began in the National Forest but, after sweeping north six or seven miles, turned east over Mount Coolidge and rolled south through Custer State Park, consuming five cabins, blackening slopes.

The dramatic changes throughout the country in recent decades are mirrored in recreational use of the Black Hills: tourism, hiking and camping, snowmobiling and skiing. Logging is no longer the economic power it once was. The Forest Service estimates that recreation, hunting and fishing in national forests nationwide contribute almost forty times as much income to the economy as logging, which has become a drain on tax revenues. In a recent five-year period the General Accounting Office reported that logging programs had cost taxpayers two billion dollars.[7]

Visionary schemes tend to blur when they encounter actualities. The Sierra Club opposes all logging on federal lands, even salvage operations, a policy impossible to implement in the Black Hills and foolish, given the increasing potential for conflagrations worse than the Jasper fire—a policy now rejected by federal law. The Forest Service's management plan outlines nine goals, including high-quality service to the public. Its governing philosophy begins by asking what the forest needs in order to be a healthy ecosystem, fifty years down the road, determining from that how much timber can be harvested, a marked change from the traditional "tree farm" system. The Illingworth photos from the Custer expedition are used as an important guide to the natural, pre-development condition of the Hills. The management plan for Custer State Park, for its part, aims to provide for both people and nature, with the natural systems predominant and the activities of management and visitors in harmony with them. It aspires to leave future generations a landscape of mixed-grass prairie along with diverse native forestlands and surface water systems hospitable to wildlife.[8]

The Forest Service makes efforts to reach out to Lakota people. The Historic Preservation Officer meets regularly with Lakota elders and safeguards the privacy of sites known to be sacred. New employees are schooled in forest history and the spiritual connections of Indian peoples with the Black Hills. Two Lakota representatives sit on the Forest's diverse new fifteen-member advisory board, which former Supervisor John Twiss will consider a success if members eventually come to respect each other's values. When he talks to Lakota people, they always tell him the Black Hills belong to the Lakotas; the elders tell them to insist on that. At the suggestion of Neal Poor Bear, an Oglala Lakota, the Forest has developed a crew of firefighters, the Tatanka Hotshots—*tatanka* for buffalo— designed to involve Lakotas and members from other tribes to train for positions in the Forest Service. A crack crew of twenty made up of white and Cherokee, Yurok, and Blackfoot as well as Lakota, the Hotshots have served with distinction in most of the Western states.[9]

A good model for efforts to preserve the natural values of the Hills can be found in the Black Hills Program of the Nature Conservancy. Launched in 1996 as a one-man operation, the Conservancy has opened fresh avenues to conservation by its non-confrontational approach, emphasizing cooperation instead of conflict. Through outright acquisition, or by establishment of easements whereby ranchers and landowners can continue operating while assured that future development will be banned, the Conservancy has established a significant footprint in the Southern Hills: the Cheyenne River Canyons Project centered in Cascade Valley, comprised of more than forty thousand acres.

Historically, homesteading and settlement have taken place not on hilltops but in riparian areas, along streams—winter range for wild- life. Cascade Creek and Cascade Spring, with its warm springs maintaining a constant flow at 68 degrees, provide a unique riverine ecosystem, ice- free year round, a microclimate that fosters southern maidenhair ferns, stream orchids, beaked spikebrush, and tulip gentians, all species not to be found elsewhere in the Black Hills or on the surrounding plains. The bird population is copious and varied. Two peregrine sightings have recently been made during breeding season. Forty-six species of butterflies have been identified. The efforts to maintain an intact ecosystem are anchored in the Nathaniel and Mary Whitney Preserve dedicated in 1999, which now, with purchase of the Hutton Ranch, conserves 17,368 acres. Land swaps with the Forest Service continue.[10]

Talk of returning federal lands in the Black Hills to the Sioux has a surreal air today. The courts have spoken. In his 1975 opinion Judge Urbom concluded that the tribe was addressing the wrong forum. At some point, conceivably, widespread public sympathy could win the day for them in Congress, remote as that seems. If such a transfer were politically feasible, to whom would the Black Hills be transferred? To the Sioux Nation, a group of allies often at odds with each other? To the Oglalas? To elected tribal governments spurned by traditionals for playing the white man's game? To a council of elders, selected by whom? If the cry is for *all*, it will surely be *nothing*. How would the principle of respect for the earth be manifested, in practical terms? What experience would Lakotas today bring to such a challenge?

The struggle over the Black Hills is hardly the only conflict between natives of the continent and the immigrant population, merely the biggest one, with the widest repercussions. Is there any hope for meaningful resolution? Perhaps yes, with goodwill and unflinching honesty. Where cultures collide, conflict can be creative. "Surprises crackle, like electric arcs, between the interfaces of culture," Robert Hughes has written. "These interfaces are where history now seeks itself; they will be the historical sites of the future. You cannot remake the past in the name of affirmative action. But you can find narratives that haven't been written, histories of people or groups that have been distorted and ignored and refresh history by bringing them in."[11]

Narratives that haven't been written? Histories that have been distorted and ignored? Certainly yes, to both, in the Black Hills. But can the present clash be called an interface when the parties scarcely talk to each other? Surprises would surely crackle if and when *their* stories truly met *ours*. A bicultural literacy campaign is clearly in order, especially among whites, because in their stories most of us are functionally illiterate. Frank Pommersheim, a calm Lakota voice, cites the importance of narrative and story. He speaks of a certain "pride" of difference, a "measured separatism," borrowing a phrase from Marsha Minow, who sees something to gain from the other's perspective: "*a corrective lens*, another partial view, not the absolute truth." And there are fundamental human considerations. Deep down, writes Vine Deloria, Jr., the cries about loss of land and way of life and the propensity of whites to shift the terms of the debate in their own favor, are "cries about dignity, complaints about the lack of respect." Deloria sums it up with Sitting Bull's observation: "It is not necessary that eagles be crows."[12]

"A people without history is like wind on the buffalo grass," goes another old Lakota saying. Here the histories diverge so sharply that no common narrative is likely to emerge, but who knows what correctives might emanate from a genuine conversation? And in a point far too often ignored, the Hills face mortal threats. A common menace can offer a common hope. Both parties here could do worse than listen to that other, that *third*, silent voice: the Black Hills themselves. In the common interest of conserving their natural and human values while fostering genuine hospitality, both parties might step back from hardened positions—from the easy "half-truth history of the celebratory mind," on the one hand, and the presenting of myth as history, on the other—to listen and reflect. "In the end," says the Senegalese conservationist Baba Dioum, "we will conserve only what we love, we will love only what we understand, and we will understand only what we are taught."[113]

Who knows but what the mountains can speak?

Connections

Why should the Black Hills have such a hold on a man who's lived half his life on the Central Coast of California? It's a fair question, and in telling this story I've tried to stay out of the way. Now let me tell you how I developed such ties, and such biases. Born on the plains, I love mountains. I've lived in mountains on several continents but always find myself drawn back to the Hills, a vital presence in my life from the beginning

The Black Hills were always the Promised Land. As Black Elk was telling John Neihardt his story back in the Thirties, I was taking my first steps on the South Dakota prairie just down the road, in Oelrichs. Black Elk's story meant nothing to me at the age of two. The Great Depression was deepening, the dust was blowing, but for one small boy the summer of 1932 had nothing to do with books or the nomination of Franklin Delano Roosevelt. The men in our family were laying the logs for our cabin. The next summer, after the logs had settled, my father finished the cabin and we spent a few weeks there.

For the two following years we spent the whole summer at the cabin. We did the things all children do. We played in the creek, charged up and down the Hills. We swung in a tire swing suspended from a limb that has held up now for three generations. Sometimes we went up to a mountain not so very far away where some man with a funny name was bossing a job blasting rock. I knew something big was going on up there. We watched the men at work, tiny men, seen from below, hanging by what looked like ropes. In the summer of 1935 came another something big. Our father took us to see the Stratosphere Bowl, a hole as big as a valley, to see a huge shiny ball. The "gondola" was attached to a gigantic bag that was supposed to lift two men high into the air. Next morning at dawn we drove to the top of Mount Coolidge to watch it go up, but nothing happened. When Explorer Two finally went up in November, we were back in Oelrichs. We loaded into the car and followed it for miles as the wind carried it east over the reservation, higher and higher, a tall, enormous balloon tapering down to a tiny ball like the marble we called a steely. Explorer II rose to 74,000 feet, a world record, and landed more than two hundred miles to the east—a pioneering first in space flight.

That pursuit was the last adventure with our father. A few weeks later we went to North Dakota for Christmas, where my uncle lay desperately ill with pneumonia. He recovered, but my father contracted the disease. In that coldest winter in decades he died on the day after New Year's, leaving a young widow with three children, our patrimony the cabin he built for us. On our long journey back to South Dakota with his body my mother chose the indirect route, through our beloved Hills. We arrived in Oelrichs to find our neighbors had gone in through an upstairs window and warmed our house, welcoming us home with a good meal.

We had to leave our little prairie town. We moved to western Nebraska and my mother's parents came to live with us. I loved sitting on my grandfather's lap in the big leather chair to hear his stories of the early days. He'd been a pioneer merchant in the Nebraska sandhills, just across the line from the Pine Ridge Reservation. He was as innocent as I in some things, but he told stories, stories about big things, things men did! He'd traded with Lakota people and could "talk Indian," as he said. He taught me to count to ten in what must have been an interesting accent. He was present during the events leading to the massacre at Wounded Knee. He would entertain us, deadpan, with the wild time they had bringing in the lambs one dark night only to discover next morning that they had corralled jackrabbits—this in the same cadence and tone he assumed in his account of the strange saga of the ghost shirts, or the "troubles" at Wounded Knee.

To me he was a man of generous instincts, yet despite daily contact with Lakotas and a limited command of their language he saw them through the prism of his own understanding and values. I can't recall his ever mentioning Indians in connection with the Black Hills.

We came to love Gering, our new home along the North Platte River. For my brother and me the river was our own little Mississippi playground. We loved the Bluff, as we called it—the Scottsbluff National Monument. I never heard of Horse Creek, where the great council had been held, or Blue Water Creek, Red Cloud's birthplace, though I lived out my remaining boyhood midway between the two. I knew the Oregon Trail, which ran along our side of the river, and Mitchell Pass, a landmark. I knew that our new home town was much too far from our cabin, but if anyone had mentioned the name Mákhpiya Lúta to me, or even Red Cloud, it would have drawn a blank. Of what had happened in my new neighborhood, or how it would affect my Black Hills, I knew nothing at all.

Nor did I have a clue as to the way railroads helped to "open the Hills." Railroads and trains, the romance of the rails: what could be more fundamental to the life of small towns in the West? The railroads made things go. They transported the mail. Children loved to wave at the engineer or go down to watch the train come in, the big event of the day, like the steamboat's arrival in Hannibal for young Sam Clemens. The locomotive with its powerful steam-belching engine, making the earth tremble, the locomotive Walt Whitman hailed in a hymn:

> Thy black cylindric body, golden brass and silvery steel,
> Thy ponderous side-bars, parallel and connecting rods
> gyrating, shuttling at thy sides . . .
> Fierce-throated beauty!

A fierce beauty it was to those of us who grew up in the West—our connection to the wider world.

In the Twenties, when my parents were engaged, my father would write a letter after work and take it down to the station to post it. The next day his sweetheart would have it, two hundred miles away. When our family moved from western Nebraska to Lincoln, four hundred and fifty miles to the east, the train was our transportation link to the Black Hills. One August night in the station, waiting for my train, I learned from a newspaper headline that my country had unleashed a frightful weapon over a faraway place called Hiroshima. Two hours after graduating from high school I boarded a train for the Pacific Northwest to begin a new phase of my life. In college I loaded mail onto trains from platforms swept by the winter winds, to the rumble now of diesel engines but still the flanged wheel and the rail, still Whitman's "emblem of motion and power—pulse of the continent."

The very name Wounded Knee evokes a chill of horror. Yet in my early years I can't recall any such chill in my grandfather's stories. I never tired of his accounts; I hear his voice forty years after it was stilled. He told about hunting antelope in Wyoming, going back to his little Pennsylvania town with his wild tales of frontier Nebraska, or alarming my grandmother by revving up their new horseless carriage to twenty miles an hour! He told about the Blizzard of '88. One of his stories had to do with The Troubles—capitalized, I understood, though I couldn't yet read or write.

"The Troubles" carried more weight than his other yarns. Folks were getting nervous, it seems, about doings on the reservation. Indians all stirred up, doing strange things—only a few miles north of town! There was talk of another uprising. The Indians had these shirts, ghost shirts, that somebody told them would stop a bullet. Ayy-y, golly! He knew Indians. Did business with them, talked Indian with them. They had their own ways; they were entitled to them. But this shirt business, that was strange.

When I try to picture that time and everything I know about its horrors, I sometimes think of my grandfather looking back from his old age. Somehow, before any explanation of those times will satisfy me, he has to be accounted for. In the motives ascribed to the new Americans, however you paint them—as hardy pioneers, greedy racists and predators, or some commonplace human mix—the pallet has to include the bland tint of naiveté. Fred Mills would never have connected The Troubles in any way with the Black Hills.

The Black Hills are one of the holy places of the earth, revered in diverse ways by various peoples. I knew that early, in ways I could never put into words. One summer, wanting to pass the knowledge on to my children, I took my eleven-year-old Erich on an overnight vigil to Bear Butte, the sacred mountain of the Cheyennes, set off just to the northeast of the Hills.

We brought sleeping bags, stopping off in Rapid City for Erich to down a hamburger. Out of respect, I fasted. As we pulled up at the visitor's center in the state park, now closed for the day, we saw not a living soul. The amber light of late afternoon washed over the short-grass slopes. It was a scene to evoke reverence. Thousands of Sioux had gathered here in 1857 for a council, rallying to halt white encroachment. Crazy Horse was believed to have been born nearby.

My son and I might be violating park rules but not, I felt, the spirit of the place. Twelve hundred feet above us stood the summit, a ridge that dipped into a canyon and rose again on the east. Dwarf pines were silhouetted along its crest. Starting for the top, we bypassed the vacant campsite reserved to the Cheyennes for religious observances. We noticed rocks wedged in the pines along the trail and tiny strips of cloth hanging from branches. We left them undisturbed.

By the time we reached the top the sun had dipped behind the Hills to the west. The plains reached into the distance on three sides. A full moon peeped over the eastern rim. We found ourselves not on a rounded summit but a spine that offered no level surface. A short distance down the ridge to the west we discovered a gentle slope where we could lay our sleeping bags out under the pines.

Erich had been unusually quiet. Now he had questions. Where was our cabin from here? he wanted to know. Hidden behind that dark mound of a ridge, I told him, pointing southwest. Those lights coming on, beyond a small lake? That was Sturgis. As I began to expand on what I knew of this part of the Hills, Erich began eyeing his sleeping bag. "I'll be right here," I told him as he crawled in. What must he think of the business his father was transacting up here? I wondered. While he slept I watched the lights glittering, fifteen or twenty miles to the west: Deadwood, where men had stampeded in search of gold, where Wild Bill Hickok had met his end; Lead, where the richest gold mine in the hemisphere was extracting treasure from deep in the earth.

Through the night, as the moon slowly arced its way across a cloudless sky, I looked out on those mountains I loved. I felt little hunger and less desire to sleep, though I dozed off briefly a time or two beside my son. At one point the lake below glistened briefly, but the dark hump of the uplift, like an immense sponge, soaked up the moon's brilliance and gave back no light at all. When the sun reappeared crimson over the eastern plains, the moon hung directly opposite—an astonishing display. On impulse I extended my arms toward both spheres and felt a current pass through me, a surge from pole to pole, a cryptic message I couldn't read and would not forget.

Wounded Knee. The name resounds in the consciousness of those who know what happened in 1890 on a little stream in South Dakota. It echoes with tones of anger, sadness, and doom, more sharply edged in English than in the softer Lakota, Cankpe Opi Wakpala, *though in either tongue the wounds go deep. In 1971 I took Erich and his sister Linda to see that place where many Minnecoujou Sioux, so many of them women and children, were cut down by Hotchkiss guns. There at the trading post featuring "Authentic Sioux Indian Arts & Crafts" I came upon a recent book by Dee Brown,* Bury My Heart at Wounded Knee. *A painstaking attempt to construct an Indian account of the American West, the book was designed to be read facing not west, but east. My thirteen-year-old Linda and I were both moved by what we read there. More than once I saw tears in her blue eyes.*

On our trip back to California we did our best to retrace the remarkable flight of the Nez Percés before units of the United States Army. Chief Joseph became Linda's hero. At the Little Bighorn Battlefield, then officially the Custer Battlefield, we saw a plaque on the museum wall that so astonished me I took it down word for word. The gist of it was that in some question not yet resolved, no one really knew, because there were no survivors. "What about the Indians?" my thirteen-year-old promptly asked.

Later I took Gabriela and Tom, my younger daughter and son, to Wounded Knee, so they could take in what had happened there. More and more, as time moved along, pesky facts and illuminations forced me to take thought. I learned that the Gordon Stockade, a symbol of pioneer heroism to me as a child, had been constructed by an outlaw bunch escorted out of the Black Hills by the army. The town of Gordon, where I was born, became the scene of a despicable racist incident. An old-timer I knew told me how he'd been driven from his ranch to make way for Custer State Park. When it seemed we were going to lose our cabin, I myself had a taste of the bitterness of dispossession suffered by the Lakotas.

Every year, somehow, I found my way back to the Hills from one place or another. One year, out there in the Hills in the off-season, I wanted an old-timer to talk to. The ones I knew were all gone. Then it registered: I had become the old-timer!

It could be worse.

Martin Luschei
Custer State Park
2006

One: Beginnings

[1] Adapted from a Lakota variation of the legend in James LaPointe, *Legends of the Lakota*, pp. 17-20. A Cheyenne version is presented by John Stands in Timber and Margot Liberty in *Cheyenne Memories*, pp. 19-24.

[2] Rodney M. Feldman and Richard A. Heimlich, *The Black Hills*, pp. 17-34, is a useful account I'm following most closely here.. John Paul Gries's thorough and authoritative *Roadside Geology of South Dakota* emphasizes the Black Hills and is clearly written in language comprehensible to the lay reader.

[3] E. Steve Cassells, *Prehistoric Hunters of the Black Hills*, pp. 30, 34. On the Bering Land Bridge theory, see the discussion of Vine Deloria, Jr.'s caustic view of white motives in the 2005 book by Charles C. Mann, *1491: New Revelations of the Americas Before Columbus*, pp. 16-17.

[4] Edwin Thomson Denig, *Five Indian Tribes of the Upper Missouri*, pp. xxx-xxxi.

[5] Frank B. Linderman, *Plenty-coups: Chief of the Crows*, p. viii.

[6] N. Scott Momaday, *The Way to Rainy Mountain,* p. 4.

[7] Mildred P. Mayhall, *The Kiowas*, p. 10; Russell C. Burnett, "Crow Indians," *The New Encyclopedia of the American West,* ed. Howard R. Lamar, p. 276.

[8] *Rainy Mountain*, p. 7.

[9] Mayhall, pp. 12-13; Momaday, p. 6.

[10] Rodney Frey, *The World of the Crow Indians: As Driftwod Lodges*, pp. 3-10; John J. Killoren, S.J., *Come Blackrobe: De Smet and the Indian Tragedy*, p. 78; Denig, pp. 137-138; Linderman, pp. 65-67.

[11] George Hyde, *Red Cloud's Folk: A History of the Oglala Sioux Indians*, p. 24.

[12] Virginia Cole Trenholm, *The Arapahoes, Our People,* pp. 3-4.

[13] Ibid., pp. 10, 38, 83, 165, 192-195.

[14] George Bird Grnnell, *The Cheyenne Indians*, p. 1. Where not otherwise indicated, the following history is taken from Grinnell, pp. 1-15.

[15] John Stands In Timber and Margot Liberty, *Cheyenne Memories*, pp. 23-24.

[16] Peter J. Powell, *Sweet Medicine: The Continuing Role of the Sacred Arrows, the Sun Dance, and the Sacred Buffalo Hat in Northern Cheyenne History*, vol. 1, pp. xxi, xxv. The parallel drawn with Judaism and the Ten Commandments is my own.

[17] *Cheyenne Memories*, pp. 27-41, gives the abbreviated account followed here.

[18] Ibid., p. 37n.

[19] Ibid., p. 40.

[20] Luther Standing Bear, *Land of the Spotted Eagle*, p. 43. In reality, all the lakes in the Black Hills have been man-made.

[21] Vine Deloria, Jr., introduction to *Black Elk Speaks*, pp. xiii-xiv.

[22] Ella Deloria, introduction to *Dakota Texts*, pp. ix-x.

[23] Doane Robinson, *A History of the Dakota or Sioux Indians*, pp. 18-20; George Hyde, *Red Cloud's Folk,* pp. 3-4; Richard White, "The Winning of the West: The Expansion of the Western Sioux in the Eighteenth and Nineteenth Centuries," *Journal of American History* 65 (September 1878), pp. 322-323. Where not otherwise indicated, my account of this Lakota migration follows White's.

[24] Hyde, p. 15.

[25] Ibid., p. 20.

[26] White, pp. 324-327.

[27] Reuben Gold Thwaites, *Original Journals of the Lewis and Clark Expedition*, 6: 98.

[28] James P. Ronda, *Lewis and Clark among the Indians*, pp. 28-30. Ronda's "full contact study," as he calls it, is an exemplary attempt to see the expedition from the Indian as

well as the white perspective. My account here follows his.

[29] Ibid, pp. 31-41.

[30] Donovin Arleigh Sprague, *Images of America: Pine Ridge Reservation*, p. 7; *Red Cloud's Folk,* pp. 21-22.

[31] "Winning of the West," pp. 320-321, 328, 338.

[32] Ibid., pp. 333-334; Elliot West, *The Way to the West*, p. 10.

[33] *Red Cloud's Folk*, pp. 41-42.

Two: Contact

[1] Moses Coit Tyler, *A History of American Literature,* 1607-1783, p. 5.

[2] Richard B. Hughes, "Legend of the Roses," reprinted in Helen Rezatto, *Tales of the Black Hills,* pp. 70-72.

[3] Watson Parker, *Gold in the Black Hills*, pp. 5-6.

[4] Edwin Thompson Denig, *Five Indian Tribes of the Upper Missouri*, p. 6.

[5] Parker, pp. 6-7. I am loosely following Parker's authoritative account of these early white explorations.

[6] Ibid., p. 8.

[7] Washington Irving, *Astoria*, pp. 205-208.

[8] James Clyman, *Journal of a Mountain Man*, pp. 9-23.

[9] Parker, p. 10.

[10] Ibid., pp. 10-11.

[11] Francis Parkman, *The Oregon Trail*, pp. 97-98; Richard White, "The Winning of the West," pp. 335-336.

[12] Martha Royce Blaine, *Pawnee Passage: 1870-1875*, pp. 100-105; White, pp. 337-339.

[13] Frederick Hoxie, *Parading Through History: The making of the Crow Nation in America 1805-1935,* pp. 55, 65.

[14] Hoxie, p. 74; Denig, p. 204.

[15] John F. Finerty, *War-Path and Bivouac, or The Conquest of the Sioux,* pp. 67-68.

[16] Frank B. Linderman, *Plenty-Coups, Chief of the Crows*, pp. 154-155, 307.

[17] LeRoy R. Hafen, *Broken Hand: The Life of Thomas Fitzpatrick: Mountain Man, Guide and Indian Agent*, p. 2.

[18] Robert M. Utley, *A Life Wild and Perilous: Mountain Men and the Paths to the Pacific,* pp 158-159; LeRoy Hafen, *Broken Hand: The Life of Thomas Fitzpatrick, Mountain Man, Guide, and Indian Agent*, p. 176.

[19] Hafen, pp. 253, 255.

[20] Robert A. Trennert, Jr., *Alternative to Extinction*, p. 162; Merrill J. Mattes, "The Sutler's Store at Fort Laramie," quoted in Martin Luschei, "Wanted—by Whom? Ben Mills As Indian Agent," *Annals of Wyoming: The Wyoming History Journal, (*Winter 1998), pp. 7-12.

[21] Merrill J. Mattes, *The Great Platte River Road*, pp. 499-500; Remi Nadeau, *Fort Laramie and the Sioux,* pp. 62, 66.

[22] Trennert, p. 165.

[23] Nadeau, pp. 67-68. Where not otherwise indicated, my account here follows Nadeau.

[24] Hafen, pp. 286-287.

[25] Ibid., pp. 290-293.

[26] *Missouri Republican*, October 29 and November 9, 1851; quoted in Trennert, p. 190.

[27] Nadeau, p. 82.

[28] Richard White, "The Winning of the West," p. 342; Trennert, p. 174.

[29] James C. Olson, *Red Cloud and the Sioux Problem,* p. 5; George Hyde, *Red Cloud's Folk: A History of the Oglala Sioux Indians*, p. 69.

[30] Robert Larson, *Red Cloud: Warrior-Statesman of the Lakota Sioux*, pp. 3-34. Larson's

life of Red Cloud is authoritative and recent, and I am following it here.

[31] Ibid., pp. 38-49, 55.

[32] Nadeau, p. 84.

[33] Ibid., p. 110.

[34] *Ibid., p 131.*

[35] *Spotted Tail's Folk*, p. 73.

[36] Ibid., pp. 74-80.

[37] Stephen E. Ambrose, *Crazy Horse and Custer: The Parallel Lives of Two American Warriors*, p. 67; Joseph M. Marshall III, "Crazy Horse (Tasunke Witko)," *Encyclopedia of North American Indians,* p. 138.

[38] Mari Sandoz, *Crazy Horse: The Strange Man of the Oglalas*, pp. 98-100.

[39] Ambrose, pp. 77-78.

[40] Larson, pp. 71-76.

[41] Merrill J. Mattes, *Indians, Infants and Infantry: Andrew and Elizabeth Burt on the Frontier*, p. 109.

[42] Olson, pp. 35-37, 49.

[43] Ralph K, Andrist, *The Long Death: The Last Days of the Plains Indians,* p. 122.

[44] Olson, p. 52.

[45] Ibid., p. 61.

[46] Ibid., pp. 69, 71.

Three: The New Eldorado

[1] Quoted in James C. Olson, *Red Cloud and the Sioux Problem*, pp. 89-92.

[2] W. F. Raynolds, U.S. Army Corps of Engineers, *Report of the Exploration of the Yellowstone River* (Government Printing Office, 1869), pp. 7, 14; Henry Nash Smith, *Virgin Land: The American West as Symbol and Myth*, pp. 123-124.

[3] Henry E. Fritz, *The Movement for Indian Assimilation, 1860-1890*, p. 109, 114-115, 118-119.

[4] Royal B. Hassrick, *The Sioux: Life and Customs of a Warrior Society,* pp. 61, 71-74.

[6] *Black Elk Speaks*, pp. 64-66, 81.

[7] Olson, *Red Cloud*, pp. 98-99. My account here, unless otherwise indicated, follows Olson, pp. 96-115.

[8] Ibid., p. 131.

[9] Robert W. Larson, *Red Cloud,* p. 150.

[10] Robert Lee, *Fort Meade & the Black Hills*, pp. 1-2.

[11] Quoted in Herbert Krause and Gary D. Olson, *Prelude to Glory: A Newspaper Accounting of Custer's1874 Expedition to the Black Hills*, p. 3.

[12] George Hyde, *Red Cloud's Folk*, p. 217; Richard Slotkin, *The Fatal Environment: The Myth of the Frontier in the Age of Industrialization, 1800-1890*, p. 330.

[13] Donald Jackson, *Custer's Gold: The United States Cavalry Expedition of 1874*, p. 5.

[14] George W. Kingsbury, *History of Dakota Territory*, p. 867.

[15] Jane Conard, "Charles Collins: The Sioux City Promotion of the Black Hills," *South Dakota History* 2, p. 134. Conard gives an extensive account of Collins' activities that I am following here.

[16] Ibid., pp. 138-141; Leland D. Case, "Where B.C. Means Before Custer," in Roderick Peattie, ed., *The Black Hills*, p. 73.

[17] Slotkin, *The Fatal Environment*, p. 327.

[18] Charles A. and Mary Ritter Beard, *The Rise of American Civilization*, p. 173.

[19] Ibid. pp. 138-141; Matthew Josephson, *The Robber Barons: The Great American Capitalists, 1861-1901,* pp. 35-36; Ellis Paxon Oberholtzer, *Jay Cooke: Financier of the Civil War*, vol. I, pp. iv-v.

[20] *The Fatal Environment*, p. 219.

[21] Josephson, p. 77-79. Josephson elaborates in detail on the reckless process employed by these holding companies, once the grant was received.

[22] Slotkin, pp. 287-288; Josephson, pp. 98-99.

[23] Slotkin, pp. 327-328.

[24] Ibid., p. 330.

[25] *Yankton Press,* March 13, 1872, quoted in James D. McLaird and Lesta V. Turchen, "Colonel William Ludlow and the Custer Expedition, 1874," *South Dakota History* 4, p. 282.

[26] Elwyn B. Robinson, *History of North Dakota,* p. 126; Robert Sobel, *Panic on Wall Street: A History of American Financial Disasters*, p. 179.

[27] Krause and Olson, *Prelude to Glory,* p. 1.

[28] Stephen E. Ambrose, *Crazy Horse and Custer: The Parallel Lives of Two American Warriors*, pp. 374-375.

[29] Jackson, p. 25.

[30] Ibid., pp. 20-21, 28-30.

[31] Krause and Olson, p. 3.

[32] Quoted in Thomas R., Buecker, ed., "'Distance Lends Enchantment to the View': The 1874 Black Hills Diary of Fred W. Power," *South Dakota History* 27, p. 198; Krause and Olson, p. 15.

[33] Buecker, pp. 214-215.

[34] Ibid., pp. 218-221.

[35] Max E. Gerber, "The Custer Expedition of 1874: A New Look," *North Dakota History*, Winter 1973, p. 12; *Custer's Gold*, p. 76. For black and white photos of Floral Valley and the wagon train passing through Castle Creek Valley, with present-day views in color on facing pages, see pp. 170-171, 174-175 in Ernest Grafe and Paul Horsted, *Exploring With Custer: the 1874 Black Hills Expedition,* a superlative recent source.

[36] Krause and Olson, pp. 87-88; Buecker, p. 224.

[37] Buecker, pp. 214-215; Krause and Olson, pp. 92, 214.

[38] *Custer's Gold*, pp. 78-81.

[39] Buecker, pp. 232-236.

[40] Jackson, p. 82.

[41] Buecker, pp. 207, 237-239.

[42] Jackson, p. 82.

[43] Buecker, pp. 236, 241, 243; Krause and Olson, pp. 92, 214.

[44] Krause and Olson, pp. 216-217, 246; Slotkin, *Fatal Environment,* p. 357.

[45] Krause and Olson, p. 26.

[46] Jackson, pp. 89-91.

[47] Slotkin, p. 356.

[48] Krause and Olson, p. 228; Slotkin, p. 364.

[49] Gerber, p. 18.

[50] Buecker, p. 244.

Four: The Rush to Gold and Grass

[1] Grant K. Anderson, "Samuel D. Hinman and the Opening of the Black Hills," *Nebraska History* 60, 1979, p. 525.

[2] Ibid., pp. 535, 524-526.

[3] Herbert Krause and Gary D. Olson, *Prelude to Glory: A Newspaper Accounting of Custer's 1874 Expedition to the Black Hills*, p. 263.

[4] Donald Jackson, *Custer's Gold: The United States Cavalry Expedition of 1874*, pp. 109-110.

[5] Richard Slotkin, *The Fatal Environment: The Myth of the Frontier in the Age of Industrialization, 1800-1890*, p. 365.

[6] Krause and Olson, p. 183.

[7] *Yankton Press and Dakotaian*, September 10, 1874, quoted in Jackson, p. 107.

[8] Quoted in James D. McLaird and Lesta V. Turchen, "Colonel Ludlow and the Custer Expedition, 1874," *South Dakota History* 4, Summer 1974, p. 314.

[9] "Report of Commissioner of Indian Affairs Edward P. Smith," November 1, 1875, reprinted Wilcomb E. Washburn, ed., *The American Indian and the United States: A Documentary History*, vol. 1, 1973, pp. 202-203.

[10] Jackson, p. 112; McLaird and Turchen, "Colonel Ludlow," p. 319.

[11] Annie D. Tallent, *The Black Hills: or, Last Hunting Ground of the Dacotahs*, pp. 13-16. Unless otherwise indicated, my account here is drawn from Tallent, pp. 1-74.

[12] Ibid., p. vii.

[13] Merrill J. Mattes, *Indians, Infants and Infantry: Andrew and Elizabeth Burt on the Frontier*, p. 198; Richard Irving Dodge, *The Plains of North America and Their Inhabitants*, p. 369; Watson Parker, "The Report of Captain John Mix of a Scout to the Black Hills, March-April 1875," *South Dakota History* 7, Fall 1977, pp. 393; Jessie Y. Sundstrom, *Pioneeers and Custer State Park*, pp. 19-22.

[14] Robert M. Utley, *A Life Wild and Perilous: Mountain Men and the Paths to the Pacific*, p. 165.

[15] Parker, p. 399.

[16] Lesta V. Turchen and James D. McLaird, *The Black Hills Expedition of 1875*, p. 1.

[17] Julia B. McGillycuddy, *Blood on the Moon: Valentine McGillycuddy and the Sioux*, pp. 33-34; James D. McLaird and Lesta V. Turchen, "The Scientists' Search for Gold, 1875: Walter P. Jenney and Henry Newton," *South Dakota History* 4, Fall 1974, pp. 413-414.

[18] Richard Irving Dodge, *The Black Hills Journals of Colonel Richard Irving Dodge*, ed. Wayne R. Kime, p. 48; McGillycuddy, p. 32. My account follows the journals closely, and observations attributed to Dodge, unless otherwise indicated, are from this source.

[19] Dodge, *The Black Hills*, p. 15.

[20] Lesta V. Turchen and James D. McLaird, pp. 12, 19; Dodge, *Black Hills Journals*, pp. 19n, 38-39.

[21] Dodge, *Black Hills Journals*, p. 58n.

[22] Ibid., pp. 8-9.

[23] McLaird and Turchen, "The Scientists' Search for Gold," pp. 416-418.

[24] Turchen and McLaird, pp. 17, 24.

[25] Dodge, *The Black Hills Journals*, p. 111.

[26] Ibid., p. 105.

[27] Ibid., pp. 60-61; Mattes, *Indians, Infants and Infantry*, p. 202.

[28] Wayne R. Kime, ed., Introduction to *The Black Hills Journals of Richard Irving Dodge*, pp. 9-10.

[29] Turchen and McLaird, *The Black Hills Expedition*, pp. 25-26, 138.

[30] Watson Parker, *Gold in the Black Hills*, pp. 35-37.

[31] For an account of the Mills episode and a portrait of this little-known figure, see Martin Luschei, "Wanted—by Whom? Ben Mills as Indian Agent," *Annals of Wyoming*, Winter 1998, pp. 8-12; Olson, *Red Cloud and the Sioux problem*, pp. 184, 187.

[32] Olson, p. 198.

[33] *Report of the Commission Appointed to Treat with the Sioux Indians for the Relinquishment of the Black Hills*, pp. 3-4

[34] George Hyde, *Spotted Tail's Folk: A History of the Brulé Sioux,* pp. 234-235.

[35] George Hyde, *Red Cloud's Folk*, pp. 242-244.

[36] *Report of the Commission*, pp. 7-8.

[37] Ibid., pp. 9-19; Olson, pp. 11-12.

[38] Dodge, *Black Hills Journals*, pp. 206-208.

[39] Parker, p. 70.

[40] Robert W. Larson, Red *Cloud: Warrior-Statesman of the Lakota Sioux*, pp. 195-198.

[41] Ibid., p. 197. The arguments swirling around motivation are developed in a collection edited by Paul L. Hedren, *The Great Sioux War, 1876-1877.*

[42] *Gold in the Black Hills*, p. 78. An extensive source on the town of Custer is Fred W. Whitley, "A History of Custer City, South Dakota, 1874-1900," *South Dakota Historical Collections*, vol. 37 (1974), pp. 234-343.

[43] Bob Lee and Dick Williams, *Last Grass Frontier: The South Dakota Stock Growers Heritage*, pp. 42-47.

Five: War

[1] Quoted in Paul Andrew Hutton, "Phil Sheridan's Frontier," *The Great Sioux War 1876-77*, ed. Paul L. Hedren, p. 98.

[2] Robert W. Larson, *Red Cloud: Warrior-Statesman of the Lakota Sioux*, pp. 199-200.

[3] Dee Brown, *Best of Dee Brown's West: An Anthology*, ed. Stan Banash, pp. 219-221, 227-228.

[4] Hutton, "Phil Sheridan's Frontier," p. 103.

[5] Larson, p. 201.

[6] James C. Olson, *Red Cloud and the Sioux Problem,* pp. 224-227. My account of the Manypenny conference is drawn from Olson.

[7] Ibid., pp. 227-229.

[8] Robert Lee, *Bob Lee's Black Hills Notebook*, pp. 26-27.

[9] Ibid., p. 29; Larson, *Red Cloud*, pp. 208-209.

[10] Nelson A. Miles, *Personal Recollections And Observations Of General Nelson A. Miles*, p. 226; Stanley Vestal, *Sitting Bull: Champion of the Sioux*, pp. 194-201; Robert M. Utley, *Frontier Regulars: The United States Army and the Indian, 1866-1891*, p. 273.

[11] Utley, *Frontier Regulars*, pp. 273-275.

[12] Ibid., p. 276; Don Rickey, Jr., "The Battle of Wolf Mountain," in *The Great Sioux War*, pp. 166-168; Miles, *Personal Recollections*, pp. 238-239.

[13] Miles, pp. 238-239; Utley, pp. 273-275.

[14] Edward Lazarus, *Black Hills/White Justice: The Sioux Nation Versus the United States 1775 to the Present*, pp. xxii, 93

[15] Lee, *Black Hills Notebook*, p. 29; Larson, *Red Cloud,* p. 209.

[16] Larson, *Red Cloud*, pp. 210-211.

[17] Charles M. Robinson III, *A Good Year to Die: The Story of the Great Sioux War,* p. 332.

[18] Stephen E. Ambrose, *Crazy Horse and Custer: The Parallel Lives of Two American Warriors,* p. 462.

[19] Larry McMurtry, *Crazy Horse,* pp. 3, 7, 117-118. In a touch of poetry McMurtry, approaching Crazy Horse Monument, eases his way through a "Black Hills buffalo herd" ten or fifteen miles from the nearest actual herd.

[20] Lee, *Black Hills Notebook,* p. 30.

[21] Catherine Price, *The Oglala People, 1841-1879: A Political History*, pp. 161, 175.

[22] McMurtry, pp. 120-126.

[23] Larson, *Red Cloud,* p. 213; McMurtry, *Crazy Horse*, pp. 70, 130, 135-140.

[24] Richard B. Hughes, *Pioneer Years in the Black Hills,* pp. 26, 191.

[25] Thomas R. Buecher, "'Can You Send Us Immediate Relief"? Army Expeditions to the Northern Black Hills, 1876-1877," *South Dakota History*, Summer 1995, p. 97.

[26] Ibid., pp. 100-106, 109-113.

[27] Richard Irving Dodge, *The Black Hills*, pp. 107-109.

[28] Fred W. Whitley, "A History of Custer City, South Dakota, 1874-1900," *South Dakota Historical Collections*, vol. 37 (1974), pp. 246-247; Tallent, *The Black Hills*, p. 123.

[29] Watson Parker, *Gold in the Black Hills*, pp. 72-74.

[30] Whitley, "A History," pp. 248-249; Tallent, *The Black Hills*, p. 199.

[31] Parker, *Gold in the Black Hills*, p. 76; Whitley, "A History," pp. 247-251.

[32] Parker, pp. 78-80.

[33] Robert J. Casey, *The Black Hills and Their Incredible Characters: A Chronicle and a Guide*, p. 139; Parker, pp. 82-83.

[34] Wallace Stegner, *Wolf Willow: A History, a Story, and a Memory of the Last Plains Frontier*, pp. 115-116.

[35] Robert M. Utley, *The Lance and the Shield: The Life and Times of Sitting Bull*, p. 189.

[36] Ibid., pp. 191-198.

[37] Olson, *Red Cloud*, pp. 247-255.

[38] Casey, p. 139.

[39] Joseph H. Cash, *Working the Homestake*, pp. 14-15; Ben Procter, *William Randolph Hearst: The Early Years, 1863-1914*, pp. 4-7; Casey, p. 213.

[40] Cash, pp. 16-18; Casey, pp. 215-216.

[41] Parker, pp. 86-87; Watson Parker and Hugh K. Lambert, *Black Hills Ghost Towns*, pp. 166-167; Richard O'Connor, *Ambrose Bierce: A Biography*, pp. 122-123; Paul Fatout, *Ambrose Bierce: The Devil's Lexicographer*, p. 124; Ambrose Bierce, *The Enlarged Devils's Dictionary*, p. 115.

[42] James C. Olson, *Red Cloud and the Sioux Problem*, p. 263.

[43] Utley, *The Lance and the Shield*, pp. 199-207; Robert E. Riegel, *The Story of the Western Railroads: From 1852 Through the Reign of the Giants*, p. 205.

[44] Brown, pp. 228-229; Utley, *The Lance and the Shield*, p. 230.

[45] Utley, *Lance and the Shield,* p. 233.

[46] *The Sixth Grandfather: Black Elk's Teachings Given to John Neihardt*, ed. Raymond J. DeMallie, pp. 163-164

[47] Utley, *The Lance and the Shield,* p. 247.

[48] Ibid., pp. 262-265; Stanley Vestal, *Sitting Bull: Champion of the Sioux*, p. 250, 255.

[49] Francis Paul Prucha, *The Great Father: The United States Government and the American Indian*, pp. 226-227; Utley, *The Lance and the Shield*, pp. 268-269, and *The Last Days of the Sioux Nation*, pp. 49-52, 55-57.

[50] Richard E. Jensen, "Another Look at Wounded Knee," in Richard E. Jensen, R. Eli Paul, and John E. Carter, *Eyewitness at Wounded Knee*, p. 5; James Mooney, *The Ghost-Dance Religion and the Sioux Outbreak of 1890, p. 771.*

[51] Mooney, p. 657.

[52] Utley, *Last Days*, 60, 77, 83.

[53] Nancy Tystad Koupal, ed., notes to L. Frank Baum, *Our Landlady*, pp. 16, 144, 160.

[54] Utley, *Last Days*, pp. 76-77.

[55] Mooney, p. 777.

[56] Utley, *Last Days,* p. 62; Jensen, p. 6.

[57] Mooney, pp. 771-772.

[58] Ibid., pp. 780-783.

[59] Jensen, pp. 6-8, 10, 12.

[60] Herbert S. Schell, *History of South Dakota*. 3rd ed., revised, p. 328; Ed Lemmon, *Boss Cowman: The Recollections of Ed Lemmon, 1857-1946*, pp. 149-150.

[61] Renée Sansom Flood, *Lost Bird of Wounded Knee: Spirit of the Lakota*, pp. 314-315n.

[62] Utley, *The Last Days*, pp. 102-108. Where not otherwise indicated, my account here follows Utley.

[63] Koupal, p. 144.

[64] Utley, *The Last Days*, pp. 111-114.

[65] John E. Carter, "Making Pictures for a News-Hungry Nation," *Eyewitness to Wounded Knee*, pp. 44-45.

[66] Ibid., pp. 47, 190-191n; Flood, p. 64.

[67] Carter, pp. 39-40, 54.

[68] Quoted in George Philip, "James (Scotty) Philip, 1858-1911," *South Dakota Historical Collections*, vol. 20 (1940), p. 383.

[69] Flood, pp. 53-54, 318, nn. 30-31.

[70] Ibid., pp. 51-52, 316, n. 13.

[71] Ibid., pp. 51-55.

[72] Elliott J. Gorn, Randy Roberts, and Terry D. Bilhartz, *Constructing the American Past: A Source Book of a People's History*, vol. 2, p. 99; Koupal, p. 147.

[73] Flood, pp. 47-50, 315, n. 6.

[74] Richard N. Ellis, "Wounded Knee Massacre," *The New Encyclopedia of the American West*, ed. Howard R. Lamar, pp. 1235-1236; Paul D. Robertson, "Wounded Knee Massacre," *Encyclopedia of North American Indians*, ed. Frederick E. Hoxie, pp. 694-697.

[75] Utley, *Frontier Regulars,* p. 408.

[76] Flood, pp. 59-60, 300-305.

Six: Preservation or Plunder?

[1] Luther Standing Bear, *Land of the Spotted Eagle*, pp. 38, 196.

[2] Joseph H. Cash, *Working the Homestake*, p. 13.

[3] Edmond Baron de Mandat-Grancey, *Cow-Boys and Colonels: Narrative of a Journey Across the Prairie and Over the Black Hills of Dakota*, pp. 176-179. On the origin myth see Patricia Nelson Limerick, *The Legacy of Conquest: The Unbroken Past of the American West*, pp. 322-323.

[4] Cash, pp. 13, 18-21; *Homestake Centennial, 1876-1976,* a publication of the Homestake Mining Company, 1976, p. 7.

[5] Richmond L. Clow, "Timber Users, Timber Savers: Homestake Mining Company and the First Regulated Timber Harvest," *South Dakota History,* vol. 22, no. 3 (Fall 1992), pp. 215-220; Martha E. Geores, *Common Ground: The Struggle for Ownership of the Black Hills National Forest*, pp. 37-38.

[6] Watson Parker, *Deadwood: The Golden Years,* pp. x-xi.

[7] Ibid., pp. ix, 99, 140-141. A paper read by Ann Heber Stanton at a historical society meeting in 1998, as yet unpublished, gives an astute appreciation of these men.

[8] Parker, pp. 111, 116-118; Cash, p. 22.

[9] Ross P. Korsgaard, "A History of Rapid City, South Dakota, During Territorial Days," *South Dakota State Historical Collections*, vol. 38 (1977), pp. 522-530, 552.

[10] Richard Irving Dodge, *The Black Hills*, p. 67; Annie B. Tallent, *The Black Hills, Or Lasting Hunting Ground of the Dakotahs*, p. 487.

[11] Suzanne Julin, "South Dakota Spa: A History of the Hot Springs Health Resort, 1882-1915," *South Dakota Historical Collections*, vol. 41 (1982), pp. 197-223.

[12] Watson Parker and Hugh K. Lambert, *Black Hills Ghost Towns*, p. 66; de Mandat-Grancey, *Cowboys and Colonels*, pp. 347-348; Robert J. Casey, *The Black Hills and Their Incredible Characters: A Chronicle and a Guide*, pp. 288-290.

[13] Mildred Fielder, *Railroads of the Black Hills*, pp. 7-9, 38-39; Parker, *Deadwood*, pp. 100-101.

[14] Edmond Baron de Mandat-Grancey, *Buffalo Gap: A French Ranch in Dakota, 1887*, p. 8.

[15] Estelline Bennett, *Old Deadwood Days*, pp. 298-300; Parker, *Deadwood*, pp. 100-101.

[16] Ed Lemmon, *Boss Cowman: The Recollections of Ed Lemmon, 1857-1946*, pp. 180-181; Bob Lee and Dick Williams, *Last Grass Frontier: The South Dakota Stock Grower Heritage*, pp. 186-187.

[17] Clow, "Timber Users," pp. 218-219; Henry S. Graves, "Black Hills Forest Reserve (South Dakota and Wyoming)," *Nineteenth Annual Report of the United States Geological Survey*, pp. 88, 97.

[18] Mitch Maloney and David B. Miller, *Centennial Mini-Histories of the Black Hills National Forest*, p. 1; Gifford Pinchot, *Breaking New Ground*, pp. 84-85.

[19] Pinchot, p. 107.

[20] Clow, pp. 220-221, 225-226.

[21] Cash, pp. 22-24; R.V. Hunkins, "The Black Hills—A Storehouse of Mineral Treasure," *The Black Hills*, ed. Roderick Peattie, p. 264.

[22] Maloney and Miller, chapter 8; Pinchot, pp. 175-176.

[23] James C. Olson, *Red Cloud and the Sioux Problem*, pp. 336-337.

[24] Robert W. Larson, *Red Cloud: Warrior-Statesman of the Sioux*, p. 294.

[25] Olson, pp. 333-334.

[26] Ibid., pp. 264-266.

[27] Marla N. Powers, *Oglala Women: Myth, Ritual, and Reality*, pp. 128-129.

[28] Ella Deloria, *Speaking of Indians*, pp. 28-29.

[29] Powers, pp. 130-131.

[30] Gordon Macgregor, *Warriors Without Weapons: A Study of the Society and Personality Development of the Pine Ridge Sioux*, pp. 37-40. My account here follows Macgregor.

[31] Luther Standing Bear, *My People the Sioux*, pp. 3, 6, 28-29. Unless otherwise stated, my account of Standing Bear's Life is taken from this source.

[32] Luther Standing Bear, *Land of the Spotted Eagle*, pp. 230-231.

[33] Standing Bear, *My People*, pp. xii, 149-152; *Spotted Eagle*, pp. 230-235, 248.

[34] Joseph Epes Brown, Interviews with Black Elk in *The Sacred Pipe*, pp. 5-6; Don Doll, S.J., *Vision Quest: Men, Women and Sacred Sites of the Sioux Nation*, p. 12.

[35] Raymond DeMallie, editor's introduction to *The Sixth Grandfather: Black Elk's Teachings Given to John G. Neihardt*, pp. 3-59.

[36] Black Elk, Nicholas, *Black Elk Speaks, Being the Life Story of a Holy Man of the Oglala Sioux*, as told through John G. Neihardt, pp. 48-49, 64.

[37] *The Sixth Grandfather*, pp. 158-163, 180-184, 193-194.

[38] Ibid, pp. 204-211.

[39] *Black Elk Speaks*, p. 231.

[40] *Sixth Grandfather*, pp. 9-11.

[41] *Black Elk Speaks*, pp. 230-238; *Sixth Grandfather*, pp. 258-259.

[42] *Black Elk Speaks*, p. 270.

[43] Michael F. Steltenkamp, *Black Elk: Holy Man of the Oglalas*, pp. 33-35, 182-183.

[44] Ibid., pp. 41, 89-90.

[45] Edward Lazarus, *Black Hills/White Justice: The Sioux Nation Versus the United States, 1775 to the Present*, p. 119. Lazarus's careful study is my source here.

[46] Ibid., pp. 120-129.

[47] Ibid., pp. 130-149.

[48] Gilbert Courtland Fite, *Peter Norbeck: Prairie Statesman*, p. 25; Edward Raventon, *Island in the Plains: A Black Hills Natural History*, p. 255.

[49] Fite, pp. 9-17.

[50] Jessie Y. Sundstrom, *Pioneers and Custer State Park*, pp. 52-55.

[51] Henry S. Graves, "Black Hills Forest Reserve," pp. 72-73, 82-83, 97.

[52] Baron Edmond de Mandat-Grancey, *Buffalo Gap: A French Ranch in Dakota: 1887*, pp. 199-201.

[53] Ibid., pp. 136-137, 203-206, 215.

[54] Ibid., pp. 205-206; Sundstrom, pp. 50-52.

[55] Cleophas C. O'Harra and Joseph P. Connolly, *The Geology, Mineralogy, and Scenic Features of Custer State Park, South Dakota*, South Dakota School of Mines Bulletin No. 14, (1926), p. 50.

[56] Raventon, pp. 171-172, 196; Sundstrom, p. 29; O'Harra and Connolly, p. 99.

[57] Robert D. Woodward, "World of Darkness: Early Explorations of the Cave," *Wind Cave National Park*, pp. 31-32; James LaPointe, *Legends of the* Lakota, pp. 79-84.

[58] Raventon, pp. 253-255.

[59] Sundstrom, p. 81.

[60] Ibid., pp. 89, 82-84.

[61] Sundstrom, p. 149; Herbert S. Schell, *History of South Dakota*, p. 269; Fite, pp. 75-76; Raventon, pp. 256-257.

[62] Donovin Sprague Hump, personal communication to the author.

[63] Robert J. Casey, *The Black Hills*, p. 17; Sundstrom, p. 83; Wayne C. Lee, *Scotty Philip, The Man Who Saved the Buffalo*, pp. 225-226, 247-248, 277-285, 308-310.

[64] Fite, *Norbeck*, p. 76; Fite, *Mount Rushmore*, pp. 131-132.

[65] Fite, *Norbeck*, pp. 76-77; Sundstrom, p. 83; Raventon, p. 258.

Seven: Monumental Dissonance

[1] Martha E Geores, *Common Ground: The Struggle for the Ownership of the Black Hills National Forest*, p. 105.

[2] Gilbert C. Fite, *Mount Rushmore*, p. 33. Where not otherwise indicated, my account follows this source.

[3] Howard Shaff and Audrey Karl Shaff, *Six Wars at a Time: The Life and Times of Gutzon Borglum, Sculptor of Mount Rushmore*, pp. 149-150, 160; Fite, p. 36.

[4] Rex Alan Smith, *The Carving of Mount Rushmore*, pp. 22-26.

[5] Fite, pp. 6, 8-9.

[6] Smith, pp. 26-27; Fite, pp. 9-11.

[7] Fite, p. 40; Shaff and Shaff, pp. 103-109, 195-198, 201; David M. Chalmers, *Hooded Americanism: The History of the Ku Klux Klan*, p. 106.

[8] Shaff and Shaff, pp. 200-203.

[9] Ibid., pp. 205-211; Smith, p. 69.

[10] Smith, pp. 71, 74; Shaff and Shaff, pp. 213-215.

[11] Smith, pp. 27-34.

[12] Ibid., pp. 79-83.

[13] Ibid., pp. 81-86.

[14] Ibid., pp. 89-96, 129-131.

[15] Fite, pp. 57-58.

[16] Fite, pp. 89-90, 106-109.

[17] Shaff and Shaff, pp. 280-281.

[18] Edward Lazarus, *Black Hills, White Justice: The Sioux Nation Versus the United States, 1775 to the Present*, pp. 160-161.

[19] Ibid., pp. 108-109; Frank Pommersheim, *Braid of Feathers: American Indian Law and Contemporary Tribal Life*, pp. 22-23.

[20] *Black Elk Speaks: Being the Life Story of a Holy Man of the Oglala Sioux*, as told through John G. Neihardt (Flaming Rainbow).

21 Ibid., Neihardt's preface to the Bison edition, pp xvi-xviii; Hilda Neihardt, *Black Elk and Flaming Rainbow: Personal Memories of the Lakota Holy Man and John Neihardt*, pp. 12-14.
22 Hilda Neihardt, *Black Elk and Flaming Rainbow,* p. 34; Raymond J. DeMallie, introduction to *The Sixth Grandfather: Black Elk's Teachings Given to John G. Neihardt*, pp. 21-23.
23 *The Sixth Grandfather,* pp. 32-39.
24 Hilda Neihardt, pp. 58-59.
25 DeMallie, *The Sixth Grandfather*, pp. 41-45.
26 *Black Elk and Flaming Rainbow*, p. 88.
27 *Black Elk Speaks*, pp. 273-274.
28 DeMallie, *The Sixth Grandfather*, pp. 51-63.
29 Paul B. Steinmetz, S. J., *Pipe, Bible, and Peyote among the Oglala Lakota: A Study in Religious Identity*, pp. 185-188; Michael F. Steltenkamp, *Black Elk: Holy Man of the Oglala*, pp. 148, 153-154.
30 Scott Momaday, "To Save a Great Vision," in *A Sender of Words: Essays in Memory of John G. Neihardt*, ed. Vine Deloria, Jr., p. 31; DeMallie, *The Sixth Grandfather*, p. 56. DeMallie's words underlined by the author.
31 Fite, pp. 136-137, 159-161; Smith, p. 314.
32 Frank Lloyd Wright, "The Bad Lands," letter to Robert D. Lusk, September 1935, *South Dakota History*, (Summer 1973), pp. 271-284.
33 Smith, pp. 364-368; *Progress*, newsletter published by Crazy Horse Memorial Foundation, vol. XXI, No. 1 (Summer 1999), p. 5.
34 Rob DeWall, *Korczak: Storyteller in Stone*, pp. 14-22.
35 Shaff and Shaff, pp. 352-355; Fite, p. 21; Smith, pp. 386-388.
36 Fite, p. 105.
37 DeWall, p. 23.
38 Lee's account, related to me in person.
39 DeWall, pp. 29-37.

Eight: Threats and Promises

1 Rolland Dewing, *Wounded Knee II*, pp. 29-31. Dewing's account is the most carefully researched and objective, and except where otherwise indicated I am following it here.
2 See definition of "event" in Marshall David Sahlins, *Islands of History*, pp. 153-154.
3 Vine Deloria, Jr., *Behind the Trail of Broken Treaties: An Indian Declaration of Independence*, pp. 23-41.
4 Paul Chaat Smith and Robert Allen Warrior, *Like a Hurricane: The Indian Movement from Alcatraz to Wounded Knee*, pp. 124-137.
5 Smith and Warrior, pp. 112-115; Russell Means, *Where White Men Fear to Tread: The Autobiography of Russell Means*, pp. 198-199.
6 Deloria, p. 45; Peter Matthiessen, *In the Spirit of Crazy Horse*, p. 60.
7 Smith and Warrior, pp. 114-116; Dewing, pp. 31-32; Means, p. 196.
8 Smith and Warrior, pp. 117-118; *Gordon Journal,* March 15, 1972.
9 Robert Burnette and John Koster, *The Road to Wounded Knee*, p. 197; Deloria, p. 44; Dewing, p. 33.
10 Smith and Warrior, pp. 138-168; Burnette and Koster, pp. 197-219.
11 Rex Weyler, *Blood of the Land: The Government and Corporate War Against the American Indian Movement,* pp. 67-68.
12 Dewing, *Wounded Knee II,* pp. 40-42; Rolland Dewing, "South Dakota Newspaper Coverage of the 1973 Occupation of Wounded Knee," *South Dakota History* 12 (Spring 1982), pp. 60-63; author interview with Jessie Sundstrom, Custer, SD, June 9, 2005.

[13] Dewing, "South Dakota Newspaper Coverage," pp. 62-63; Means, p. 243.

[14] Hobart Gates, "Narrative of February 6, 1973 in Custer, South Dakota," pp.1-2, unpublished manuscript lent to me by Gates; Lyn Gladstone, "Gates outlines basis for manslaughter charge in death," *Rapid City Journal*, February 7, 1973.

[15] *Like a Hurricane*, p. 183.

[16] Dewing, *Wounded Knee II*, pp. 42-43; author interview with Jessie Sundstrom, June 9, 2005; Mary Crow Dog, with Richard Erdoes, *Lakota Woman*, pp. 118-120.

[17] Crow Dog, pp. 112, 118-122; Gates, "Narrative of February 6, 1973," p. 2; Dewing, *Wounded Knee II*, pp. 43-44; Means, p. 244.

[18] Lyn Gladstone, "Confrontation first, then 'everything broke loose,'" *Rapid City Journal*, February 7, 1973; Matthiessen, p. 64.

[19] Crow Dog, p. 122; Dewing, "South Dakota Newspaper Coverage," pp. 59-60.

[20] Harold Higgins, "Mayor vows action on racial complaints," *Rapid City Journal*, February 8, 1973; Smith and Warrior, pp. 188-189.

[21] Dewing, *Wounded Knee II*, pp. 46-48; *Sturgis Tribune*, February 14, 1973; Gates, "Narrative of February 6, 1973," p. 3.

[22] Smith and Warrior, p. 198. Unless otherwise indicated, I am following this source.

[23] Michael F. Steltenkamp, *Black Elk: Holy Man of the Oglalas*, p. 155.

[24] Terri Schultz, "Bamboozle Me Not at Wounded Knee," *Harper's*, June 1973, p. 56; "The Continuing Massacre at Wounded Knee," *Harper's*, June 1974, p. 32.

[25] Smith and Warrior, p. 228. Jefferson's view is from "Query XVIII: Manners," *Notes on the State of Virginia*.

[26] "Remarks by James R. Smith, Assistant Secretary – Water and Power Development, Department of the Interior, Washington, D. C. to Major Electric Power Suppliers of Northcentral United States, Omaha, Nebraska, May 26, 1970," news release of the Department of the Interior.

[27] Quotations taken from Sally Jacobsen, "The Great Montana Coal Rush," special report of *Bulletin of the Atomic Scientists* 29: 37-42 (April 1973).

[28] U. S. Department of the Interior, *North Central Power Study: Report of Phase 1*, Volume 1, October 1971, pp. 2-22; Richard L. Gilluly, "A home on the range for a vast industry," *Science News*, vol. 101 (March 4, 1972), pp. 157-158; "Plains energy complex: Debate quickens," *Science News*, vol. 102 (October 14, 1972), pp. 244-245; Jacobsen, p. 40; Peter Matthiessen, *Indian Country*, p. 204.

[29] *In the Spirit of Crazy Horse*, pp. 56, 105-106.

[30] John William Sayer, *Ghost Dancing the Law: The Wounded Knee Trials*, pp. 49-50.

[31] Smith and Warrior, pp. 275-276.

[32] Schultz, p. 56.

[33] Sayer, pp. 69-70, 195-196.

[34] Thurman Wilkins, *Cherokee Tragedy: The Ridge Family and the Decimation of a People*, p. 222; Sayer, pp. 204-205; Edward Lazarus, *Black Hills/White Justice: The Sioux Nation Versus the United States, 1775 to the Present*, pp. 375, 401.

[35] Matthiessen, *In the Spirit of Crazy Horse*, pp. 105-107, 413-415, 588.

[36] David Dinsmore Covey, "The legacy of uranium tailings," *Bulletin of the Atomic Scentists*, September 1975; Matthiessen, *Indian Country*, p. 207.

[37] Means, pp. 400-401.

[38] Author interviews with Marvin Kammerer, Rapid City, SD, June 9, 2000 and June 10, 2001.

[39] *Rapid City Journal*, July 18, 1980; Molly Ivins, "An Eclectic Crowd Gathers to Save the Black Hills," *New York Times*, July 28, 1980.

[40] Author interviews with Marvin Kammerer, June 9, 2000 and June 10, 2001, Rapid City, SD; *Rapid City Journal*, July 19-28, 1980.

[41] Means, pp. 337-339, 407-408.

⁴² *Rapid City Journal*, April 5-8, 1981; Matthiessen, p. 530.
⁴³ *Rapid City Journal*, April 12, 1981; Means, pp. 408-413.
⁴⁴ Donald Worster, "The Black Hills: Sacred or Profane?" in *Under Western Skies: Nature and History in the American West*, pp. 108-109; author interview with Paul Ruder, District Ranger, Custer, SD, May 20, 2001. In a personal letter June 23, 2006, Watson Parker leans to the latter view.
⁴⁵ Means, pp. 411-412; Matthiessen, p. 532; author interview with Kammerer.
⁴⁶ Bill Bradley, *Time Present, Time Past: A Memoir*, pp. 290-316.
⁴⁷ Lazarus, p. 17.
⁴⁸ See Chapter Four of this book.
⁴⁹ Worster, pp. 136, 142.
⁵⁰ Cited in Peter Nabokov, *Where the Lightning Strikes: The Lives of American Sacred Places*, p. 218.
⁵¹ *The Sixth Grandfather*, pp. 309-310.
⁵² Charlotte Black Elk, "Black Hills Place Names," testimony on Senate Bill 1453, pp. 205-210, July 16, 1986; Linea Sundstrom, "Native American Cultural Properties," *Black Hills National Forest Cultural Resources Overview*, Vol. 2, p. 3a-3, 1996; Andrew Gulliford, *Sacred Objects and Sacred Places: Preserving Tribal Traditions*, pp. 119, 144-148; Linea Sundstrom, *Storied Stone: Indian Rock Art of the Black Hills*.
⁵² Author interview with Dave McKee, Historical Preservation Officer, Custer, SD, May 14, 2001.

Prospects

¹ Pommersheim made the observation in a keynote address at Augustana College in Sioux Falls, South Dakota, May 24, 2001.
² Donald Worster, "The Black Hills: Sacred or Profane?" in *Under Western Skies: Nature and History in the American West*, p. 153.
³ Luther Standing Bear, *Land of the Spotted Eagle*, pp. 196-197.
⁴ Bruce Catton, *The Coming Fury*, p. 219.
⁵ Ronald Wright, *Stolen Continents: The "New World" Through Indian Eyes*, p. 5.
⁶ Martha E. Geores, *Common Ground: The Struggle for Ownership of the Black Hills National Forest*, pp. 122, 128.
⁷ Sierra Club factsheet, downloaded from Internet, June 21, 2001.
⁸ Author interview with John Twiss, Supervisor, Black Hills National Forest, Custer, South Dakota, May 21, 2001; author interview with Ron Walker, Resource Program Manager, Custer State Park, Custer, South Dakota, June 7, 2001
⁹ Frank Carroll, "The Enduring Forest," *The Black Hills National Forest: A History Primer for New Employees*, 2004, pp. 3-6.
¹⁰ Bob Paulson, "Cascade Valley 70+ Years Later," epilogue to reprint of *The Black Hills Engineer, Hot Springs Number: Biologic Features of Cascade Valley and Vicinity*, January 1928; author interview with Bob Paulson, Rapid City, South Dakota, June 11, 2001 and June 16, 2003.
¹¹ Robert Hughes, *Culture of Complaint: The Fraying of America*, p. 121.
¹² Frank Pommersheim, *Braid of Feathers: American Indian Law and Contemporary Tribal Life*, pp. 2-3, 199-200.
¹³ Epigraph to William Dietrich, *Northwest Passage: The Great Columbia River*. The "half-truth history" is Donald Worster's phrase from *Under Western Skies*, p. 107. The thoughtful reader will find amplication of the phrase in Patricia Nelson's *The Legacy of Conquest: The Unbroken Past of the American West*, pp. 322-323.

Bibliography of Works Cited

Ambrose, Stephen E. *Crazy Horse and Custer: The Parallel Lives of Two American Warriors.* Anchor Book. New York: Doubleday, 1996. Hardcover originally published: New York: Doubleday, 1975.

Anderson, Grant K. "Samuel D. Hinman and the Opening of the Black Hills." *Nebraska History* 60 (1979).

Andrist, Ralph K. *The Long Death: The Last Days of the Plains Indians.* New York: The Macmillan Co., 1964.

Baskett, Tom, Jr., and Jerry Sanders. *An Introduction to Custer State Park and the Southern Black Hills.* Billings, MT: RAWCO, 1977.

Baum, L. Frank. *Our Landlady.* Edited and annotated by Nancy Tystad Koupal. Bison Book. Lincoln: University of Nebraska Press, 1996.

Beard, Charles A.and Mary Ritter Beard. *The Rise of American Civilization.* Revised and enlarged. 2 vols. New York: Macmillan, 1959. Originally published: New York: Macmillan, 1930.

Bennett, Estelline. *Old Deadwood Days.* Reprint. Bison Book. University of Nebraska Press, 1982. Originally published: New York: J. H. Sears, 1928.

Bierce, Ambrose. *The Enlarged Devil's Dictionary.* Doubleday, 1967.

Black Elk, Charlotte. "Black Hills Place Names," testimony on Senate Bill 1453, July 16, 1986.

Blaine, Martha Royce. *Pawnee Passage: 1870-1975.* Civilization of the American Indian, vol. 202. Norman: University of Oklahoma Press, 1990.

Bradley, Bill. *Time Present, Time Past.* Vintage edition, revised. New York: Random House, 1997. Originally published: New York: Alfred A. Knopf, Inc., 1996.

Brown, Dee. *Best of Dee Brown's West: An Anthology.* Ed. Stan Banash. Santa Fe, NM: Clear Light Publishers, 1998.

Brown, Joseph Epes. Notes to *The Sacred Pipe: Black Elk's Account of the Rites of the Oglala Sioux.* Recorded and edited by Joseph Epes Brown. Baltimore: Penguin Books, Inc., 1971. Originally published in The Civilization of the American Indian Series, vol. 36. Norman: Oklahoma University Press, 1953.

Buecker, Thomas R. "'Can You Send Us Immediate Relief'? Army Expeditions to the Northern Black Hills, 1876-1877." *South Dakota History* 25 (1995).

____. Ed., "'Distance Lends Enchantment to the View': The 1874 Black Hills Diary of Fred W. Power." *South Dakota History* 27 (1997).

Carroll, Frank. "The Enduring Forest." *The Black Hills National Forest: A History Primer for New Employees.* Custer, SD: Black Hills National Forest, 2004.

Case, Leland D. "Where B.C. Means Before Custer," in Roderick Peattie, ed., *The Black Hills.* New York: The Vanguard Press, Inc., 1952.

Casey, Robert J. *The Black Hills and Their Incredible Characters: A Chronicle and a Guide.* Indianapolis: The Bobbs-Merrill Company, Inc., 1949.

Cash, Joseph H. *Working the Homestake.* Ames, IA: Iowa State University Press, 1993.

Cassells, E. Steve. *Prehistoric Hunters of the Black Hills.* Boulder, CO: Johnson Books, 1986.

Catton, Bruce. *Gettysburg: The Final Fury.* Garden City, NY: Doubleday, 1974.

Chalmers, David M. *Hooded Americanism: The History of the Ku Klux Klan.* New York: F. Watts, 1981.

Clow, Richmond L, "Timber Users, Timber Savers: Homestake Mining Company and The First Regulated Timber Harvest." *South Dakota History*, vol. 22 (1992).

Clyman, James. *Journal of a Mountain Man.* Edited with Introduction by Linda M. Hasselstrom. Classics of the Fur Trade Series, Winfred Blevins, General

Editor. Missoula: Mountain Press Publishing Co., 1984.

Conard, Jane. "Charles Collins: The Sioux City Promotion of the Black Hills." *South Dakota History* 2 (1971).

Crow Dog, Mary, with Richard Erdoes. *Lakota Woman.* New York: Grove Weidenfeld, 1990.

Deloria, Ella C. Introduction to Ella C. Deloria, *Dakota Texts*, ed. Agnes Picotte and Paul N. Pavich. Vermillion, SD: Dakota Press, 1978.

____. *Speaking of Indians.* Introductory notes by Agnes Picotte and Paul N. Pavich. Vermillion, SD: State Publishing Company, 1983.

Deloria, Vine, Jr. *Behind the Trail of Broken Treaties: An Indian Declaration of Independence.* Austin: University of Texas Press, 1985.

____. Introduction to *Black Elk Speaks: Being the Life Story of a Holy Man of the Oglala Sioux as told through John G. Neihardt.* Reprint. Bison Book. Lincoln: University of Nebraska Press, 1988. Originally published: New York: Morrow, 1932.

DeMallie, Raymond. Editor's introduction to *The Sixth Grandfather: Black Elk's Teachings Given to John G. Neihardt.* Bison Book. Lincoln: University of Nebraska Press, 1985.

Denig, Edwin Thompson. *Five Indian Tribes of the Upper Missouri: Sioux, Arickaras, Assiniboines, Crees, Crows.* Edited with an introduction by John C. Ewers. The Civilization of the American Indian Series, vol. 59. Norman: The University of Oklahoma Press, 1961.

DeWall, Robb. *Korczak: Storyteller in Stone.* Revised edition. Crazy Horse, SD: Korczak's Heritage, Inc., 1994.

[DeWall, Robb?], *Progress,* newsletter published by Crazy Horse Foundation, vol. XXI (Summer 1999).

Dewing, Rolland. "South Dakota Newspaper Coverage of the 1973 Occupation of Wounded Knee," *South Dakota History* 12 (Spring 1982), pp. 60-63.

____. *Wounded Knee II.* Chadron, NE: Great Plains Network, 1995.

Dietrich, William. *Northwest Passage: The Great Columbia River.* New York: Simon & Schuster, 1995.

Dodge, Richard Irving. *The Black Hills. A Minute Description of the Routes, Scenery, Soil, Climate, Timber, Gold, Geology, Zoology, etc. With an Accurate Map, Four Sectional Drawings, and Ten Plates from Photographs Taken on the Spot.* Facsimile edition. Minneapolis: Ross & Haines, 1965. Originally published: New York: James Miller, 1876.

____. *The Black Hills Journals of Colonel Richard Irving Dodge.* Ed. Wayne R. Kime. The American Exploration and Travel Series, vol. 74. Norman: University of Oklahoma Press, 1996.

____. *The Plains of North America and Their Inhabitants.* Ed.Wayne R. Kime. Newark: University of Delaware Press, 1989.

Doll, Don, S. J. *Vision Quest: Men, Women and Sacred Sites of the Sioux Nation.* Photographs by Don Doll. Introduction by Vine Deloria, Jr. New York: Crown Publishers, Inc., 1994.

Ellis, Richard N, "Wounded Knee Massacre," *The New Encyclopedia of the American West*, ed. Howard R. Lamar. New Haven: Yale University Press, 1998.

Fatout, Paul. *Ambrose Bierce: The Devil's Lexicographer.* Norman: University of Oklahoma Press, 1951.

Feldman, Rodney M. and Richard A. Heimlich. *The Black Hills.* K/H Geology Field Guide Series. Dubuque, IA: Kendall/Hunt Publishing Company, 1980.

Fielder, Mildred. *Railroads of the Black Hills.* Deadwood, SD: Dakota Graphics,

1985. Reprint. Originally published: Seattle, WA: Superior Publishing Company, 1964.

Finerty, John F. *War-path and Bivouac, or, The Conquest of the Sioux, a narrative of stirring personal experiences and adventures in the Big Horn and Yellowstone Expedition of 1876, and in the campaign on the British border in 1879.* Introduction by Oliver Knight. Norman: University of Oklahoma Press, 1961.

Fite, Gilbert Courtland. *Peter Norbeck: Prairie Statesman.* Afterword by R. Alton Lee. Pierre, SD: South Dakota Historical Society, Press, 2005. Originally published as vol. 22 of The University of Missouri Studies. Columbia, MO: 1948.

____. *Mount Rushmore.* Norman: University of Oklahoma Press, 1952.,

Flood, Renée Sansom. *Lost Bird of Wounded Knee: Spirit of the Lakota.* New York: Da Capo Press, 1998. Originally published: New York: Scribner, 1995.

Frey, Rodney. *The World of the Crow Indians: As Driftwood Lodges.* Civilization of the American Indian Series, vol. 185. Norman: University of Oklahoma Press, 1987.

Fritz, Henry E. *The Movement for Indian Assimilation, 1860-1890.* Philadelphia: University of Pennsylvania Press, 1963.

Gates, Hobart, "Narrative of February 6, 1973 in Custer, South Dakota." Unpublished manuscript. Copy in author's possession.

Geores, Martha E. *Common Ground: The Struggle for Ownership of the Black Hills National Forest.* Lanham, MD: Rowman & Littlefield Publishers Inc., 1996.

Gerber, Max E. "The Custer Expedition of 1874: A New Look." *North Dakota History* 40. Bismarck, ND: State Historical Society of North Dakota,1973.

Gorn, Elliott J., Randy Roberts, and Terry D. Bilhartz, *Constructing the American Past*: *A Source Book of a People's History*, vol. 2. New York: HarperCollins Publishers, 1991.

Grafe, Ernest and Paul Horsted. 2d ed. *Exploring with Custer: The 1874 Black Hills Expedition.* Custer, SD: Golden Valley Press, 2002.

Graves, Henry S. "Black Hills Forest Reserve (South Dakota and Wyoming)," *Nineteenth Annual Report of the United States Geological Survey.* Washington: U. S. Government Printing Office, 1899.

Gries, John Paul. *Roadside Geology of South Dakota.* Missoula, MT: Mountain Press Publishing Co., 1996.

Grinnell, George Bird. *The Cheyenne Indians: Their Histories and Ways of Life.* 2 vols. New introduction by Mari Sandoz. New York: Cooper Square Publishers, Inc.., 1962.

Gulliford, Andrew. *Sacred Objects and Sacred Places: Preserving Tribal Traditions.* Boulder: University Press of Colorado, 2000.

Hafen, LeRoy. *Broken Hand: The Life of Thomas Fitzpatrick, Mountain Man, Guide, and Indian Agent.* Bison Book. Lincoln: University of Nebraska Press, 1981. Reprint. Originally published: Denver: Old West Publishing Co., 1931.

Hassrick, Royal B. *The Sioux: Life and Customs of a Warrior Society.* The Civilization of the American Indian Series, vol. 72. Norman: University of Oklahoma Press, 1964.

Hedren, Paul L., ed. *The Great Sioux War 1876-77: The Best from Montana The Magazine of Western History.* Helena: Montana Historical Society Press, 1991.

Hoxie, Frederick. *Parading through history: The making of the Crow nation in America 1805-1935.* Cambridge and London: Cambridge U. Press, 1995.

Hughes Richard B. "Legend of the Roses." Reprinted in Helen Rezatto, *Tales of the Black Hills.* Aberdeen, SD: North Plains Press, 1983.

____. *Pioneer Years in the Black Hills.* Edited by Agnes Wright Spring. Glendale, CA: A. H. Clark Co., 1957.

Hughes, Robert. *Culture of Complaint: The Fraying of America.* New York: Warner Books, Inc., 1994.

Hunkins, R. V., "The Black Hills—A Storehouse of Mineral Treasure," *The Black Hills*, ed. Roderick Peattie. New York: The Vanguard Press, Inc., 1952.

Hutton, Paul Andrew, "Phil Sheridan's Frontier," *The Great Sioux War 1877: The Best from Montana The Magazine of Western History*, ed. Paul L. Hedren. Helena: Montana Historical Society Press, 1991.

Hyde, George. *Red Cloud's Folk: A History of the Oglala Sioux Indians*, with foreword by Royal B. Hassrich. The Civilization of the American Indian Series, vol. 15. Norman: University of Oklahoma Press, 1975.

_____. *Spotted Tail's Folk: A History of the Brulé Sioux*, 2d ed. Foreword by Harry H. Anderson. Civilization of the American Indian Series, vol. 57. Norman: University of Oklahoma Press, 1974.

Irving, Washington. *Astoria.* Clatsop Edition. Portland, OR: Binfords & Mort, Publishers, 1967. Originally published 1836; rev. 1849.

Jacobsen, Sally, "The Great Montana Coal Rush," *Bulletin of the Atomic Scientists* 29 (April 1973).

Jackson, Donald Dean. *Custer's Gold.* Yale Western Americana Series. New Haven: Yale University Press, 1966.

Jensen, Richard E., "Another Look at Wounded Knee," in Richard E. Jensen, R. Eli Paul, and John E. Carter, *Eyewitness at Wounded Knee.* Great Plains Photography Series. Lincoln: University of Nebraska Press, 1991.

Josephson, Matthew. *The Robber Barons: The Great American Capitalists, 1861-1901.* A Harvest Book. San Diego and New York: Harcourt Brace & Company, 1995. Originally published: 1934.

Julin, Suzanne, "South Dakota Spa: A History of the Hot Springs Health Resort, 1882-1915," *South Dakota State Historical Collections*, vol. 41. Pierre, SD: State Publishing Company, 1982.

Killoren, John J., S.J. *Come Blackrobe: De Smet and the Indian Tragedy.* Norman: University of Oklahoma Press, 1994.

Korsgaard, Ross P., "A History of Rapid City, South Dakota, During Territorial Days," *South Dakota State Historical Collections*, vol. 38. Pierre, SD: State Publishing Company, 1977.

Koupal, Nancy Tystad. Annotations in L. Frank Baum, *Our Landlady*, ed. Nancy Tystad Koupal. Lincoln: University of Nebraska Press, 1996.

Krause, Herbert and Gary D. Olson. *Prelude to Glory: A newspaper accounting of Custer's 1874 Expedition to The Black Hills.* Sioux Falls, SD: Brevet Press, 1974.

LaPointe, James. *Legends of the Lakota.* San Francisco: The Indian Historical Press, 1976.

Larson, Robert W. *Red Cloud: Warrior-Statesman of the Lakota Sioux.* Norman: University of Oklahoma Press, 1997.

Lazarus, Edward. *Black Hills/White Justice: The Sioux Nation Versus the United States, 1775 to the Present.* New York: HarperCollins Publishers, 1991.

Lee, Robert. *Bob Lee's Notebook.* A collection of Lee's columns appearing in Dickson Media weekly publications, 1997-1998. N.p.: 1998.

_____. *Fort Meade & the Black Hills.* Bison Book. Lincoln: University of Nebraska Press, 1996.

Lee, Bob [Robert] and Dick Williams, *Last Grass Frontier: The South Dakota Stock Grower Heritage.* Sturgis, SD: Black Hills Publishers, Inc., 1964.

Lee, Wayne C. *Scotty Philip, the Man Who Saved the Buffalo.* Caldwell, ID: Caxton Printers, Ltd., 1975.

Lemmon, Ed. *Boss Cowman: The Recollections of Ed Lemmon 1857-1946.* Edited by
Nellie Snyder Yost. Bison Book. Lincoln: University of Nebraska Press,
1974. Originally published: Lincoln: University of Nebraska Press, 1969.

Lewis, Meriwether. *Original Journals of the Lewis and Clark Expedition, 1804-1806.*
Vol. 6. Edited and with introduction by Reuben Gold Thwaites. New York:
Antiquarian Press, 1959.

Limerick, Patricia Nelson. *The Legacy of Conquest: The Unbroken Past of the American
West.* New York: W. W. Norton & Company, inc., 1987.

Linderman, Frank B. *Plenty-coups: Chief of the Crows.* 1930. Bison Book New
Edition. Lincoln: University of Nebraska Press, 1962.

Luschei, Martin. "Wanted—by Whom? Ben Mills as Indian Agent." *Annals of
Wyoming* (Winter 1998).

Magregor, Gordon, with the collaboration of Royal B. Hassrick and William E.
Henry. *Warriors Without Weapons: A Study of the Society and Personality
Development of the Pine Ridge Sioux.* Chicago: University of Chicago Press, 1946.

Maloney, Mitch and David B. Miller. *Centennial Mini-Histories of the Black Hills
National Forest.* Custer, SD: Black Hills National Forest, 1997.

McGillycuddy, Julia B. *Blood on the Moon: Valentine McGillycuddy and the Sioux.*
Introduction by James C. Olson. Reprint. Bison Book. Lincoln: University of
Nebraska Press, 1990. Originally published as *McGillycuddy, Agent*: Stanford,
CA: Stanford University Press, 1941.

McLaird, James D. and Lesta V. Turchen. "Colonel Ludlow and the Custer
Expedition." *South Dakota History* 4 (1974).

____. "The Scientists' Search for Gold, 1875: Walter P. Jenney and Henry Newton."
South Dakota History 4 (Fall 1974).

McMurtry, Larry. *Crazy Horse.* A Penguin Life. New York: Viking Penguin, 1999.

Mandat-Grancey, Edmond Baron de. *Buffalo Gap: A French Ranch in Dakota: 1877.*
Edited by Keith Cochran, with research assistance by Dave Strain. Hermosa,
SD: Lame Johnny Press, 1981. Originally published as *La Breche Aux Buffles*:
Paris: Librarie Plon, 1889.

____. *Cow-boys and Colonels: Narrative of a Journey Across the Prairie and Over the
Black Hills of Dakota.* Translation of *Dans les Montagnes Rocheuses.* Bison
Book. Lincoln: University of Nebraska Press, 1984. Originally published:
London: Griffith, Farran, Okeden & Welsh, 1887.

Marshall, Joseph M III. "Crazy Horse (Tasunke Witko)." *Encyclopedia of North
American Indians,* ed. Howard R. Lamar. New Haven: Yale University Press,
1998.

Matthiessen, Peter. *In the Spirit of Crazy Horse.* New York: The Viking Press, 1983.

____. *Indian Country.* New York: The Viking Press, 1984.

Mattes, Merrill J. *The Great Platte Rive Road: The Covered Wagon Mainline
Via Fort Kearney To Forth Laramie.* Reprint. Bison Book. Lincoln: University
of Nebraska Press, 1987. Originally published, Nebraska State Historical
Publications Series. Lincoln: Nebraska State Historical Society, 1969.

____. "The Sutler's Store at Fort Laramie," quoted in Martin Luschei, "Wanted—by
Whom? Ben Mills as Indian Agent." *The Wyoming History Journal* (Winter 1998).

____. *Indians, Infants and Infantry: Andrew and Ellizabeth Burt on the Frontier.*
Bison Book. Reprint. Lincoln: University of Nebraska Press, 1988.
Originally published: 1960.

Mayhall, Mildred P. *The Kiowas.* The Civilization of the American Indian Series,
vol. 63. Norman: University of Okalahoma Press, 1962.

Means, Russell, with Marvin J. Wolf. *Where White Men Fear to Tread: The
Autobiography of Russell Means.* New York: St. Martin's Press, 1995.

Miles, Nelson A. *Personal Recollections And Observations Of General Nelson A. Miles*. New introduction by Robert M. Utley. New York: Da Capo Press, 1969.

Momaday, N. Scott, "To Save a Great Vision," A *Sender of Words: Essays in Memory of John G. Neihardt*, edited by Vine Deloria, Jr. Salt Lake City: Howe Brothers, *1984*.

____. *The Way to Rainy Mountain*. Albuquerque: University of New Mexico Press, 1969.

Mooney, James. *The Ghost-Dance Religion and the Sioux Outbreak of 1890*. Introduction by Raymond J. DeMallie. Reprint. Bison Book. Lincoln: University of Nebraska Press, 1991. Originally published as Part 2, *Fourteenth Annual Report of the Bureau of Ethnology, 1892-1893*: Washington: Government Printing Office, 1896.

Nabokov, Peter. *Where the Lightning Strikes: The Lives of American Indian Sacred Places*. New York: Viking Penguin, 2006

Nadeau, Remi. *Fort Laramie and the Sioux*. Reprint. Bison Book. Lincoln: University of Nebraska Press, 1982. Originally published: *Fort Laramie and the Sioux Indians*. American forts series. Englewood Cliffs, NJ: Prentice-Hall, *1967*.

Neihardt, Hilda. *Black Elk and Flaming Rainbow: Personal Memories of the Lakota Holy Man and John Neihardt*. Lincoln: University of Nebraska Press, 1995.

Neihardt, John G. *The Sixth Grandfather: Black Elk's Teachings Given to John G. Neihardt*. Edited with an introduction by Raymond J. DeMallie. Bison Book. Lincoln: University of Nebraska Press, 1985.

____. *Black Elk Speaks: Being the Life Story of a Holy Man of the Oglala Sioux* as told through John G. Neihardt. Reprint. Bison Book. Lincoln: University of Nebraska Press, 1988. Originally published: William Morrow & Company, 1952.

Oberholtzer, Ellis Paxon. *Jay Cooke: Financier of the Civil War*. Reprint. 2 vols. New York: B. Franklin, 1970. Originally published: Philadelphia: G. W. Jacobs, 1907.

O'Connor, Richard. *Ambrose Bierce: A Biography*. Boston: Little, Brown, 1967.

O'Harra, Cleophas C. and Joseph P. Connolly. *The Geology, Mineralogy, and Scenic Features of Custer State Park, South Dakota*. Rapid City, SD: *South Dakota School of Mines Bulletin No. 14* (1926).

Olson, James C. *Red Cloud and the Sioux Problem*. Reprint. Bison Book. Lincoln: University of Nebraska Press, 1975. Originally published: Lincoln: University of Nebraska Press, 1965.

Parker, Watson. *Gold in the Black Hills*. Reprint. Bison Book. Lincoln: University of Nebraska Press, 1982. Originally published: Norman: University of Oklahoma Press, 1966.

____. "The Report of Captain John Mix of a Scout to the Black Hills, March-April 1875." *South Dakota History* 7 (Fall 1977).

Parker, Watson and Hugh K. Lambert. *Black Hills Ghost Towns*. Athens, OH: Swallow Press/Ohio University Press, 1980.

Parkman, Francis. *The Oregon Trail*. Reprint. Garden City, NY: Garden City Publishing Co., 1948. Originally published: Boston: Little, Brown, and Co., 1897.

Philip, George, "James (Scotty) Philip, 1858-1911," *South Dakota Historical Collections*, vol. 20. Pierre, SD: State Publishing Company, 1940.

Pinchot, Gifford. *Breaking New Ground*. New York: Harcourt Brace and Company, Inc., 1947.

Pommersheim, Frank. *Braid of Feathers: American Indian Law and Contemporary Tribal Life.* Berkeley: University of California Press, 1995.

Powell, Peter J. *Sweet Medicine: The Continuing Role of the Sacred Arrows, the Sun Dance, and the Sacred Buffalo Hat in Northern Cheyenne History.* 2 vols. The Civilization of the American Indian Series, vol. 100. Norman: University of Oklahoma Press, 1969.

Powers, Marla N. *Oglala Women: Myth, Ritual, and Reality.* Chicago: The University of Chicago Press, 1986.

Price, Catherine. *The Oglala People, 1841-1879: A Political History.* Lincoln: University of Nebraska Press, 1996.

Procter, Ben. *William Randolph Hearst: The Early Years, 1963-1914.* New York: Oxford University Press, 1998.

Prucha, Francis Paul. *The Great Father: The United States Government and the American Indian.* Abridged edition. Lincoln: University of Nebraska Press, 1986.

Raventon, Edward. *Island in the Plains: A Black Hills Natural History.* Boulder, CO: Johnson Books, 1994.

Raynolds, W. F., U.S. Army Corps of Engineers. *Report of the Exploration of the Yellowstone River.* Washington: Government Printing Office, 1869.

Report of the Commission Appointed to Treat with the Sioux Indians for the Relinquishment of the Black Hills. Washington: Government Printing Office, 1875.

Rickey, Don, Jr., "The Battle of Wolf Mountain," in Hedren, ed., *The Great Sioux War: The Best from Montana The Magazine of Western History.* Helena: Montana Historical Society Press, 1991.

Riegel, Robert E. *The Story of the Western Railroads: From 1852 Through the Reign of the Giants.* Reprint. Lincoln: Nebraska University Press, 1963. Originally published: New York: Macmillan, 1926.

Robertson, Paul D., "Wounded Knee Massacre," *Encyclopedia of North Ameriocan Indians,* ed. Frederick E. Hoxie. Boston: Houghton Mifflin Company, 1996.

Robinson, Charles M. III. *A Good Year to Die: The Story of the Great Sioux War.* Norman: University of Oklahoma Press, 1996. Originally published: New York: Random House, 1995.

Robinson, Doane. *A History of the Dakota or Sioux Indians: From their earliest traditions and first contact with white men to the final settlement of the last of them upon reservations and the consequent abandonment of the old tribal life.* N.p.: State of South Dakota, 1904. Reprint. Minneapolis: Ross & Haines Inc., 1956.

Robinson, Elwyn B. *History of North Dakota.* Lincoln: University of Nebraska Press, 1996.

Ronda, James P. *Lewis and Clark among the Indians.* Bison Book. Lincoln: University of Nebraska Press, 1988.

Sahlins, Marshall David. *Islands of History.* Chicago: University of Chicago Press, 1985.

Sandoz, Mari. *Crazy Horse: The Strange Man of the Oglalas.* Bison Book. 50th Anniversary Edition. Introduction by Stephen B. Oates. Lincoln: University of Nebraska Press, 1992. Originally published: New York: A. A. Knopf, 1942.

Sayer, John William. *Ghost Dancing the Law: The Wounded Knee Trials.* Cambridge: Harvard University Press, 1997.

Schell, Herbert S. *History of South Dakota.* 3rd edition, revised. Bison Book. Lincoln: University of Nebraska Press, 1975.

Shaff, Howard and Audrey Karl Shaff. *The Life and Times of Gutzon Borgrlum, Sculptor of Mount Rushmore.* Foreword by Mary Ellis Borglum Vhay. Sioux

Falls, SD: The Center for Western Studies, in cooperation with Permelia
　　Publishing, Darien, CT, 1985.

Slotkin, Richard. *The Fatal Environment: The Myth of the Frontier in the Age of
　　Industrialization 1800-1890*. Reprint. Harper Perennial Edition. New York:
　　HarperCollins, 1994. Originally published: New York: Atheneum, 1985.

Smith, Edward P. "Report of Commissioner of Indian Affairs Edward P. Smith
　　November 1, 1875." Reprinted Wilcomb E. Washburn, ed., *The American
　　Indian and the United States: A Documentary History*, vol. 1. New York:
　　Random House, 1973.

Smith, Henry Nash. *Virgin Land: The American West as Symbol and Myth*. Vintage
　　Book. New York: Alfred A. Knopf, Inc. and Random House, 1950. Reprint.
　　Originally published: Cambridge: Harvard University Press, 1950.

Smith, James R., "Remarks by James R. Smith, Assistant Secretary – Water and
　　Power Development, Department of the Interior, Washington D.C. to Major
　　Electric Power Suppliers of Northcentral United States, Omaha, Nebraska,
　　May 26, 1970." News release of the Department of the Interior.

Smith, Paul Chaat and Robert Allen Warrior. *Like a Hurricane: The Indian Movement
　　from Alcatraz to Wounded Knee*. New York: The New Press, 1996.

Smith, Rex Alan. *The Carving of Mount Rushmore*. New York: Abbeville Press,
　　1985.

Sobel, Robert. *Panic on Wall Street: A History of American Financial Disasters*.
　　New York: Macmillan, 1968.

Sprague, Donovin Arleigh. *Images of America: Pine Ridge Reservation*. Charleston, SC:
　　Arcadia Publishing, 2004.

Standing Bear, Luther. *Land of the Spotted Eagle*, with foreword by Richard N. Ellis.
　　Reprint. Bison Book. Lincoln: University of Nebraska Press, 1978.
　　Originally published: Boston: Houghton Mifflin Company, 1928.

____. *My People the Sioux* . Edited by E. A. Brininstool, with introduction by Richard
　　N. Ellis. Reprint. Bison Book. Lincoln: University of Nebraska Press, 1975.
　　Originally published: Boston: Houghton Mifflin Company, 1928.

Stands In Timber, John and Margot Liberty, with the assistance of Robert M. Utley.
　　Cheyenne Memories. New Haven: Yale U. Press, 1967.

Stegner, Wallace. *Wolf Willow: A History, a Story, and a Memory of the Last Plains
　　Frontier*. New York: Penguin Books, 1990. Originally published: New York:
　　The Viking Press, Inc., 1962.

Steinmetz, Paul B., S.J. *Pipe, Bible, and Peyote Among the Oglala Lakota: A Study
　　in Religious Identity*. Knoxville: The University of Tennessee Press, 1990.

Steltenkamp, Michael F. *Black Elk: Holy Man of the Sioux*. Norman: University of
　　Oklahoma Press, 1993.

Sundstrom, Jessie Y. *Pioneers and Custer State Park: A History of Northcentral
　　Custer County*. Custer, SD: Jessie Y. Sundstrom, Publisher, 1994.

Sundstrom, Linea, "Native American Cultural Properties," *Black Hills National Forest
　　Cultural Resources Overview*, Vol. 2 (1996).

____. *Storied Stone: Indian Rock Art of the Black Hills Country*. Norman: University of
　　Oklahoma Press, 2004.

Tallent, Annie D. *The Black Hills: or, The Last Hunting Ground of the Dakotahs: A
　　Complete History Of the Black Hills of Dakota from their First Invasion in
　　1874 to the Present Time, Comprising a Comprehensive Account of How They
　　Lost Them; of Numerous Adventures of the Early Settlers; Their Heroic
　　Struggles for Supremacy against the Hostile Dakotah Tribes, and their Final
　　Victory;The Opening of the Country to White Settlement, and its Subsequent
　　Development*. Reprint. 2d ed. Sioux Falls, SD: Brevet Press, 1974.

Trenholm, Virginia Cole. *The Arapahoes, Our People*. The Civilization of the American Indian Series, vol. 105. Norman: University of Oklahoma Press, 1970.

Trennert, Robert A., Jr. *Alternative to Extinction: Federal Indian Policy and the Beginnings of the Reservation System, 1846-51.* Philadelphia: Temple U. Press, 1975.

Turchen, Lesta V. and James D. McLaird. *The Black Hills Expedition of 1875.* Mitchell, SD: Dakota Wesleyan University Press, 1975.

U. S. Department of the Interior. *North Central Power Study: Report of Phase I,* vol.1. Prepared Under the Direction of the Coordinating Committee, North Central Power Study. Washington: Department of the Interior, October 1971.

Utley, Robert M. *Frontier Regulars*. New York: Macmillan, 1973.

____. *The Lance and the Shield: The Life and Times of Sitting Bull.* A John Macrae Book. New York: Henry Holt and Co., 1993.

____. *The Last Days of the Sioux Nation.* Yale Western Americana Series. New Haven: Yale University Press, 1963.

Vestal, Stanley. *Sitting Bull: Champion of the Sioux: A Biography.* The Civilization of The American Indian Series, vol. 46. Norman: University of Oklahoma Press, 1957. Originally published: Boston: Houghton Mifflin Co., 1932.

Weyler, Rex. *Blood of the Land: The Government and Corporate War Against the American Indian Movement.* New York: Everest House Publishers, 1982.

White, Richard. "The Winning of the West: The Expansion of the Western Sioux in The Eighteenth and Nineteenth Centuries." *Journal of American History* 65 (September 1978).

Whitley, Fred W. *"A History of Custer City, South Dakota, 1874-1900."* *South Dakota State Historical Collections*, vol. 37. Pierre, SD: State Publishing Co., 1974.

Wilkins, Thurman. *Cherokee Tragedy: The Ridge Family and the Decimation of a People*. 2d. edition, revised. The Civilization of the American Indian Series, vol. 169. Norman: University of Oklahoma Press, 1986.

Woodward, Robert D. "World of Darkness: Early Explorations of the Cave," *Wind Cave National Park*, *South Dakota*. National Park Service Handbook 104. Washington: National Park Service, 1979.

Worster, Donald. *Under Western Skies*. New York: Oxford University Press, 1992.

Wright, Frank Lloyd, "The Bad Lands," letter to Robert D. Lusk, September 1935, *South Dakota History* (Summer 1999).

Wright, Ronald. *Stolen Continents: The "New World" Through Indian Eyes*. A Peter Davison Book. Boston: Houghton Mifflin Company, 1992.

ACKNOWLEDGMENTS

My deepest gratitude goes to my brother, Gene Luschei, who supported this endeavor from the outset, without whose help it would never have seen light, and to Ellen, my wife, whose love sustained me through the long process required.

This book has only been possible because of the faithful labors of so many who have gone before. Among those who personally helped me along the way, I want especially to thank Lyle Clifford, Mike Foscha, Dave McKee, Ann Neumann, Bob Paulson, Jessie Sundstrom, John Twiss, and Ron Walker. My profound thanks to those who reviewed the entire manuscript: Bob Lee, Frank Carroll, Donovin Sprague Hump, and Marvin Kammerer, who did their best to keep me on the right path.

Finally, a particular salute to that rare duo, Watson Parker, whose suggestions have been crucial, and the late Bob Lee, a friend whose door was always open.

Index

Sioux Act of 1888: carves out six reservations, 105; and fear of the incomprehensible, 105
Sioux City, IA, 38, 46, 65, 66, 68, 79
Sioux Falls, SD, 148, 188
Sioux Falls Daily Argus-Leader, 148
Sioux Indians: xii, 23, 24, 25, 26, 29, 67, 93 111, 112, 120-121, 147, 148, 168, 189, 195; assigned Black Hills by 1851 treaty, 27; awarded seventeen and a half million dollars for loss of Black Hills, 185; "best Indians on the prairie," 22; Black Hills best home for, 65; Black Hills seized from, 92; and Bradley bill, 189; cautioned about regaining Black Hills, 136; denied right to counsel, 135-136; as dependents, 80; dialect groups of, 11; divided on sale of Black Hills, 81; and extinction as their fate, 65; and extinguishment of title, 64-65; and factionalism among tribes, 105 ; first encountered by French in Minnesota, 11; frozen in place by Army, 5; Kiowas and Crows driven out by, 26; Kiowas driven out by, 6; most feared enemy of other tribes, 13; railroads, and death of free life on the plains, 44; as savages, 66; signatures of three-fourths of adult white males required, 82, 83; as stewards of Black Hills, 200; on ten thousand years' occupancy, 190; as valiant and warlike, 9; violating treaty, 78; violations to be punished, 65; and white advocate, 126. *See also* individual tribes.
Sioux Jurisdictional Act, 136
Sioux Nation Black Hills Act: *see* Bradley bill
Sioux Park, 189
Sioux, Teton or Western, 10. *See* Lakotas
Sitting Bull: 9, 39, 44, 47, 58, 85, 89, 90, 93, 94, 95, 107, 109, 112, 132; calls off war and moves to Canada, 92; demands whites leave his country, 91; description of, by Col. Miles, 91; on eagles becoming crows, 200; joins Wild West show, 105; killing of, 111, 126; as magnet for discontented, 103; and old free life in Canada, 99-100; poverty exacted by virtue of generosity, 104; song of, 104; surrender of, 103-104; with Gen. Terry, 100; with Maj. Walsh, 99-100; would never talk to white man, 81
Sitting Bull (Oglala), 89
Sixth Grandfather, The, 191
Slotkin, Richard: on financing of railroads, 47; on Indian grand race war, 64; on promoters masking reality of actions from themselves, 49; on secret history of Custer expedition, 45
Smith, Comm. Edward P.: on Black Hills as best region for Sioux, if, 65; on fair equivalent for loss, 65; issues ultimatum to tribes, 84-85
Smith, Henry Nash, 38
Smith, Henry W. "Preacher," 96
Smith, James R., 180
Smith, Jedediah, 18, 20, 147
Smith, Capt. John, 15
Smith, Co. Atty. Mike: 170; charges Hare brothers with manslaughter, 170; gains conviction, 171; investigates Yellow Thunder death, 170
Smith, Paul Chaat: 168, 170, 172; on South Dakota, 174; and traditional wisdom, 178
Smith, Rex Alan, 152, 163
Snakes: *see* Shoshones
Song of the Messiah, The, 156
South, the, 146, 148, 152, 196
South Dakota: 106, 120, 122, 123, 141, 147, 148, 150, 151, 161, 163, 171, 176, 182, 185, 189; backlash against AIM, 182-183; as racist, 174; response to Bradley bill,190; South Dakota vs. Georgia, 152
South Dakota Highway Patrol, 176
South Dakota Peace and Justice, 185
Southern Hills: 1; description of, 137-138, 140-141; and footprint in, 199; and gold, paucity of, 137-138; spared worst of environmental destruction, 137
Southern Plains, 88
Soviet Union, 180
Spearfish, SD, 19, 85, 96, 124
Spearfish Canyon, 96, 161
Spotted Tail: 63, 72, 84, 93, 94, 103, 131; death of daughter, 33; finds troops mingling with miners, 81; and high price for Black Hills, 80; jealous of Crazy Horse, 94, 95; as leader of "friendlies," 40; made leader of Oglalas, 91; moved to Missouri River, 101; murdered by Lakota rival, 126; as peace chief, 96; signs Treaty of 1868, 34; transformed by imprisonment, 31; wants money left with President, 82, 190; at White House dinner, 41
Spotted Tail Agency, 54, 91, 95
Spring Creek, 97, 99, 102, 132
Spring Valley, 121
Spurlock, 139
St. Louis, 12, 18, 65
St. Paul, 57
St. Paul Daily Press, 53
Stands in Timber, John, 8
Standing Bear, 157
Standing Bear, Henry: 136; asks Ziolkowski to carve Indian figure, 162; touches off charge on memorial, 165; writes Borglum a letter, 154-155
Standing Bear, Luther: 136, 154; on being, vs.